RESTLESS HISTORY

Restless History

Political Imaginaries and Their Discontents in Post-Stalinist Bulgaria

ZHIVKA VALIAVICHARSKA

McGill-Queen's University Press
Montreal & Kingston • London • Chicago

ISBN 978-0-2280-0582-7 (cloth)
ISBN 978-0-2280-0583-4 (paper)
ISBN 978-0-2280-0782-1 (ePDF)
ISBN 978-0-2280-0783-8 (ePUB)

Legal deposit second quarter 2021
Bibliothèque nationale du Québec

Printed in Canada on acid-free paper that is 100% ancient forest free (100% post-consumer recycled), processed chlorine free

Publication of this book was made possible, in part, by a grant from the First Book Subvention Program of the Association for Slavic, East European, and Eurasian Studies, as well as a grant from the School of Liberal Arts and Sciences and the Department of Social Science and Cultural Studies at Pratt Institute.

Library and Archives Canada Cataloguing in Publication

Title: Restless history: political imaginaries and their discontents in post-Stalinist Bulgaria/Zhivka Valiavicharska.

Names: Valiavicharska, Zhivka, author.

Description: Includes bibliographical references and index.

Identifiers: Canadiana (print) 20200398342 | Canadiana (ebook) 20200398423 | ISBN 9780228005827 (hardcover) | ISBN 9780228005834 (softcover) | ISBN 9780228007821 (ePDF) | ISBN 9780228007838 (ePUB)

Subjects: LCSH: Socialism—Bulgaria—History—20th century. | Political theory/political philosophy; Balkans. | LCSH: Socialism—Europe, Eastern—History—20th century. | LCSH: Communism—History.

Classification: LCC HX363.5 .V35 2021 | DDC 335.4309499—dc23

This book was typeset by Marquis Interscript in 10.5/13 Sabon.

Contents

Acknowledgments vii

Figures xv

Introduction: Post-Stalinism in the Folds of Humanism 3

1 Journeys of the *1844 Manuscripts*: Historiographic Shifts in Marxist Thought 27

2 Gender and Social Reproduction the Socialist Way 57

3 In the Darkness of Humanism 89

4 Stalinism to Post-Stalinism: Shifting Histories, Shifting Readings 122

5 Violent Revivals 149

6 Uncanny Symbioses: Ethnonationalism and the Global Orientations of Bulgarian Socialism 170

Conclusion: In the Haunted Landscapes of Post-Socialism 189

Notes 203

Bibliography 227

Index 265

Acknowledgments

Restless History turns to the former socialist world in light of the realities of the last thirty years of post-socialist development. It offers a rethinking of that past in the hopes for a different future. As such, this book is but one piece of a larger collective effort that I hope will take diverse intellectual, material, cultural, and political forms. I have great appreciation for the friends and colleagues with whom I share in this collective project. Among them are Raia Apostolova, Arto Artinian, Konstantin Bobotsov, Tsvetelina Hristova, Mariya Ivancheva, Nikolay Karkov, Ognian Kasabov, Rositsa Kratunkova, Philipp Lottholz, Polina Manolova, Georgi Medarov, Madlen Nikolova, Stanimir Panayotov, Daniel Petrov, Bozhin Traykov, Jana Tsoneva, Lea Vajsova, and many others, including the LevFem, DVersia, KOI, and LeftEast collectives. Martin Marinos has been a treasured companion throughout the process. Our conversations have given me a much-needed space in which to explore these ideas in their earliest and most unstable forms. My deep gratitude goes Momchil Khrisov, whose brilliance, insight, and generosity over the years has enriched my work and thinking beyond measure. Neda Genova's thought and praxis continues to inspire me. She has engaged my work in profound ways on multiple occasions, including through the process of translation, and her feedback has added strength, accuracy, and subtlety to it. Polina Mukanova has made a significant contribution to this book with her experience in library and archival research, especially the chapter on gender and social reproduction. Thank you to Boryana Rossa and Oleg Mavromati, and to the lovely and fierce diasporic feminists Nina Georgieva, Assia Nakova, Velina Manolova, Deliana Simeonova, and Shirly Bahar, without whom I would not be able to survive the rewarding yet often grueling experiences of displacement across continents and oceans.

This project owes so much to the conversations at various conferences and public events with my colleagues working on the former socialist countries and the post-colonial world. Special thanks to Marina Antić, Joseph Feinberg, Katarina Kušić, Ivan Landa, Danijela Majstorović, Jan Mervart, Suzana Milevska, Djordje Popović, Lela Rekhviashvili, Piro Rexhepi, James Robertson, Jiří Růžička, Ovidiu Ţichindeleanu, and Ana Vilenica. I have endless respect for Rossen Djagalov – for his generosity and contributions to forging open, diasporic intellectual and political spaces, discussions, and collectivities, and for his work on bridging worlds and forging new futures out of them. Special thanks to Chavdar Marinov, who read and commented on large parts of the manuscript with great care and responsibility and gave me valuable and reassuring feedback at a crucial time. Deian Deianov and Liliana Deianova have generously shared their time, materials, analyses, and lived experiences. I would like to thank Kevin Anderson, Teodora Dragostinova, and Maria Todorova for their serious engagement at various public events. Their feedback, questions, and productive critiques have brought clarity and precision and have helped me add layers of complexity. Todorova's work has had a profound impact, and her colossal legacy in the critical study of the Balkans remains a foundational influence on my thinking.

Pratt Institute, where I have been teaching for most of the time it has taken me to write *Restless History*, provided a uniquely creative environment, one that expanded the contours of this project and its critical methodologies. I want to thank my colleagues at Pratt, and especially Andrew Barnes, Francis Bradley, Jayna Brown, Ric Brown, Josiah Brownell, Caitlin Cahill, Lisabeth During, Nurhaizatul Jamil, Ann Holder, Paul Haacke, Jeffrey Hogrefe, Gregg Horowitz, Arlene Keizer, Ira Livingston, Luka Lucić, Jennifer Miller, Wendy Muñiz, Darini Nicholas, Johanna Oksala, Minh-Ha Pham, Uzma Rizvi, Jennifer Telesca, Helio Takai, Kumru Toktamis, Karin Shankar, Iván Zatz-Díaz, and Carl Zimrung, as well as my lovely, creative, and brilliant students, who continue to energize my thinking and social practice. I have deep appreciation for May Joseph – I find so much inspiration in her writing praxis, a synthesis of lyrical prose and sharp analysis that speaks from multiple embodied, counterhegemonic places. I always derive a sense of hope from our journeys into reviving lost and forgotten transcontinental and transoceanic connections as we continue to make sense of our personal and social histories. An enormous thank you, as well, to Macarena Gómez-Barris for her sustained support over the years, for bringing so much energy, creativity, and vision into our worlds, and for retrieving the views submerged beneath the waters. Amanda Davidson's editorial work and her creative suggestions have helped me rebuild each chapter almost from scratch. Jeanne Landers and Kathrine Fetizanan have also participated in this editorial work. I thank Pratt's interlibrary loan librarians Caroline Skelton and Nicholas Dease for pulling together with the greatest precision my calls for sources in four languages in different alphabets from various far-flung places. Pratt's School of Liberal Arts and Sciences and the Department of Social Science and Cultural Studies have provided crucial financial and material support for the research, writing, and publication of the book.

The rather strewn trajectories I have followed as a migrant person in the hold of larger social and political forces have accumulated into a disorderly, fragmented bundle of locales, incompatible social contexts, and intersecting temporalities, each following their own life and rhythm. Without this mesh of experience, much of which remains unprocessed, this book could not have been written in the same way – its spatial and temporal warps have added to the macroscopic stretches and disjointed parts that may appear here, in ways that are perhaps unknown to me. Many friends, colleagues, and comrades I met during my years spent in Chicago, Oakland, Berkeley, and New York have enriched my visions through their intellectual, emotional, and creative energies. I am forever grateful and indebted to Wendy Brown, whose lasting influence remains, and whose brilliance, wisdom, and support have lifted me at key moments of my intellectual journey. I thank as well Amanda Armstrong, Cinzia Arruzza, Fadi Bardawil, Banu Bargu, Matt Bonal, Kaeshi Chai, Chris Chen, Yasmeen Daifallah, Dace Dzenovska, James Elkins, Samera Esmeir, Silvia Federici, Roxana Galusca, Cindy Gord, Adam Hefty, Larisa Kurtović, Satyel Larson, Zachary Levenson, Munira Lokhandwala, George Ciccariello-Maher, Caitlin Manning, Francesca Manning, James Martel, Eli Meyerhoff, Salar Mohandesi, Paul Nadal, Dan Nemser, Trevor Paglen, K-Sue Park, Praba Pilar, Jay Rehm, Suzana Sjeničić, Bettina Stoetzer, Michael Taussig, Cassandra Troyan, Dennis O'Brien, Olivia Taussig-Moore, Tom Rees, Yuri Slezkine, Anuj Vaidya, Susanne Wengle, Brian Whitener, Alexandria Wright, and Aleksei Yurchak. Much warmth and gratitude to Hale Thompson, whose work and practice has influenced mine in profound ways. Kelly Gawel, my dear friend and colleague, has engaged my worlds in multiple ways and has read various drafts of this book at crucial moments. Thank you for the work of care, the profound insights birthed together, and the power that we conjure, all of which become possible only in the deep collective spaces of feminist process and practice. Much love to Kelly as well as to Esra Atamer, Melissa Buzzeo, and the spectre of the wondrous Care Cadre, in which collective feminist practice crossed into magical realms.

In Sofia and Plovdiv, I hold continual respect and admiration for the lasting contributions of Ruzha Marinska, a treasured interlocutor and my former mentor at the National Academy of Arts in Sofia, who has always been a source of determination and deep historical reflection. I also feel tremendous gratitude for Petur-Emil Mitev, as this project owes so much to his historical knowledge and his intellectual and social contributions during the post-Stalinist years in Bulgaria and the socialist world more broadly. Our conversations have been important markers and events for me because they have shifted my historical awareness in profound ways. I want to extend my appreciation and gratitude as well to Stefka Delkinova, Nedialka Khristonova, Dimitrina Vangelova, and the late Detelin Delkinov and Docho Tsanev. All of them, along with Mitev, have accompanied my journey into my next long-term research commitment, the history of the social movements and land communes influenced by Russian writer and social thinker Lev Tolstoy in Bulgaria, Russia, Eastern Europe, and beyond. My own family history and social environment while growing up on the edges of Plovdiv, Bulgaria, connects me to this piece of world history in deeply formative ways.

I am always grateful to Emil Mirazchiev, who took some of the photos, advised me to retake others, and edited most of the images that appear in this book, sharing his stunning visual thinking and precision along the way. His astonishing energy, creativity, and generous spirit continues to energize our worlds and make them thrive. Galina Dimitrova-Dimova, Suzana Karanfilova, Svetlana Kuyumdzhieva, Maria Mirazchieva, Nikolina Parikian, Kamen Starchev, and Khristo Tanev have helped with research and access to the visual materials published here, and each has shared their knowledge, experience, and expertise with so much generosity. Special thanks to Asen Krustenov, who took the cover photo along with Emil Mirazchiev, for responding with generosity and openness. Stefan Shivachev and Nedelcho Nedelchev at the Regional History Museum, Plovdiv, have kindly assisted me with access to the Bratska Mogila, which is now closed to the public. The fate of this extraordinary anti-fascist monument from 1974, a highlight of socialist urban planning nested in one of the greenest areas of the city, is currently uncertain, dwarfed as it is by aggressive real-estate development. It will hopefully see a much-needed restoration and reopening someday. Thanks go to the Regional History Museum, Plovdiv, as well for permission to publish the cover image: Ustrem (1974), sculptural composition by Liubomir Dalchev, Ana Dalcheva, and Petur Atanasov, Bratska Mogila, Plovdiv.

I owe much to the Public Library Ivan Vazov in Plovdiv, one of the most remarkable public institutions in the world, where I have spent significant stretches of my life since my teenage years, always in a state of altered temporality. Each time I pass through these doors I give up my ordinary coordinates in order to enter a heterotopic space of infinite worlds. I am always impressed by the work and spirit of the librarians there, mostly women, who have dedicated their labour to making publicly accessible a unique trove of resources, thereby enabling the intellectual and creative work of countless people. On many occasions I have worked closely with the reference desk librarians on duty at the Plovdiv Public Library and the National Library St. St. Cyril and Methodius in Sofia, who have guided me through their labyrinthine collections. Their enormous erudition and experience inspires great respect and admiration. Special gratitude goes to the now retired librarians Snezhka Neshkova, Filka Litovoiska, and Reni Panaiotova at the Plovdiv Public Library. At the National Library in Sofia, Maia Peovska and Maia Dimitrova have assisted my research at crucial junctures, and the staff in the photocopy room there has enabled my work, perhaps most significantly.

My work would not be the same without the incredible generosity, collaborative energy, and expertise of all these colleagues – their contributions further underscore the collective nature of research, of creative and intellectual work, and make visible the contradictions contained in projects undertaken under individual authorship. I am hoping for many more years of creative and inspiring work with these colleagues and many others, and for material and social practices that open new worlds and possibilities.

The majority of this book was written between 2015 and 2018, in New York, Plovdiv, and Sofia, although I began researching and collecting archival and historical materials many years earlier; indeed, the interpretations I am offering here have been germinating for a decade or more and have appeared before in earlier versions. I have presented pieces of this work at various stages at a number of public events and conferences, including the different gatherings of post-colonial and post-socialist scholars to which I have contributed, several meetings of the *Historical Materialism* conference in New York City, and the annual summer conventions of the Association for Slavic, East European, and Eurasian Studies (ASEEES). I appreciate the intellectual spaces and communities sustained by ASEEES, whose conventions provide the occasion for the most stimulating discussions. The association has also provided support for the publication of this book. Some ideas explored in the introduction and chapter 1 appear in my 2017 article "Herbert Marcuse, the Liberation of 'Man,' and Hegemonic Humanism" (*Theory and Event* 20, no. 3). Chapter 2, which focuses on social reproduction, grew out of an accumulation of thinking and writing that began as a collaboration with Brian Whitener and continued in collective form with many colleagues and friends. Some of this prior work has appeared in *Viewpoint Magazine* and in the article "Social Reproduction in the Making: Recentering the Margins, Expanding the Horizons," part of a special issue of *Comparative Literature and Culture* edited by Kelly Gawel and Cinzia Arruzza on social reproduction (20, no. 2 [2020]). An early version was also presented at ASEEES in November 2017. Parts of chapters 3, 4, and 5 were presented at various stages at different venues and public events, including the Institute of Philosophy of the Czech Academy of Sciences in Prague in June 2018; I would like to thank the generosity and warm hospitality of my colleagues and collaborators there. Chapter 6, revised and updated here, has appeared earlier as an article in the special issue of *DVersia*, "Decolonial Theory and Practice in Southeast Europe" (March 2019). I want to thank the editors of that special issue, Katarina Kušić, Polina Manolova, and Philipp Lottholz, as well as the *DVersia* editorial collective, for their extensive feedback and engagement with my arguments. Parts of this research were also published in 2018 under the title "Rethinking East-European Socialism: Notes toward a Decolonial, Anti-Capitalist Methodology," an article co-authored with Nikolay Karkov that appeared in *Interventions: International Journal of Postcolonial Studies* (20, no. 5). Some portions of the conclusion draw on my 2014 article "How the Discourse of Totalitarianism Appeared in Late Socialist Bulgaria: The Birth and Life of Zheliu Zhelev's Book

Fascism," which appeared in *Kritika: Explorations in Russian and Eurasian History* (15, no. 2).

I thank McGill-Queen's University Press for welcoming this manuscript in a rather wobbly state and for walking me with great care and professionalism through the multiple stages it took to bring it to completion. This book is now out in the world in great part due to the remarkable foresight and experience of my editor, Richard Ratzlaff. He guided me through the process in a positive, careful, and engaging way, and I thank him for his trust, patience, and openness, and for his truly inspiring work in the publishing world. I appreciate the thorough and rigorous feedback of the two anonymous reviewers – their critical engagement was absolutely crucial and helped make this book much more complex. It was an honour to work with Ryan Perks – I thank him for his subtle, thorough, and professional copy-editing. Sergey Lobachev shared his marvelous skills in the art of indexing. I also thank Kathleen Fraser for coordinating the multiple moving pieces during the production process, and the marketing department at MQUP for releasing this book into the world.

Across the continents, I have been blessed with my parents, Elena and Venelin. Their generosity, intelligence, and beautiful connection to each other and the world have been a guiding light in my life. My dear sister, Vessela, and her family, David and Anna-Elena, have been a solid support throughout the years. To Kostadin, Kalina, Stefka, Milen, Milko, Mikhaela, Vasilena, Vladi, and everyone else, and to Filip, Tania, *lelia* Danche and *chicho* Petur – thank you all for your support. My grandparents, all of whom also raised me, and who are no longer in this world – my grandmother, Vasilka Katsarova-Valiavicharska, my great-aunt, Nadezhda Katsarova, my grandfather, Stoichko Valiavicharski, and my great-uncle, Virginii Katsarov – I carry the memory of their lives and work always, their strong and beautiful spirits, and the history they have gifted to the world.

Figures

1.1. The catalogue entry for Marx and Engels's *Iz pannikh proizvedenii* (1956) in the Plovdiv Public Library Ivan Vazov. Photo by author. 37

1.2 "Socialism and the Human," article in *Zhenata dnes* 8 (1974): 16–17. Published with permission. 53

2.1 "The Other Mothers of Our Children," article by Rositsa Boseva and Varvara Kirilova in *Zhenata dnes* 11 (1968): 12–13. Published with permission. 76

2.2 *Family* (1981), sculptural composition by Nikolina Parikian, near the Wedding Ritual Hall, Plovdiv. Photo by and courtesy of Emil Mirazchiev, October 2020. 79

2.3 "Unity of form and content," satirical drawing by Zhivko Ianchev, *Narodna mladezh* (10 March 1968), 4. 84

3.1 1,300 Years Bulgaria in its original condition, Sofia, 1981; view from the north. Personal archive of Valentin Starchev; courtesy of the Starchev family. 90

3.2 Past, Present, Future (1981) by sculptor Valentin Starchev. Sculptural compositions from the 1,300 Years Bulgaria monument as of May 2008. Photo by author. 92

3.3 Detail from the mural *The Fire* (1981) by artist Khristo Stefanov, with a portrait of Liudmila Zhivkova, at Auditorium No. 7, National Palace of Culture, Sofia, in 1981. Source: Khristo Stefanov and Maksimiliian Kirov, eds, *Suvremenno bulgarsko monumentalno izkustvo 1956–1986* (Sofia: Durzhavno izdatelstvo D-r Petur Beron, 1986), 228–9.

Photos in the book were taken by a collective at Natsionalna Fotografska Agentsiia, and by Sava Boiadzhiev, Iliia Zinoviev, and Nedialko Krustev. 98

3.4 1,300 Years Bulgaria in its original condition, designed by a collective of architects, engineers, and sculptors, Sofia, 1981, seen from the west. 119

4.1 The first page of a letter of complaint sent to the government in April 1960 by an anonymous citizen about the 1959 education reform. Central State Archive, Sofia. Photo by author, 2018; published with permission. 123

4.2 Nâzim Hikmet's selected poems translated into Bulgarian by Nikolai Tsonev, with cover design and illustrations by Boris Angelushev. Nazum Khikmet, *Izbrani stikhotvoreniia* (Sofia: Bulgarski pisatel, 1952). Library copy of the Public Library Ivan Vazov, Plovdiv. 137

6.1 "Welcome, Angela!," an article celebrating the arrival of Angela Davis in Sofia in September 1972, published in the youth newspaper *Narodna mladezh* (18 September, 1972), 1. 171

6.2 Political cartoon commenting on the arrest of Angela Davis by Ivan Stoichev, *Komsomolska iskra* (Plovdiv; 11 January 1971), 4–5. 173

6.3 *Robstvo* (Yoke) from the Bratska Mogila, Plovdiv (1974), in its original state by sculptors Liubomir Dalchev, Ana Dalcheva, and Petur Atanasov. Source: Veneta Ivanova, *Bulgarska monumentalna skulptura: razvitie i problemi* (Sofia: Bulgarski khudozhnik, 1978), 188. Photo by Mikhail Enev. 187

6.4 The Bratska Mogila, Plovdiv (1974) by architects Liubomir Shinkov and Vladimir Rangelov, and sculptors Liubomir Dalchev, Ana Dalcheva, and Petur Atanasov. Photo by and courtesy of Emil Mirazchiev, October 2020. 188

7.1 A protest action against the demolition of the monument 1,300 Years Bulgaria, Sofia, July 2017. Photo by author, 2017. 196

7.2 The central figure of the Memorial to the First Sofia Division of the Bulgarian Army from 1934 (the Lion), June 2018. Photo by and courtesy of Maria Mirazchieva, October 2020. 197

RESTLESS HISTORY

INTRODUCTION

Post-Stalinism in the Folds of Humanism

Post-Stalinist political thought in Eastern Europe and the Soviet Union has a rich and nuanced history, but few theorists and intellectual historians have taken it seriously. This is in part because of the overbearing legacy of the Stalinist intellectual tradition, in part because of monolithic and ahistorical renditions of the socialist period as a whole, and in part because of the overall devaluation and erasure of the socialist world and its contributions to political alternatives. This book delves into the world of political ideas and political life during the post-Stalinist period in Bulgaria (roughly the last three decades of socialism) and places them in the open and dynamic context of the East European and global radical movements of the 1960s and '70s. When we unsettle monolithic narratives, the socialist past appears as a restless history that bears on the present in both galvanizing and disturbing ways. Against those who have discarded it as a failed experiment, as an attempt at utopia gone terribly wrong, this book pries open its complexity. It invites the reader to inhabit the uneasy tension between its radical political practices and its terrifying moments, to bear the strain of its structuring contradictions, to hold together the multiplicity of meanings that leave a complex, ambivalent, and radically unfinished legacy.

Much of the history of political ideas and political life during the post-Stalinist era in Eastern Europe unfolded on the terrain of Marxist humanism, or at least had to contend with the Marxist-humanist tradition in some way or another. Because of its anti-Stalinist orientation, humanism became a defining framework in the socialist countries during the post-Stalinist period, yet it took root among diverse political communities on the left far beyond the socialist world. The ideas generated in the socialist "East" during this time continually reconfigured the political and intellectual terrain in the West and on the formerly colonized continents. In fact, the 1960s became legible as a "global" political era to a great extent due to the rise of humanism. Ideas about human liberation and human freedom swept political communities across geopolitical divides, promising a common critical perspective for the Left under a humanist rubric on both sides of the Iron Curtain and on the colonized continents. If we can speak about the 1960s and '70s as a global era that shook the world in a wave of protests, demonstrations, revolts, and anti-colonial liberation struggles, these political contexts and localities were so distant from one another that it was mainly through the left-humanist lens, and the universal dimensions to which it aspired, that they could be seen as a distinct, if multi-faceted, political period with a common political logic.

The Frankfurt School, to which Herbert Marcuse and Erich Fromm belonged, was perhaps the most visible cluster of thinkers to embrace these humanist values while restoring the lost trajectory that linked Marx and Hegel. In the United Kingdom, prominent figures such as E.P. Thompson, John Saville, and others used a Marxist-humanist lens to critique Stalinist Marxism and the Stalinist state, giving rise to what is known as the British New Left. In the United States, Marcuse's critique of the technological and administrative apparatuses of industrial society articulated a powerful perspective, grounding the anti-war movements in a critique of capitalism and reimagining them as a left political project. The work of C.L.R. James, Raya Dunayevskaya, Grace Lee Boggs, and others – a cluster of radicals known as the Johnson-Forest Tendency in the 1940s – contributed immensely to the Marxist-humanist tradition. In addition to translating into English and popularizing hitherto unknown works by Marx and Lenin, their writings focused on relationships between race and working-class struggle and offered a revolutionary and anti-capitalist perspective rooted in the Black liberation struggles in the United States and the anti-colonial liberation movements in Africa. Writing and organizing out of Detroit, a city that concentrated some of the largest industries in the United States, they reported on a wide range of struggles while exploring complex crossovers between the labour movement in the Midwest, women's liberation, and the struggles against racism, segregation, and discrimination across the United States, drawing direct lines between these and the anti-authoritarian movements in Eastern Europe and China, the anti-colonial liberation movements in Africa, and more. In a searing critique of the war in Vietnam, Fidel Castro called US imperialism "the most serious danger that humanity faces today"; US interference in Cuba, he continued, cannot be seen as an isolated case but as part of the American intervention in Laos and Cambodia, the support for reactionary governments and coups d'états in Latin America and Africa, and acts of aggression against the Arab peoples.[1]

Anti-colonial liberation movements throughout the twentieth century similarly embraced a range of humanist discourses. A humanist theme framed the Bandung Conference of 1955, the first meeting of the newly independent Asian and African nations that laid the grounds for the formation of the Non-Aligned Movement several years later. African and Caribbean anti-colonial intellectuals such as Aimé Césaire, Frantz Fanon, and Amilcar Cabral gave birth to their own radical humanist ideas, developing critiques of the Eurocentric and racist notions of the "human" that drove much of European colonialism, while offering alternative and much more politically capacious, as well as militant, formulations of human liberation. Across the Atlantic, Malcolm X spoke from the Audubon Ballroom in Washington Heights in Manhattan, linking Black Power movements in the US to the anti-colonial revolutions on the African continent. "You can't understand what is going on in Mississippi if you don't understand what is going on in the Congo," he stated. "Today, real power is not local. The only power that can help you and me is international power, not local power."[2]

In this sense, although culturally and geographically disparate writers and movements embraced the term, the Marxist-humanist "era" should not be seen as a homogeneous phenomenon with a singular political logic, but rather as a complex terrain of antagonistic and overlapping positions that reflected the larger political upheavals of the Left, from decolonization and the politics of non-alignment in the global South to Black liberation movements in the United States to the anti-authoritarian and "third way" socialism movements in Eastern Europe.[3]

But even considering this diverse and contradictory legacy, it is hard to understand the pervasive global turn to humanism in the radical political imaginary from the 1960s and '70s without tracing its relationship to political developments in the socialist countries. What transpired in the socialist countries during the post-Stalinist years and how it impacted the rest of the world needs to be revisited with more nuance. There has been some work, rather outdated now, on Central Europe and Yugoslavia.[4] The developments in the Soviet Union, which were central to the rise of humanism, have been left untouched in anglophone scholarship, but also within Eastern Europe itself. This is, of course, partially the result of linguistic and cultural barriers of various sorts. But this invisibility is also an effect of the rigid division that pervades our understanding, a division that stems from the most right-wing and authoritarian tendencies on each side of the Cold War political divide.

Further, the influence of East European political thought during the post-Stalinist era has remained suppressed by a monolithic understanding of the intellectual history of twentieth-century socialism, a framework that subsumes these movements' political diversity and dynamic historical development under the paradigm of "totalitarianism." Privileging dissidents as the main historical subjects of political struggle, the totalitarian framework reduced a complex spectrum of political ideas and a diversity of social movements under socialism to a dichotomy of dissidents versus allies of the regimes. The totalitarian states were seen as static monoliths averse to historical change, located somewhere outside of history, insulated from the rest of the world.

This kind of invisibility or absence is also the effect of the continuous dismissal of the socialist countries, their erasure from the intellectual and political understanding of history, as they were proclaimed by Western liberals and leftists alike as failures, the historical experience of which was unworthy of serious consideration. Even in their most radical formulations, the Left in Western Europe and the United States dismissed from afar the socialist countries in the "Soviet orbit" as totalitarian and authoritarian, corroborating Western mainstream liberal and right-wing arguments. Yet, most liberals and leftists in the West who considered these countries a failure never set foot in them, and, speaking none of their languages, never attempted independent historical or ethnographic research. They relied on dissident Soviet and East European voices that were pro-Western, liberal, and anti-communist, and later, openly pro-capitalist. But while critical of the "totalitarian" states, East European dissidents (most of whom were Eurocentric and oriented toward the West) often supported or collaborated with state power in the "democratic" ones. In other words, the "Western Left" never took the social realities of socialist societies on their own terms, thereby erasing their historical and social specificity and remaining blind to the diversity of social life and the radically communal and autonomous social forms that thrived under socialism.

But even post- and decolonial critiques of global dynamics from the 1980s onwards, which have recentred the formerly colonized countries and the global South, have mostly neglected the role of the socialist countries in the anti-colonial liberation movements and in forging distinct economic, social, and cultural alternatives to global capitalist development and resistant to Western hegemonies. Focused exclusively on "First World"/"Third World" geopolitical dynamics, post-colonial critiques from the 1980s and '90s rarely mention the socialist countries, rendering invisible the geographies of the "Second World" and subsuming them under the frameworks of Western modernity. Much of this disavowal is due to the rigid binaries pervading our understanding of the global political context of the post-Stalinist era, including analyses focusing on East–West, North–South, and even South–South global mobilities and encounters.

EAST EUROPEAN HUMANISM OVER AGAINST STALINISM

Marxist-humanist ideas in Eastern Europe mobilized currents of social and political change. They became the backbone of the anti-Stalinist movements, which called for democracy, political reform, and for a "third way" for socialism's future. "Socialism with a human face" was a common rallying point in many of the protests against authoritarianism and bureaucracy, including the Hungarian uprising of 1956 and the Prague Spring of 1968. In fact, beginning with the early 1960s, almost every socialist country developed its own Marxist-humanist movements and intellectual traditions. In Yugoslavia, the Praxis School gained international prominence, spearheading dialogues on critical issues specific to socialist countries and the international Left more broadly. The local journal *Praxis* (1964–74) published conversations on a number of pressing questions, ranging from the critique of socialist political hierarchy and bureaucracy, to worker-controlled management of production, to the promises and risks of embracing automation, to questions of socialist subjectivity and personhood.[5] In Hungary, a distinct tradition of thought, known as the Budapest School, coalesced around the students and followers of György Lukács. In Czechoslovakia, Karel Kosík's 1963 study *Dialectics of the Concrete*, as well as the work of Ivan Sviták, Robert Kalivoda, and others, energized left intellectuals at roughly the same time that Leszek Kołakowski published *Towards a Marxist Humanism* in Poland. From the 1950s to the 1980s, a new generation of scholars of Marx appeared in the Soviet Union; these included Nikolai Lapin, Georgii Bagaturiia, Merab Mamardashvili, Evald Ilyenkov, Viktor Vaziulin, Genrikh Batishchev, and many others still barely known to readers outside the former socialist world. Many of them were involved in the collective labour of transcribing, translating, and republishing the entire corpus of Marx's writings, including the influential early work known as the *Economic and Philosophical Manuscripts* from 1844, which came out in Russian in 1956. In the People's Republic of Bulgaria, a cluster of progressive sociologists and researchers coalesced around the sociology of youth, a revisionist movement which, informed by humanist ideas and renewed methodologies, took up the task of critiquing socialist society from within, and used their analyses to push for social changes in multiple spheres of life and governance.

These humanist frameworks opened terrains for radical shifts in political organizing and social reform from the 1960s to the end of the 1980s in Eastern Europe. In socialist countries such as Czechoslovakia, Hungary, and Yugoslavia, they gave language to protests against the formation and entrenchment of political elites, the bureaucratization of the system, state repression, the hierarchies of government, and against the alienation of urban life in the socialist city. They took the form of direct oppositional movements, mobilizing collective protest in the streets. In the Soviet Union, Bulgaria, and other socialist countries, humanism provided the political foundation for reforms within the structures of state administration. They changed some entrenched models of the Stalinist system and ushered in social reforms in many spheres of life and governance toward a participatory political and social life.

It is only by turning to the developments under Stalinism that we can understand why the return to the idea of the "human" became so appealing during the post-Stalinist years, and what discursive and political conditions gave rise to it. Marxism-Leninism, the product of Stalinism, was an oversimplified and reductive reading of both Marx and Lenin based on narrow and selective segments of their work, dehistoricized to the extreme. It had an ambitious vision to rewrite the world's knowledge in revolutionary ways, but as a doctrine based on several axioms or unquestionable "rules," it made possible only very limited forms of inquiry and reached many dead ends. Some of these "principles" included the dichotomous base-superstructure model, the basis of Stalinist economic determinism; the "advanced detachment of the Party," the vanguardist and hierarchical relationship between party and masses; and the evolutionary and teleological views of the historical past and future. All these rendered ordinary people passive subjects with no political or historical agency and placed the "arrival of communism" in the hands of the political vanguard.

Considering the structuring limitations of Stalinist thought, the turn to humanism in the 1960s was, at its core, "a revolt against Stalinism," an anti-Stalinist pivot with a "militant, polemic character," in the words of Yugoslavian Praxis philosopher Mihailo Marković.[6] The West European Left understood the turn in similar terms: in the first issue of the *New Reasoner*, a front-line journal for the British humanists that later became known as the *New Left Review*, E.P. Thompson argued that in "Russia the struggle against Stalinism [was] at one and the same time a struggle against the bureaucracy, finding expression in the various pressures for de-centralization, economic democracy, [and] political liberty."[7] It was also a theoretical revolution against the "false consciousness" of Stalinist orthodoxy and intellectual dogmatism, a revolt against its "inhumanity" – "against administrative, bureaucratic, and twisted attitudes towards human beings." Denying creative human agency, Stalinism had turned ordinary people into an "appendage to the instruments of production."[8] In this sense, Thompson argued, the socialist-humanist movement was a "return to man: from abstractions and scholastic formulations to real men ... It is humanism because it places once again real men and women at the centre of socialist theory and aspiration ... It is socialist because it reaffirms the revolutionary perspectives of communism, [and] faith in the revolutionary potentialities ... of real men and women."[9] Thompson asserted that Stalinism tried to suppress the fact that "the 'end' of Communism is not a 'political' end but a human end: or rather, the end of man's transition from the animal, the beginning of man, the assertion of his full humanity."[10]

Dialectical totality, alienation, reification, praxis, and freedom from the realm of necessity – these became central categories in Marxist-humanist thought, which Stalinist Marxism had expelled from its conceptual apparatus. And most importantly, the "human" emerged as a new political subject and an agent of a universal struggle for freedom. Human liberation, human freedom, and human agency became central organizing problems for many post-Stalinist Marxist thinkers and activists, and the assertion that "humans" are creators of their own history found reverberations among the anti-Stalinist Left across geopolitical divides and on multiple continents.

In other words, to imagine an ordinary, everyday subject as an active agent of historical change was quite a remarkable shift from the Stalinist era. Against the economic determinism of previous frameworks, an element of historical contingency reappeared to restore the lost relationship between historical change and collective social agency. This element reinvented ordinary people as active historical subjects and placed them at the centre of historical understanding. In socialist Bulgaria, leading Marxist-humanist philosopher and social theorist Petur-Emil Mitev pointed out that "a new perception begins to establish itself" – namely, "that [in our society] the social world is a product of human activity, that humans can change and improve [their social conditions] as a result of [their] own activity, and that personal contribution and initiative is a necessary element in collective endeavor of group, class, and social activity."[11] To the west, across the Berlin Wall, E.P. Thompson affirmed the vision that "men make their own history: they are part agents, part victims: it is precisely the element of agency which distinguishes them from the beasts, which is the human part of man, and which is the business of our consciousness to increase."[12]

Yet, as much as this new subject – "man" or the "human" – became the foundation for new and radical visions for liberation, it also laid the groundwork for reactionary political developments. By endorsing the opposition, initially present in Marx's early works, between "man" and "animal," "man" and "beast," and "man" and "nature," many of the humanist traditions embraced the evolutionary developmentalism and anthropocentrism of bourgeois and European Enlightenment thought. Often converging with Eurocentric frameworks, they reproduced the colonial premises, anthropocentric binaries, and patriarchal logics of European humanist thought. These ideas form the core of what I will refer to as *hegemonic humanism*. In its hegemonic formulations, post-Stalinist humanism continued to use general, universalizing notions of the human, which remained blind to gender, sexual, racial, and ethnic difference, and adhered to universal notions of "human need" and "human oppression."

Humanists in Eastern Europe and the Soviet Union present similar tendencies. From Mihailo Marković and Gajo Petrović in Yugoslavia, to Petur-Emil Mitev in Bulgaria, to Bronisław Baczko in Poland, the dialectical method and humanist ideas became core conceptual elements in a shared vision of socialist universalism. The socialist "human" was a creature with universal proportions and subsumed various forms of social difference into its sweeping logic; it was a kind of universalism that presumed a male and ethnocentric subject as the subject of universal human emancipation. It also remained blind to the colonial and teleological premises of European knowledge.

Among the Western Marxist philosophers, Louis Althusser was the most unapologetic antagonist of this abstract, universal concept of "man" as the subject of freedom, and his searing critique emerged precisely in this context. For him, addressing the political and philosophical limitations of Stalinist Marxism was an urgent political task of the Left. However, embracing the "human" as a subject of liberation was a tendency he called politically dangerous. The return to the abstract and general concept of the human or "man" (in the singular), ironically and sadly, could only lead to another dead end. In it, he saw the return of bourgeois liberalism and argued that there is a structural juncture between bourgeois liberalism and Marxist humanism. Politically, this kind of "theoretical revisionism" was an anti-militant, reformist tendency that had to be combatted by all means.[13] The concept of "man" was not only liberalism in disguise, but also became a function of a dominant human subject that produced its own exclusions and marginalizations.[14]

Further, hegemonic humanism, even in its left formulations, contained Eurocentric and colonial elements. Anti-colonial and, later, decolonial thinkers showed that Western constructions of "man," premised on regimes of racism and white supremacy and buttressed by Eurocentric notions of civilization and progress, have been central to establishing and maintaining colonial domination. The Western humanist traditions therefore were deeply entangled in the history of colonialism and racism. Their concepts of humanity were central instruments in the production of colonized subjects and regimes of racial superiority. It is not surprising that in the context of anti-colonial liberation struggles, African and Caribbean political thinkers and activists were, in a sense, preoccupied with the theme of the human, deploying it against colonial and racist forms of violence and degradation. In the writings of anti-colonial liberation writers such as Aimé Césaire, Frantz Fanon, and Amilcar Cabral, colonial domination figures as a deeply dehumanizing force, one that strips the colonized of their humanity in a fundamental way. Recuperating the othered subject from the West's underworld, anti- and decolonial visions of humanity became active weapons of resistance against annihilation and historical erasure.[15] This is why Caribbean decolonial philosopher Sylvia Wynter saw the human subject as a historical configuration whose empirical and historical parameters became a terrain of ideological inscription and political reckoning. Her work focused on the intellectual and political traditions of non-Eurocentric humanisms; it called for disrupting orders of knowledge that render the human synonymous with Western "man" and insisted on the open-ended and pluralist meanings of the human.[16]

MAPPING THE BOOK'S TRAJECTORIES

Bulgaria's layered historical experience offers a rich picture as a meeting point of distinct geographies and histories, a context that decentres dominant geographies and complicates homogenous narratives. While unfolding the historical depth and political specificity of Bulgarian post-Stalinism, I found myself at the point of several converging contexts and intersecting bodies of literature: Balkan history and critical Balkan studies, which centre on the shared Ottoman historical legacy of the Balkans and on the region's different movements for national independence; scholarship on Yugoslavian socialism and post-socialism; the vast and rich literature on Soviet socialism; and the literature on Central and East European socialism, with its distinct post–World War II history and a post-socialist fate within the context of the European Union.

Socialist and post-socialist Bulgaria is ambiguously positioned on the cusp of each of these historical and political contexts. Situated on the margins of several geopolitical formations, in the shadow of their historical legacies or political influences, Bulgaria casts a unique light on the worlds it is enmeshed in but never entirely belongs to. The country's ethnic, religious, and gender configurations, its relationship to European fascist and anti-fascist history, and its close but not uncomplicated relationship with the USSR illuminate larger trends in the Balkans, Eastern Europe, the Soviet Union, and beyond. In other words, geography itself becomes a guiding methodology for a post-colonial reassessment that takes as its starting point the peripheries and the margins. Often at the thresholds of multiple worlds, these marginal geographies contain dense historical and cultural layerings, what May Joseph has called "amalgamated" and "synchretic" environments, which disrupt the coherence of homogenous and monochromic narratives.[17]

Throughout the socialist period Bulgaria remained a firm political ally of the Soviet Union and was tethered to it economically. The country's "official course" never had a break with the USSR, like Yugoslavia or Albania did, and never experienced open civil unrest in opposition to Soviet political control, as in the case of Czechoslovakia or Hungary. Yet it is not exactly the case that socialist Bulgaria was a "sixteenth republic," as Bulgarian pro-Western liberals and anti-communists used to call it. Political relations with the Soviet Union were subject to a careful dance. For one, Bulgaria was a small country rich in resources but with limited capacities to develop economies of self-reliance, at least for its ambitious projects of industrial development, and its economies and markets were largely entangled with the economic infrastructure of the USSR, while participating vigorously in the formation of alternative global socialist markets and economies in the socialist and post-colonial worlds. Unlike Yugoslavia, it did not have the political influence to be a major player in global politics; it therefore developed a sort of self-awareness as a "minor" nation and country on the geopolitical stage. The sentiment that the country was doomed to be in the shadow of other superpowers and rely on paternalistic alliances with larger and more powerful siblings has deep roots in Bulgarian national consciousness. Yet in the context of the USSR's direct political control or soft hegemony, Bulgarian socialist society had its own forces of resistance to the Soviets and strong anti-Soviet sentiments were expressed in various ways by dissident and critical voices.

When it comes to national, religious, and ethnic minorities, Lenin's principles of national self-determination and autonomy were adopted during the early socialist period in Bulgaria, yet the country's demographic, historical, and cultural context was very different from the USSR's federal model. Because of a shared Ottoman history, the history of national independence movements, the local histories of fascism and anti-fascism during the interwar period, and various cultural, demographic, and religious affinities, the new socialist country shared more in common with socialist Yugoslavia. But because of frictions over each country's political relations with the Soviet Union, as well as over territories with predominantly Macedonian populations, the socialisms in each of these countries made rather different political journeys. Tensions between nationalist and federalist visions played a role in Bulgaria's soured relationship with Yugoslavia in the years after World War II as much as the two countries' diverging political histories when it comes to the Soviet Union (Yugoslavia's breakup with the Soviet Union and Bulgaria's continued loyalty to it). Instead, Bulgaria built cultural relations and cultural exchanges with the Central Asian republics, and in the early years of socialism the country imported cultural production from Azerbaijan for its Muslim and Turkish-speaking minorities.

The critical analyses developed here speak to these larger and different socialist geographies, but they speak out of the situated historical and political experience of Bulgarian socialism. Because of the imbrications of multiple histories with their own worldly entanglements, the Bulgarian context is quite dense. In it, entwined and colliding worlds coexist in ways that present zones of illegibility or dissonance that are too much to unpack, so this context often suffers either marginalization or simplification. But it also offers a synthesis that disrupts and reorients our navigational tools from the margins of multiple worlds.

Chapter 1 frames the rise of Marxist humanism within the larger intellectual and social context of Eastern Europe and the Soviet Union while taking into account the different "shapes" of socialism. While post-Stalinist socialism cannot be defined entirely in terms of or equated with the humanist turn, humanist discourses and politics had a deep influence on the socialist experience in the Soviet Union, the Balkans, and the East European socialist countries. The chapter traces the intellectual and political work of Soviet, Bulgarian, and Yugoslavian scholars during the post-Stalinist era as they worked to liberate Marx's thought from the fixed, ahistorical renditions of the Stalinist doctrine. As a contribution to Marxist historiography, leading anti-Stalinist Marxists in the Soviet Union and other socialist countries recovered and published Marx's early works, which had been marginalized during the formation of the Marxist-Leninist canon. In particular the chapter traces the historiography of the *Economic and Philosophical Manuscripts* (otherwise known as the *1844 Manuscripts*), Marx's most influential early philosophical work. Scholars and activists were familiar with the text after it was published, first in a partial Russian translation from 1927, part of the first series of Moscow's *Marx-Engels Archive*, and then in a full publication of the German original from 1931. The Russian text omitted crucial parts of the manuscript, including the chapters on alienation, and misidentified it as the preparatory notes to *The Holy Family*, Marx's work from 1845. The first full version of the *1844 Manuscripts* in the Russian language appeared in 1956 in a special volume forming part of the second, post-Stalinist edition of the *Collected Works of Marx and Engels*. That volume, *Iz Rannikh Proizvedenii* (*From the Early Works*), was intended for specialists and published in limited numbers, yet it circulated with great speed across borders and communities. Soon after that the *1844 Manuscripts* came out in the German original, followed by several translations into English, French, and other languages.

Through the *1844 Manuscripts*, post-Stalinists were able to trace the genealogy of materialist critique and reconstruct the historical origins of its formation, bringing to light the conceptual and historical links between Hegelian dialectical thought and Marx's materialist method. Other previously unpublished and unstudied works helped them develop holistic and historically contextual readings of Marx's entire oeuvre, reconstructing the internal structural links in the trajectory of his thought.

The chapter offers new readings of socialist political writings and their contributions to Marxist historiography as post-Stalinist thinkers polemicized their contemporaries from the West and other parts of the world. It reads Soviet, Bulgarian, and Yugoslavian Marxist-humanist writings in comparison and in dialogue, both with each other and with political writers and figures outside the socialist world. While keeping sight of their shared concerns and interests, the chapter discusses the different interpretations and uses of Marx's early works, and their travels and encounters with radical ideas and contexts from other parts of the world. Against dismissive renditions of socialist scholarship from the period, the chapter reconstructs, through a careful comparative analysis, a complex polemical environment that gave birth to a set of political categories unique to the socialist traditions. Along with concepts such as praxis, alienation, dialectical totality, and youth, the "holistically developed person" (*vsestranno razvita lichnost*) became a central concept in East European humanist visions of socialist time, freedom, personhood, democracy, and social integrations. The socialist person was a "holistically" and "harmoniously" developed person: embodying a social micro-universe of sorts, this person overcame dichotomies between private and public, personal and collective, work and leisure, production and social reproduction, and became the subjective expression of developed socialist relations. Under conditions that made possible the full expression of their social, intellectual, and creative potential, the holistically developed person was the living embodiment of a socialist modernity and a socialist way of life. At the same time, the chapter highlights the universalist, monistic, and teleological elements present in the formulations of these categories as a way of foregrounding the core of my critique – it is these elements that enabled humanism's political uses in service of ethnonationalist and pro-nativist visions of socialism.

Chapter 2 revisits the debates on social reproduction from the 1970s and centres them on the contributions from the socialist countries. The concept of social reproduction played a prominent role in the work of anti-Stalinist Marxist humanists in the socialist countries, from studies on gender inequality to education, leisure, the "socialist family," and the "socialist way of life." To a degree that has perhaps gone under-recognized, "reproduction" generally, and "social reproduction" in particular, were central concepts of non-orthodox and anti-Stalinist Marxist thought in Eastern Europe as well as in the West. The range of writings on social reproduction, which appeared more or less coevally in the late 1960s and '70s, including the work of Marxist feminists, Althusser's work on the reproduction of the relations of domination under capitalism, autonomist Marxists in Italy, and others, all came to the concept of social reproduction at the particular juncture of the crisis of Stalinist Marxism in order to criticize its analyses of labour and exploitation and expose the blind spots in its conceptions of working-class struggle.[18]

Inspired by waves of feminist and queer organizing in the streets and on the campuses of the United States, recent scholarship on social reproduction has revisited Marxist-feminist arguments and debates from the 1970s onwards, focusing mainly on work coming from the West European and North American contexts.[19] Less attention has been accorded to contributions around social reproduction coming from the socialist and post-colonial worlds.

Post-colonial feminists showed that Western feminist organizing and theorizing around gender, unwaged labour, and reproduction perpetuated Western capitalist cultural norms and colonial frameworks, othering non-Western social and material practices, rendering them backward and undeveloped. By taking the economic norms and political values of Western capitalist societies as the starting point of their critiques of patriarchal relations in non-Western contexts, they implicitly embraced capitalist development as the vehicle for reforms in the global South.

Similarly, Western Marxist feminism, following a certain kind of scholarly inertia and without serious empirical, ethnographic, or historical research, abounds with simplistic readings of socialist societies and gender relations under socialism. We often encounter reductive pictures of the political economies of socialism: the Western imaginaries see them as productivist and labour- and industry-centric. Socialist society is "work society perfected, with its labors rationally organized, equally required, justly distributed" – a picture that renders the socialist economy as an extension of capitalism, as derivative of the capitalist mode of organization, as capitalism rationalized differently.[20]

But if socialism placed emphasis on industrial development and labour, this was to a large extent a Stalinist paradigm. Post-Stalinist humanists were able to marginalize these frameworks as part of their critiques. They centred their analyses of social relations as well as their visions of "developed" socialism on the problems of free time and leisure, social reproduction and care work, social mobility and social self-realization. In fact, socialist-humanist notions of labour and work (*trud*) departed starkly not only from Western capitalist notions, but also from their formulations during the Stalinist period. Post-Stalinist concepts of work were subordinated to principles of community, leisure, socialist personhood, and to the goals of personal and creative self-realization. They contained strong tendencies toward the abolition of dichotomies between work and leisure. Most importantly, this shift in emphasis on social reproduction and the reproduction of social relations at large meant that the socialist environments from the post-Stalinist period were already open to feminist visions and feminist practices.

Chapter 2 explores the rich contributions of post-Stalinist scholarship to questions of social reproduction, gender relations, sexuality, and socialist constructions of "womanhood" in comparative perspective with Western Marxist-feminist, Black feminist, and post-colonial feminist writings on the subject. While Western feminists picked up the concept in the 1970s, anti-Stalinist Marxist humanists in Eastern Europe had already been talking about it for at least a decade. Their work not only historically preceded Western debates on social reproduction, but also presented a solid theoretical tradition, which evolved from within the specific discursive and social contexts of the post-socialist period and offered its own distinct formulations. With their focus on community, leisure, rest, and socialist personhood, as well as the reproduction of social relations at large, leading post-Stalinist social thinkers and activists radically redefined the meanings of social reproduction. They turned the reproduction of social relations into a major terrain where patriarchal relations could be abolished and where society could be remade according to socialist visions of democracy, equality, and communal forms of life.

Much of their practical efforts were focused on socializing reproductive, domestic, and care work to allow women to pursue realization in the professional and public spheres. Kristen Ghodsee's work offers a detailed account of the extensive social support socialist women received in Bulgaria during the 1970s and '80s, including paid parental leave, free kindergartens and daycare centres, free reproductive health care, communal kitchens, after-school programs, and various in-kind benefits. Contrary to common assumptions that these social and material infrastructures of support were simply "handed down" to women from above, they became a reality thanks to women's relentless organizing and a history of struggle that spans several decades.[21] The work and organizing of these women made social reproduction the centre of their new visions of socialism. They opened new terrains for communal and collective forms of social life and succeeded in socializing and communizing social-reproductive labour in ways that remain unparalleled.

But this legacy had its undersides, which can be seen only if we go beyond the feminist scholarship that stays within heteronormative frameworks or that takes for granted the sweeping generality of the category "women," of heterosexuality and the gender binary. Much of the work on gender from socialist Bulgaria naturalized motherhood and found in women's "nature" a social function central to the building of socialist society. It made women's bodies and lives not only central to the project of building a socialist society, but also placed them at the centre of the ethnonationalist politics of the period. Thus, socialist women's work from the 1970s became deeply embedded in the biopolitical logics of the socialist states, which took a pro-nativist turn while embracing ethnonationalist visions of socialist society. The most active members of the movement generally supported the pro-nativist turn in the 1970s and lent their work to population-management projects.

Chapters 3, 4, and 5 descend deep into the darkest moments in the history of post-Stalinist Bulgaria, showing how the rise of humanism during the post-Stalinist era opened the discursive and political conditions for the rise of ethnonationalism – a historical fate shared by other Balkan and East European socialist countries. These chapters examine the epistemic logics that enabled the ethnonationalist turn and trace their historical manifestations in post-Stalinist Bulgaria. They explore the peculiar convergence between the nationalist and socialist-humanist political projects – a sort of symbiosis championed as the culmination of human struggle and the apex of human freedom.

The analysis in this chapter bears comparative relevance to the political experience of other socialist countries in Eastern Europe, such as socialist Yugoslavia. In a comparative study of socialist Yugoslavia and Bulgaria, Nikolay Karkov and I have already explored how Marxist-humanist discourses in these countries colluded with the ethnic assimilation campaigns and ethnic violence from the period.[22] As Karkov shows, Praxis School members in the former Yugoslavia turned to nationalist ideas and joined "the rising tide of Serbian pan-nationalism" to become "champions of Greater Serbia."[23] Mihailo Marković, one of the Praxis School's most prominent members, became the ideological architect of Milošević's nationalist offensive. Mobilizing civilizational discourses against non-Serbian ethnicities, they saw the principles of ethnic and cultural pluralism espoused by the Yugoslav Federation as the "chief obstacle to the development of socialism," and some of them helped to formulate Milošević's Serbo-centric visions of Yugoslavia.[24] Karkov traces the theoretical continuities that "make manifest the deeply hidden logic" of the relationship between violent ethnonationalism and universal humanism embedded in Praxis's philosophical modalities.[25] The philosophy of Praxis," he states, "never managed to free itself from its colonialist dispositions, from the developmentalist fallacy that pitted its own humanism against the presumed inhumanity of others."[26] This is because Yugoslavian humanists, while resistant to the "West," were still rooted and invested in notions of "man," progress, and rationality, ultimately endorsing the premises of Western modernity and becoming subsumable by its frameworks.

In a similar move, the post-Stalinist government in Bulgaria abandoned earlier models of national, linguistic, and religious pluralism and diversity from the early years of socialism to begin various ethnic assimilation campaigns, which culminated in the so-called "Revival

Process" (*Vuzroditelen protses*). Beginning in the late 1950s and early '60s, the campaigns forced ethnic and cultural assimilation on Turkish, Roma, and Pomak populations by suppressing the practice of their cultures, faith, rituals, and languages, and by forcibly renaming hundreds of thousands of people. By 1989, after a decade marked by demonstrations and unrest, the Revival Process had escalated to the expulsion of several hundred thousand Turkish-identifying Bulgarian citizens into neighbouring Turkey, amounting to the biggest ethnic purge in Bulgaria's modern history. Born and raised for generations in Bulgaria, hundreds of thousands of people left their homes to seek asylum in Turkey, enduring displacement, material dispossession, loss of familial and communal bonds, and a profound disruption of the historical coordinates that anchored their sense of community, belonging, and identity.

While in the former Yugoslavia ethnonationalist politics resulted in inter-ethnic war and the disintegration of the multi-ethnic federal state, the Bulgarian state delivered its political assault on Turkish, Roma, Pomak, and other minorities mainly through assimilationist and social-integrationist agendas that aimed to "modernize" them culturally and historically, causing mass displacement, dispossession, historical erasure, and loss of community. In some sense, these political damages cannot be compared because they took very different political forms. But the ethnonationalist politics of these post-socialist countries in the region, some of which erupted in unforeseen ethnic conflict, were not a product of the 1990s, as is commonly assumed, but rather the continuous effect of the ethnocentric politics of the socialist governments, which began to take shape in the 1960s within a humanist and anti-Stalinist framework.

This is not to imply a simple causal relationship between humanism and ethnonationalism. Yet it was not an accident that Marković and other members of the Yugoslavian Praxis group turned to pan-Serbian nationalism, or that some Bulgarian historians used the new terminology of socialist humanism to formulate a novel ethnonationalist doctrine. These historical turns, while not inevitable, were nevertheless contained as a possibility in the epistemic logics of humanism's dominant tropes, rooted in monistic and universal notions of "man" and the "human," in social progress and social integration, and in the anthropocentric, androcentric, and ethnocentric biases that their conceptual frameworks allowed. In this sense, Marxist humanism was less a rhetorical cover for ethnonationalism than a political discourse containing uncritical ethnocentric notions of "socialism," "society," and the "human."

Chapter 3 studies closely the post-Stalinist doctrine of Bulgarian ethnonationalism in its conceptual or theoretical specificity. It argues that the doctrine emerged from within the specific logics of Marxist humanism and its ideas of freedom, democracy, peoplehood, social mobility, and social integration. The ethnonationalist doctrine was an ideology of ethnic monism. The concept of unity and the thesis of "the common roots" of the Bulgarian people (*obshti rodovi koreni*) became the backbone of humanism's drive toward ethnic homogeneity. Wedded to ideas of historical progress and monistic ideas of the "people," it helped construct a continuous historical narrative of a unified "Bulgarian people" throughout the ages. The suffering and oppression of the people, as well as their struggle for liberation, was to culminate in the socialist present, which carried in itself all the progressive elements of past struggles. Further, socialist discourses on modernization subscribed to notions of socio-economic backwardness and underdevelopment, which were uncritically transported from Western thought, or were part of the imaginaries of a socialist modernity.[27] These notions provided the backbone of the state's developmentalist projects among ethnic and religious minorities, and rendered the Ottoman past a sort of cultural anachronism that socialist modernization and democratization was to overcome.

Chapter 4 builds on the work of historians of nationalism in the Balkans to trace continuities and discontinuities with earlier articulations of ethnonationalism in the region, back to the national independence movements of the nineteenth century. It spells out important and under-theorized differences between the minority politics of the Stalinist and post-Stalinist governments in socialist Bulgaria. As the details around the Revival Process continue to emerge, the majority of existing research has underscored continuities with earlier waves of ethnic assimilations, expulsions, and population exchanges in the Balkans during the late nineteenth and early twentieth centuries. The Revival Process is indeed part of a continuous history of ethnic, linguistic, and religious homogenization in the Balkans dating back to the nation-state-formation projects of the early twentieth century. The ethnonationalist doctrine of the Revival Process adopted earlier uses of language and ethnicity in a return to the pre-socialist period of national independence in an attempt to order national identities rather simplistically along the continuous axis of ethnicity–language–religion. Even as it insisted on the freedom of religious conscience, it triumphantly collapsed religion, language, and "ethnic origin" into a singular measure of difference. This singular continuity was incorporated into the vision of socialist society and became a central vehicle of the effort to accomplish the social integration and mobility that socialist humanism had imagined. Further, consistent with earlier ideas of national consciousness, it reinforced a pre-existing, already antagonized Christianity-Islam dichotomy, and continued to marginalize ethnic, religious, and cultural communities that did not fit neatly within the binary logics of this order.

The historical developments from the 1956–89 period, however, present a kind of specificity shaped by the unique social conditions of the post-Stalinist socialist nation-state, and they follow a distinct historical and political logic. The vast majority of literature on the minority politics of socialist Bulgaria and the Balkans neglects this important difference. Even studies critical of anti-communist and totalitarian frameworks remain hostage to sweeping periodizations and often perceive the "regime" as a single historical monad with a unified political logic. Clumping together earlier and later socialist periods, they fall short in registering not only subtle but also drastic shifts in political orientation. This is a general tendency, but it is even more the case when it comes to minority politics. Most often, the history of socialism is narrated as a single continuum that gradually escalated to the assimilationist politics of the 1980s, and although some nuance is registered in some studies, as in the work of Ulrich Büchsenschütz, the "communist regime" is still seen in monolithic terms.[28]

But further inquiry reveals that the early socialist period in Bulgaria – the years between 1945 and 1956 – marks a radical shift from earlier, pre-socialist policies toward ethnic, cultural, linguistic, and religious minority groups, as well as from the nationalist turn during the later post-Stalinist government. The "new times" (*novoto vreme*), as people used to call the first decade of socialism, represented a brief opening for minorities, subsequently obliterated during the post-Stalinist years. In fact, Bulgarian ethnonationalism was mounted as a resistance to the affirmative model on the national question during Otechestven Front, the first socialist government in power, and framed as its alternative. It also emerged in the wake of the Otechestven Front regime to enact a kind of cultural emancipation from Soviet hegemony.

The 1947 Constitution of the People's Republic of Bulgaria, the first socialist constitution (known as the "Dimitrov Constitution"), was also an anti-fascist constitution. The socialist government ended the persecution and assimilation of national and religious minorities by the pro-fascist governments from the interwar period. The first socialist constitution gave minorities the right to national, linguistic, and cultural self-determination, as well as the right to education and press in minority languages. While the early socialist government experimented with the administrative governance of its own minorities in harmful ways, causing much dispossession and displacement in the process, its politics were generally oriented toward adopting models of socialism that embraced national, linguistic, cultural, and religious pluralism and that looked toward the political experience and the multinational model of emerging socialist Yugoslavia. In the wake of World War II, the two countries explored the possibility of forming a Balkan federation to strengthen local ties and gain more political autonomy in the region.[29]

Leaders of the post-Stalinist government found Otechestven Front's stance on cultural diversity and national self-determination not only untenable for the Bulgarian context but rather dangerous for the national security and territorial integrity of the country. When General Secretary Todor Zhivkov came to power in 1956, one of his first tasks was to dismantle national, cultural, and linguistic self-determination policies and statutes, and later, to introduce radical changes in the constitution (in effect from 1971 to 1990). This was a reactionary setback from the earlier model. The reading offered here challenges established narratives and opens avenues for a difficult reassessment. Seen from the perspective and the historical experience of national, ethnic, and religious minorities, the dominant narrative of the socialist regimes, which frames the transition from Stalinism to post-Stalinism to late socialism as a shift from repression to liberalization, is turned upside down and completely inverted.

Chapter 5 chronicles the events of the Revival Process and the heroic histories of resistance, including several village uprisings in communities that were turned into autonomous zones of sorts. It recounts the brutal repression of these movements, as well as the multiple forms of refusal, negotiation, and survival that the people engaged in while coming to terms with the monstrous proportions of this campaign and navigating its contradictions. The chapter describes the ethnocentric and assimilationist politics of the post-Stalinist state, which

I call "ethno-statism." Using existing research, primary documents, and first-person accounts, I show that the institutions of population management, social welfare, education, health care, and housing – the very institutions that ensured social mobility and democratic access to resources, labour, education, health, and the infrastructure of social services – also became the most powerful instruments of ethnic assimilation.

The question of state power is important here, and indeed throughout the book, as the socialist models of the twentieth century have been appropriately called statist or *étatist* forms of socialism. For the most part, humanists in Western as well as Eastern Europe had no radical critique of the state, remaining pro-statist in some form or another or implicitly endorsing the state, even in their autonomist currents. Although developed as a left critique and an alternative to the Stalinist state and its administrative hierarchies, the humanist movements remained state-centric, foreclosing the possibility of imagining autonomous forms of communism that transcend or abolish the state form. They did not consider a radical critique of the state, but celebrated state power and state-centric historical narratives, positing the state as the privileged point of historical origin for the "people." A critique came largely from the dissident, anti-communist tendencies, and they used mainly liberal concepts of totalitarian power to explain and critique the socialist state. Yet, in post-Stalinist Bulgaria, other non-Marxist, anti-statist traditions were able to regain some strength, including anarchist movements, the social movements and land collectives influenced by the Russian writer and social thinker Lev Tolstoy, and various egalitarian mysticisms, such as the movements influenced by mysticist philosopher Petur Dunov. These social phenomena are under-studied – they require further research and deserve the focus of a separate study.

The embrace of ethnonationalism stood in stark contrast to the politics socialist Bulgaria forged in the global sphere. The socialist global imaginaries from the 1960s and '70s were built on anti-colonial, anti-imperialist, and anti-racist principles that aimed to reorder the geographies of power and the circulation of knowledge away from the Euro-American capitalist world. A growing body of research has returned to these marginalized cross-continental histories in new ways. It has challenged existing narratives and offered new methodologies, opening yet wider horizons for decolonizing the historiographies of radical political movements during the 1960s and '70s.[30] The picture that emerges out of this collective research suggests that the relations between the formerly colonized countries and the socialist world, although deeply entangled in Cold War politics, cannot be easily explained through the main tropes of Cold War political rationality – economic interest and gain, spheres of political and economic influence, imperial expansion, and geopolitical competition. These relations were not unidirectional but multi-faceted, marked by what David Engerman has called a "multipolarity" of interactions and dynamics, including Sino-Soviet, pan-African, Sino-African, and Afro-Asian relations, and more. Instead, as Rossen Djagalov and Masha Salazkina argue, the socialist countries were situated at the intersection of multiple hegemonies. The global convergences they made possible on their terrains and globally, through substantial material, cultural, and political support, destabilized fixed dynamics and opened new possibilities.[31] The bridges between the socialist East and the global South built during and after decolonization became a way of uprooting the colonial legacy and resisting the reproduction of colonial power in the post-colonial nations – all the while bringing political energy and inspiring social radicalism in the socialist East. These connections forged alternative global alignments and worldly imaginaries for the socialist youth resistant to capitalist and Western hegemonies.

Chapter 6 explores the perplexing overlaps between socialist Bulgaria's anti-colonial politics in the global context of the 1960s and '70s and the country's embrace of ethnonationalism domestically. The chapter follows the coverage of international events during this period in progressive youth journals and newspapers, including the civil rights and Black Power movements in the United States, anti-colonial independence struggles against the Portuguese in Africa, and the war in Vietnam and the protests against it in the United States and internationally. At the same time, the international support for the people struggling against colonialism, imperialism, and racism that socialist Bulgaria projected in the global sphere converged in the most uncanny ways with the ethnic assimilation campaigns within the country.

These discordant moments, the chapter argues, are embedded in the specific political logics of Bulgarian nationalism from the post-Stalinist period. With its subaltern and revolutionary elements, its global-humanist orientations, and its commitment to socialist modernization and social progress, the nationalist imaginaries of the post-Stalinist period constructed analogies and political links between nineteenth-century Bulgarian struggles for national independence from the Ottoman Empire and the anti-colonial national liberation movements and the nation-building projects in the post-colonial context. These were often discursive metaphorical formations that stretched incompatible historical realities. They make the post-Stalinist decades in Bulgaria a manifold environment in which subaltern and decolonial elements cohabitated with quasi-colonial and Eurocentric logics, and in this way opened the way for different and conflicting political agendas.

These tensions can also be seen as the different facets of what Michael David-Fox has called "multiple" modernities and their transcontinental "entanglements," which the socialist worlds have been enmeshed in and have set in motion in the global sphere.[32] Socialist modernities were organized around distinctly socialist concepts of equality, community, leisure, public access, and social mobility, all these woven around legacies of anti-capitalist, anti-fascist, anti-colonial, and national liberation movements. At the same time, they were committed to social progress, modernization, and industrial and infrastructural development with their own teleologies and universals.

With all their contradictions, the persistence of the socialist countries throughout the twentieth century produced a kind of historical and temporal displacement that disrupted the totalizing spatial movement of capitalism and its unified world history – and reordered the world with a force. Their radical political promises, as well as the disturbing political directions that they took, leave an uneven historical legacy, a legacy rife with tensions and ambivalent moments. Yet it is a troubled history whose ghostly and material presence continues to haunt the post-socialist present and shape the spectrum of forces that unfolded in Bulgaria and Eastern Europe after 1989. The conclusion, then, dwells on the contested meanings of the socialist period in post-socialist political life, on the continuities and ruptures with the socialist past. It discusses emergent and historical possibilities for building an alternative politics after the end of twentieth-century socialist projects.

1

Journeys of the *1844 Manuscripts*: Historiographic Shifts in Marxist Thought

Iz rannikh proizvedenii (*From the Early Works*) is a rare book in the former socialist world.[1] In Bulgaria, the physical copy of the book is hard to come by – even backup library copies are missing. One's best chance of getting a hold of it is to know the people who have a copy in their personal libraries and to hope that they'll have enough trust in you to lend it. Published in 1956, this was the first book in the socialist world to make available a significant number of Marx's early works. It also contains the first full version of Marx's *Economic and Philosophical Manuscripts*, known as the *1844 Manuscripts*, which were translated into Russian directly from the handwritten German-language manuscript. This "odd" volume, part of the second and complete edition of the *Collected Works of Marx and Engels* yet separate from the numerical series, was printed in significantly reduced numbers and was meant only for readers with scholarly interest in Marx and Engels. Yet despite the projections of the editors and its reduced print run, during the post-Stalinist years it became one of the most influential of Marx's philosophical works, a text that defined the era in significant ways. Written between April and August 1844, it was partially published in Russian in 1927 and appeared in full in the German original in 1932. But it wasn't until the latter part of the 1950s and the early 1960s that, together with other early works by Marx and Engels, it gained wider circulation through publication in Russian, German, English, French, and other languages.

The humanism of the *1844 Manuscripts* became a defining framework for the radical political imaginaries of the post-Stalinist period in Eastern Europe and beyond. The publication of Marx's early works significantly changed established historiographical narratives of

Marxist thought and opened possibilities for new forms of organizing and global solidarities for struggles against authoritarianism, racism, colonialism, and capitalist exploitation in North America, Eastern Europe, and the global South.

This chapter traces the publications, translations, and journeys of the *1844 Manuscripts* and situates the significance of Marx's early works in light of the political context of the 1960s and '70s, both in the socialist countries and globally. Centring on the Bulgarian, Soviet, and Yugoslavian Marxist-humanist traditions in a global-comparative perspective, the chapter reconstructs the diverse uses of Marx's humanist thought and the political critiques it mobilized in the Soviet and East European contexts. The *1844 Manuscripts* shed new light on Marx's revolutionary thought and his writings on political economy and radically revised the canonical interpretations of both the earlier and later works in circulation. Through the *1844 Manuscripts*, post-Stalinist scholars in the socialist countries reconstructed the genealogy of materialist critique and the historical origins of its formation, bringing to light the conceptual and historical links between Hegelian dialectical thought and Marx's materialist method. Other previously unpublished or marginalized works, such as *The Grundrisse* and *Theories of Surplus Value*, also emerged during this period. These works gave socialist scholars access to Marx's creative laboratory and helped them gain a larger and more holistic sense of the trajectory of his thought and thereby reconstruct previously unexplored links and continuities.

Against Stalinist renditions of Marx's work, humanists insisted on the emancipatory powers of concepts such as alienation, reification, praxis, human freedom, and human self-realization. Concepts such as production, labour, and class – the language of orthodox and Stalinist Marxism – gave way to interest in social reproduction, free time, and socialist subjectivity and personhood, all subordinated to the needs of community, leisure, creative work, and personal and social self-realization. Most importantly, the "human" emerged as a new political subject and an agent of struggle for freedom, and human liberation, human freedom, and human agency became central organizing problems in much post-Stalinist Marxist thought. The "holistically developed person," a leading concept in East European Marxist humanism, was a kind of socialist-humanist subject who organized the political imaginary and became the measure of social relations at large, a micro-universe of sorts and a reflection of the totality of social relations.

While these concepts played a central organizing role in post-Stalinist political thought, their interpretations, meanings, and political uses were nonetheless diverse. Tracing debates among and points of divergence between the Soviet, Yugoslavian, and Bulgarian humanist traditions, this chapter seeks to ground the political meanings and uses of these terms within the particular socio-political contexts they spoke to. At the same time, the chapter explores the ambivalent political effects of humanist thought in the socialist countries, which left a historical legacy strained by the tensions of its own contradictions. In their hegemonic formulations, I argue, the humanist traditions subscribed to totalizing visions of society, monistic concepts of the social whole, and universalizing notions of humanity, which converged with ethnocentric and ethnonationalist visions of socialism. The turn toward ethnonationalism during the post-Stalinist period was, while not historically inevitable, by no means accidental. It was contained as a possibility within the epistemic logics of the humanist traditions, at least within their hegemonic versions. As subsequent chapters will show, humanist notions of social mobility, social emancipation, and democracy became a vehicle for the integrationist and ethno-assimilationist politics of the post-Stalinist governments from the 1960s on.

The dominant versions of these humanisms were also manifestly male-centric and patriarchal, as the languages capture the easy convergences and slippages between "man" and the "human." As they adhered to universal notions of human freedom and socialist personhood, many of the writings discussed in this chapter remained blind to gender, sexual, racial, and ethnic difference, imagining a human subject who stood for men – of the dominant ethnicity, race, and sexuality. Yet as chapter 2 shows, humanist visions were also picked up by socialist women activists, who moved them in feminist directions and found in them the open spaces to transform gender relations in profound ways.

THE *1844 MANUSCRIPTS* IN PRINT AND TRAVEL

The majority of Marx's early manuscripts are held in the Institute of Marxism-Leninism in Moscow. They were obtained in the early 1920s by what was then called the Institute of Marx-Engels. Founded in 1921, the institute was the first and largest research facility dedicated to the collection, preservation, study, research, and publication of the work of Marx and Engels, and the history of Marxism and the revolutionary movements more generally. It was later renamed twice and eventually became the Institute of Marxism-Leninism at the Central Committee of the Communist Party of the Soviet Union (TsK na KPSS). By 1921, the institute had begun building an archive pertaining to the lives and work of Marx and Engels and the revolutionary movements from the nineteenth and early twentieth centuries, obtaining a large number of original manuscripts, archival documents, historical materials, and collections of nineteenth-century radical literature on the bourgeois revolutionary, anarchist, utopian socialist, and proletarian movements from England, France, Germany, the United States, Russia, Eastern Europe, and other parts of the world. In addition to the vast collection of books on history, philosophy, and political economy, which included large parts of the personal libraries of Marx and Engels and other revolutionaries, the archive collected troves of pamphlets, periodicals, fliers, books, and underground publications, which by the beginning of the 1930s amounted to 45,000 titles, 15,000 original documents, and 175,000 photocopies organized in five different sections.[2]

In the meantime, the institute had formed a team of researchers solely for the purpose of "deciphering" Marx and Engels's handwritten texts, "a gigantic and complex task requiring tremendous erudition, marvelous command of European languages, and the skills of deciphering Marx's extremely small and difficult handwriting, with which he managed to fill one sheet of paper with up to ten regular pages of text."[3] By 1928, the institute had launched several ambitious projects aimed at translating and publishing the writings and correspondence of Marx and Engels. Of particular significance were the first multi-volume series of collected works in Russian, *Works* (*Sochineniia*), and in German (*Marx-Engels-Gesamtausgabe*, or MEGA), which over the years appeared in two subsequent editions. In addition, the institute published *Arkhiv K. Marksa i F. Engel'sa* (*The Marx-Engels Archive*), designed to accompany the collected works and aid the work of Russian-speaking researchers and specialists in the field (rather than to reach a wider readership), and *Letopisi Marksizma* (*Annals of Marxism*), which collected mostly correspondence related to on-the-ground revolutionary and organizing work, including but not limited to Marx and Engels's correspondence.[4]

The *Marx-Engels Archive* featured the first (and incomplete) publication of the *1844 Manuscripts*, which came out in 1927 in volume 3 of the series.[5] Published in Russian translation, together with the first publication of Marx's *Critique of Hegel's Philosophy of Right*, it was misidentified and titled as "Preparatory Notes for the 'Holy Family.'" The publication omitted many parts of the text, including the chapter on alienation, and included chapters on private property and labour and private property and communism, along with Marx's critique of Hegel's dialectical philosophy. In the context of the late 1920s, when abolishing private property and establishing new regimes and categories of ownership were pressing political tasks, these selections made sense.

Five years later, in 1932, the Marx-Engels Institute published the full text in the German original in the first edition of the *Marx-Engels Gesamtausgabe* (MEGA). Between 1924 and 1973, the *Marx-Engels Archive* published twenty volumes of Marx and Engels's manuscripts, preparatory notes, and historical studies in two series. Following Stalin's reforms of the institute in the early 1930s, David Riazanov, a Marxist philosopher, historian, and organizer who edited the first five volumes of the series (1924–30), was purged, and the editorial team was completely reshaped. The institute resumed the *Marx-Engels Archives* under a different editorial team (volumes 1–15, 1933–73), marginalizing the first sequence and erasing continuities with it. Thus for thirty years, Marx's early works, although partially available, were stored away and ignored.[6]

STALINISM AS A DOCTRINE

The revival of interest in the early works during the mid-1950s can best be understood within the context of Stalinist Marxism and its structuring limitations for social inquiry and critique. The doctrine of Marxism-Leninism didn't cohere until the early 1930s, and was only fully elaborated in the *History of the Communist Party of the Soviet Union (Bolsheviks)*, known as the *Short Course* – what one could call the exemplary work of high or mature Stalinism. The book, an ambitious project, came out in multiple editions between 1938 and 1956 and was reprinted over three hundred times. It was translated into sixty-seven languages and widely disseminated around the world. It provided a narrative of the history of the communist movement in Russia and also the foundations and the general methodology for the natural sciences and the historical and social disciplines – Dialectical Materialism and Historical Materialism, or *Diamat* and *Istmat*, as they were often called (abbreviated from *Dialekticheskii materializm* and *Istoricheskii materializm*).

Diamat and *Istmat*, the main philosophical subfields that organized the Stalinist epistemologies of knowledge, constructed a rigid dichotomy between the economic and material organization of life, or the "base," and the "superstructure," which included knowledge, consciousness, and political institutions. All that belonged to the "superstructure" was considered secondary to the "base." Even though it called itself "dialectical," the Stalinist philosophical system thus affixed a two-dimensional, non-dialectical relationship of representation between "base" and "superstructure," where the "superstructure" was derived from the primary economic, material relations.

Further, *Diamat* and *Istmat* skillfully eliminated the knowing subject from the study of social processes in order to establish the positivist methodologies of its knowledge systems. All social and historical processes were objectively knowable by means of scientific method, and thereby, in Stalin's words, "the history of society ceases to be an agglomeration of 'accidents'; [it] becomes a development of society according to regular laws, and the study of the history of society becomes a science."[7] Because it was scientifically knowable, historical progress could be studied with recourse to a science of social phenomena and with the aid of a systematic methodology, which identified the "correct" vanguard historical elements, analyzed them, transformed them into normative instruments, and redeployed them back onto historical reality to accelerate its movement.[8] According to a projected historical teleology, then, historical contingencies became "deviations" and departures from the "correct" and "truthful" line of development; the multiplicity of social forces were turned into contaminations; the spectrum of available political discourses, identities, and configurations were mapped onto an evolutionary plane of retrograde and vanguard forces, where "being a reformist means to be on the bad side of history," and where all critique and interpretation is a threat, an enemy, a deviation.[9]

The only active agent in history became the party, whose legitimacy was grounded in the teleological inevitability of historical development. Perhaps the most defining feature of Stalinist theory, the "advanced detachment of the party," was a vanguardist concept that rendered the "masses" a sort of backward, unknowing subject that had to be "led" into the right course of history.

All these points had the status of doctrinaire axioms, which were not subject to questioning or critique. Their simplicity and rigidity also generated many inconsistent moments and logical contradictions within the doctrine. These contradictions were left over as remnants of an obliterated dialectical method, which grasped the manifest contradictions of social forces as the enabling conditions for historical change while relocating history's metabolic force in the practical activity of the people.

Henri Lefebvre, in his book *Dialectical Materialism*, thoroughly critiqued this move. This small and now marginalized study seems to be one of the earliest humanist critiques of the Stalinist doctrine. Lefebvre published parts of his critique as early as 1935, which put him in sharp conflict with the French Communist Party. His study contains an astute diagnosis of Stalinism's reductive rewritings of Marx. In the foreword to the fifth edition of the book, published in 1961, he noted that we are just "beginning to see and know better what took place" under Stalinism.[10] Marxism-Leninism's drive toward a positivist methodology, even if it called itself "dialectical," had developed tremendous hostility to the dialectic: "[Stalinists] became more contemptuous than ever of Hegel and Hegelianism, they rejected Marx's early writings as being tainted with idealism and as having preceded the formulation of dialectical materialism, they drew a line between Marx and his predecessors and another one between the so-called philosophical and so-called scientific works in the Marxian corpus."[11]

Lefebvre saw that Stalinist philosophy had declared a war on Hegel and the Hegelian aspects of Marx's thought, suppressing the deep continuities and complex junctures that define the relationship between Marx and Hegel, Feuerbach, and other young Hegelians in the early writings. At a time when "dogmatism is crumbling and dissolving," he wrote, "the early writings of Marx have become of the first importance."[12] He devoted a significant number of years to restoring Hegel's influence on Marx and Lenin in the French-language historiography on Marx, publishing the first French translation of Lenin's *Philosophical Notebooks* in 1938.[13]

Similar critiques appeared in the socialist world: in Yugoslavia, Praxis group philosopher Mihailo Marković wrote that the doctrine, while paying lip service to the dialectical method, in fact reduced the dialectic to simplistic dichotomies and dogmatic formulations. "The use of dialectical phraseology created an illusion of continuity and method," he claimed, but the elimination of the dialectical method had "fatal consequences": it prevented the grasp and analysis of social contradictions within socialism itself, seeing all undesirable social phenomena manifest in the new social order as part of reactionary, bourgeois forces. "When everything negative is construed as only a 'remnant of bourgeois and petty-bourgeois consciousness in the heads of people,' it is impossible for any new contradictions to arise in the process of socialist development."[14] In other words, Stalinism disabled the power of Marxist critique to engage self-reflectively in social reality in the present, to deliver a critical analysis of social relations in the new socialist societies then being constructed. "On the one hand," Marković remarked,

> there was a society in which all important decisions were said to follow from scientific insights into social necessity, which was so rational that no errors were possible; and on the other hand, there was the same society ruled by the arbitrary decisions of a few leaders, without social sciences in the proper sense, i.e. without objective and critical examination of its structure, its centers of power, its inner tensions and conflicts, and the way of life, attitudes, and morals of its various social groups.[15]

Perhaps most aware of these limitations were Soviet scholars themselves, who worked directly with the manuscripts and primary materials. In 1954, soon after Stalin's death, the institute moved to publish a new edition of the collected works of Marx and Engels, although preparations had begun almost a decade earlier.[16] Consisting of twenty-eight volumes (1928–46), the first Stalinist edition was still considered the result of a great collective scholarly effort, yet in the postwar years Soviet scholars conceded that it had "a number of flaws": some of these included inaccuracies in the translations and in the prefaces; an incomplete reference apparatus (for example, the volumes contain no annotations); texts that were wrongly attributed to Marx and Engels; and works of "great political and scholarly interest" that were omitted.[17] Further, new and unknown works, letters, and documents were continually emerging. In the decade following World War II, the institute obtained a large number of originals and photocopies of letters, manuscripts, and historical documents from France, England, Italy, Austria, Czechoslovakia, Hungary, and the Netherlands – none of which were included in the first edition of the *Collected Works*.[18] The need for a second edition had already emerged while the first one was still in the process of being completed.[19]

POST-STALINIST REVISIONS

The second Russian edition, known as the *Complete Works of Marx and Engels*, consisted of fifty volumes and a scholarly apparatus of six additional books. The first volumes began to appear as early as 1955 and the series was completed over a stretch of three decades (1955–86). For years, it was the most complete – indeed, the only – scholarly publication of Marx and Engels's body of work in Russian translation. To this day it is succeeded only by the second edition of MEGA in the original languages, which was launched much later, in 1975, as a collaboration between Moscow and East Berlin. The second Russian edition included a number of Marx and Engels's writings that were omitted, unknown, suppressed, or heavily edited and mistranslated during the publication of the first edition.[20] In addition, new and unknown manuscripts, letters, and other materials continued to emerge after the series had already been mapped out and launched. At first the series was projected at thirty volumes, yet as soon as the first books began to appear, it became clear that the process of selection was highly "subjective"; it would be impossible to predict which documents would be of interest to a larger audience, and which ones to "a narrow circle of specialists." To address this potentially varied readership, the institute extended the series with another nine volumes.[21]

The editorial team decided that the *1844 Manuscripts* and a few other early works, including Marx's doctoral dissertation and the preparatory notes for it, would be of interest only to a specialized audience, and so excluded these from the numerical series; instead, these were compiled into a separate volume of selected early works.[22] Thus the first full Russian version – of the *1844 Manuscripts* came out in 1956 in an "odd" volume called *Iz rannikh proizvedenii* (*From the Early Works*), separate from the *Collected Works*, and was released in significantly reduced numbers – 60,000 copies, compared to the usual 200,000 for each numerical volume. Appearing after most early works had already been published in the first four volumes of the *Collected Works*, Marx and Engels's *Iz rannikh proizvedenii* occupies an ambiguous status as both separate and inseparable from the series. The result of a strange displacement or aberration, it is still frequently considered part of the series and sometimes referred to as "volume 0."

By 1965, the institute had completed the projected thirty-nine volumes and several other stand-alone collections of selected works, similar to *Iz rannikh proizvedenii.* In the ensuing years, the institute extended the series with another eleven volumes (volumes 40–50, 1970–86) under a new team of anti-Stalinist Marxist scholars. These last publications were meant to incorporate missing or new material – such as the *Grundrisse* and the *1844 Manuscripts* – not originally included in the series. Thus a second Soviet edition of the complete *1844 Manuscripts* came out almost two decades later, this time fully integrated into the *Collected Works* (volume 42, 1974).

Back in the 1950s, socialist scholars seized on the "odd" volume immediately, and even though the book came out in more limited numbers, it began circulating widely in the Soviet Union and beyond.[23] Within the next several years, Soviet and socialist scholars produced numerous interpretations of the early works. They traced the genealogy of materialist critique and reconstructed the historical origins of its formation, shedding the Stalinist legacy and re-historicizing Marx's work. By recovering the continuous evolution, dynamism, and instability of his thought, they decanonized it and liberated it from the fixed, ahistorical renditions produced under Stalinism.[24]

One of the earliest interpretations of the *1844 Manuscripts* belongs to Soviet scholar Nikolai Lapin, a student of the prominent Soviet philosopher Teodor Oizerman.[25] A detailed historical reconstruction of the philosophical context of the early 1840s, his book *Molodoi Marks* (*The Young Marx*), with its extensive analysis and historical detail, remains to this date one of the most marvelous interpretations of the early works of Marx to come out of the Soviet and socialist worlds. Lapin studied the *1844 Manuscripts* in the context of Marx's "Contribution to the Critique of Hegel's Philosophy of Right," "Introduction to the Critique," and the "Jewish Question" as they led to his "Theses on Feuerbach" and *The German Ideology.*

Soviets were well acquainted with the latest debates in the West and engaged forcefully with these polemics – especially the so-called "continuity-discontinuity" debates opened by the publication of the *1844 Manuscripts* and other early works. What was the relationship between the early and the later works, the "young" and the "mature" Marx? To some, especially in the West, Marx's early "philosophical" and "humanist" writings were so surprising in light of the later work, which appeared more like "political economy," that it almost seemed as if they were written by two different people. In Althusser and

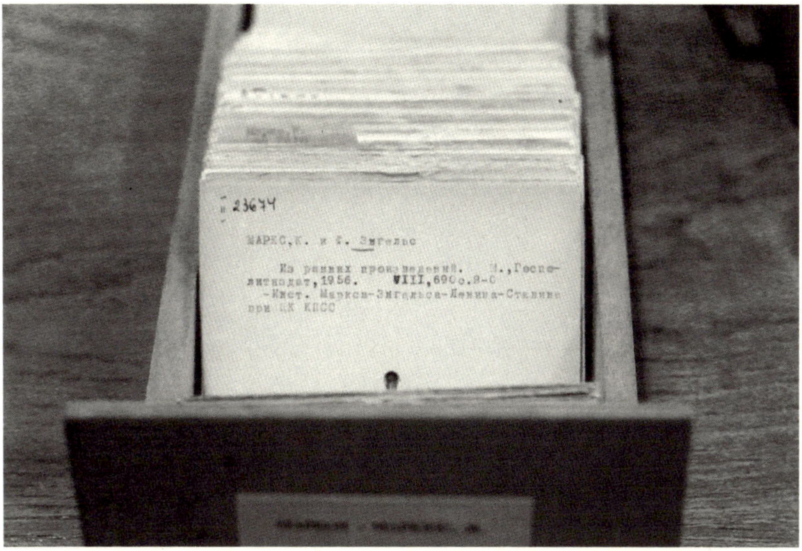

Figure 1.1 The catalogue entry for Marx and Engels's *Iz pannikh proizvedenii* (1956) in Plovdiv's Public Library Ivan Vazov, which contains the full version of the *1844 Manuscripts*. Because the book was in high demand, library copies are often missing; such is the case in Plovdiv, where the copies have been lost.

Balibar's interpretation, there was a "radical break" between the two.[26] The Soviets came to dismantle this Western "myth of the two Marx's." It contained hidden political agendas that needed to be exposed.[27] According to Lapin, liberals, reformists, and anti-communists in the West used the *1844 Manuscripts* to privilege the young Marx and claim that the later Marx abandoned his humanist foundations, thus neglecting his critique of capitalist relations and its mediating social forms as they mystified class domination.[28] Soviet Marxists considered these "bourgeois left" and "bourgeois revisionist" moves, which used the young Marx against the later one to marginalize the importance of his critique of capitalist relations. Others, like Louis Althusser, pushed hard against the tendency to privilege the early works to the point of renouncing them, arguing that they showed Marx as a hostage to bourgeois idealist philosophy.

Against the first tendency – to depoliticize Marx and tame the class struggle – but without resorting to Althusser's manoeuvre of disowning the early works, Soviet thinkers developed a holistic and historically contextual reading of the *1844 Manuscripts*. Lapin used the *1844 Manuscripts* as a window into the historical formation and internal development of Marx's entire oeuvre, reconstructing the internal structural continuities in the trajectory of his thought.[29] He identified the "consecutive nodes" that led Marx to the formation of his later critique of political economy and traced the uninterrupted structural continuities that tied them together.

These studies became possible because over the next two decades several other major works, which gave the Soviets access to Marx's "creative laboratory," were made available for the first time. Between 1960 and 1962 the institute published the full version of all three volumes of *Capital* (volumes 23–25, part 1 and 2), followed by the full version of the *Theories of Surplus Value*, the draft of the fourth volume of *Capital*, published between 1962 and 1964 (volume 26, parts 1–3); in 1968–69, the *Grundrisse*, or the first draft of *Capital*, came out (volume 46, parts 1 and 2), followed by the *Economic Manuscripts* between 1961 and 1963, the second draft of *Capital* (volumes 47 and 48), chapter 6 of volume 1 of *Capital*, which Marx had taken out of the text (volume 49) and the first version of volume 2 of *Capital* (volume 49).[30] Thus, against established readings arguing that Marx abandoned his interest in philosophy and his humanist views to venture into the world of political economy and privilege the structural logics of capitalism over the agency of the people, Soviets interpreted the *1844 Manuscripts* as a work of political economy and *Capital* as a work of dialectical-materialist philosophy, and a profoundly humanist one at that.[31] Soviet philosopher Georgii Bagaturiia, who spearheaded much of the second edition of the *Collected Works* of Marx and Engels, found in the *1844 Manuscripts* the first synthesis of Marx's philosophical, political-economic, and communist ideas: "It was the first economic work by Marx, the starting point of a long process that led him to *Capital*." In actuality, he continues, "the *1844 Manuscripts* appear as the philosophical preface to his critique of political economy."[32]

Similar arguments appeared in Bulgaria. Petur-Emil Mitev, prominent Bulgarian philosopher, social theorist, and sociologist, argued against "bourgeois claims" that the mature Marx underestimated the question of individual, personal, and human freedom and insisted that Marx's greatest contribution in his later life was in fact "real" humanism.[33] "At a certain time," wrote Mitev, "the human factor becomes defining. The intellectual and creative force of humans becomes the primary importance to all production. Alienation comes forth as a barrier for human development."[34] Mitev saw Marx's categorical apparatus as having a "synthetic" character, and he argued that, holistically speaking, his work could be defined variously as philosophy, sociology, political economy, or scientific communism, because it contained all of these.[35]

In the meantime, the *1844 Manuscripts* had been slowly making inroads into the West as scholars gained partial access to earlier versions of the manuscript. In the United States, Marxist-humanist philosopher and activist Raya Dunayevskaya had translated parts of the text on her own; she worked for years to persuade publishers of academic and left literature to publish the work, yet under the weight of McCarthyism, she had little success. "For fifteen long years," she wrote to Erich Fromm, "I tried in vain to get a publisher and couldn't."[36] She translated the work from the incomplete 1927 Russian edition and had Marcuse compare the translation to the original German text – so she only included the chapters "Private Property and Communism" and the "Critique of the Hegelian Dialectic." She finally published these two chapters in 1958 as part of the appendix to her first book, *Marxism and Freedom*, together with parts of *Philosophical Notebooks*, Lenin's extensive notes on Hegel.[37] Even then, as she reports later, "they did not become available to a mass audience."[38]

By 1959, Moscow had published an English translation of the full version of the *1844 Manuscripts* through their Foreign Languages Publishing House (later renamed Progress Publishers).[39] Two years later, Erich Fromm included another translation of the *Manuscripts* as part of his 1961 book *Marx's Concept of Man*, and it wasn't until then, Dunayevskaya observes, that the work "reached [a] mass audience in the United States and received widespread attention in American journals."[40] But even though she took credit for the years of work that went into making it available to English-speaking readers, Dunayevskaya did not engage in the "intellectual arrogance of [West] European Marxologists" who claimed to have originated the discussions and generated interest in the work through their scholarship alone. Against such intellectual elitism, she argued that the political and historical relevance of the work was made possible only through a series of upheavals in the 1960s, including the Hungarian Revolution of 1956, the rise of automation in US factories, and anticolonial struggles in Africa. It is only in the context of these events that "the discussion of humanism reached the level of either concreteness or urgency."[41]

In the early 1960s, dialogues began to form among West European Marxist humanists, Marxist humanists from the Praxis School in Yugoslavia, humanists from other East European socialist countries, and revolutionaries from the formerly colonized world and the global South. These dialogues appeared in the Yugoslavian journal *Praxis* and in several stand-alone volumes, such as Erich Fromm's *Socialist Humanism* (1965) and Carl Oglesby's *The New Left Reader* (1969), and through the voices of Frantz Fanon, Fidel Castro, Malcolm X, Huey Newton, Léopold Senghor, Herbert Marcuse, Erich Fromm, Karel Kosík, Ivan Sviták, Raya Dunayevskaya, Bronisłav Baczko, Iring Fetscher, and others. They shaped a new global imaginary that connected movements on the left across continents and transcended Cold War antagonisms, bringing together struggles against racism in the United States, domestic and international opposition to US imperialism, anti-colonial liberation movements in Africa, pro-democracy and "third way" socialism movements in Eastern Europe, and working-class struggles in the developed capitalist world.[42]

ALIENATION A THOUSAND WAYS

Alienation became a powerful critical concept in these writings and dialogues. In light of the contemporary political moment and the social contexts that it spoke to, its meaning was an object of intense contestation. Was it a kind of social condition specific to capitalist societies, with their liberal, democratic governments? Or could we speak about alienation in socialist societies? Was it a product of a kind of modernity and the modernization of life shared by both socialism and capitalism, through industrial development, urbanization, and all these seemingly similar features of the modern age?

Western humanists thought the concept made the Stalinists particularly vulnerable as it promised to expose the "ideological and political alienations inside socialism."[43] They found the notion flexible and open enough to escape the confines of bourgeois society, a concept that offered a valuable tool for a critical analysis of material and social relations within the socialist systems. In Western Europe and the United States, alienation therefore served as a vehicle for a critique of social relations in developed industrial societies that transcended Cold War oppositions between socialism and capitalism. It was a concept that promised a common ground for the anti-Stalinist Left on both sides of the Iron Curtain. In the words of E.P. Thompson,

> the ideologies of capitalism and Stalinism are both forms of "self-alienation": men stumble in their minds and lose themselves in abstractions: capitalism sees human labor as a commodity and the satisfaction of his "needs" as the production and distribution of commodities. Stalinism sees labor as an economic physical act in satisfying economic-physical needs. Socialist humanism declares: liberate men from slavery to things, to the pursuit of profit or servitude to "economic necessity." Liberate man, as a creative being – and he will create, not only new values, but things in super-abundance.[44]

Tempted by these analogies, Western Marxists, from C.L.R. James and Raya Dunayevskaya, to Marcuse and the Frankfurt School, to the British New Left, reduced, often dismissively, "actually existing socialism" to a version of capitalist relations – the Johnson-Forest Tendency called it a form of "state capitalism" that mirrored monopoly capitalism in the West, failing to reorganize the process of production and the organization of labour, failing to abolish the logic of capitalism's accumulation of surplus as well as the commodity and the wage labour form.[45] They saw global industrial development, which included the social welfare regimes in the West as well as the industrialized socialist countries in the East, as a third stage of world or global capitalism, extending Lenin's thesis on state monopoly capitalism but subsuming, in a somewhat totalizing fashion, the socialist economies into its imperialist, profit-driven, and extractivist logics.

But "state capitalism" critiques were made from afar, without empirical or ethnographic studies, and without taking into account the lived experiences of the people. Even if they were engaged by some East European humanists, they remained Western-centric as they saw the socialist economies as entirely derivative of capitalism. Their accounts of socialism transposed the logic and the structure of capitalist relations onto the realities of socialist life.

Marxist humanists from the Soviet Union and Bulgaria rejected this comparison, arguing for the irreducibility of the socialist historical experience to "capitalism." On the contrary, they claimed, socialist economies were oppositional, and even if their industries retained some elements that resembled capitalist industry and economy, as Dunayevskaya insisted, they moved toward their abolition and gradual dissolution. This included the function of money and the wage, the networks of sharing and distribution, categories of ownership and their administrative regimes. The organization of industry and labour was different, the machines were different – they were machines and it was industry, indeed, but they were socialist machines and the industry was socialist. Not to mention the sense of collective and personal ownership, community relations among workers – all these were so uniquely shaped, together with the fabric of socialist societies, that they were incompatible with the logics of capitalist production and reproduction, and with capitalist relations more generally. In this sense, to place class struggles under capitalism in the same category as workers' self-management movements in Yugoslavia, workers' demands for more wages in Poland, and the hostility of the socialist people toward the "red bourgeoisie" was to miss the radicality of these struggles in the socialist contexts, the radicality of what was perceived as social privilege and inequality.[46]

Anti-Stalinist sociologists and social theorists in socialist countries such as Bulgaria and the Soviet Union were eager to develop critical analyses of socialist societies by accounting for these societies' problems on their own terms. After several decades of life, socialist societies, through what they called "developed" socialist relations, created something unknown, a social reality that raised a lot of question marks. These new societies presented a unique set of historical experiences and social problems that needed to be studied from within, and there was much research and work to be done.

The category of alienation offered ambivalent promises in the socialist traditions. "We need to reject the unruly use of the category with respect to the social phenomena that pertain to socialism and communism, which many revisionists share," some Soviet voices argued.[47] Socialism was, for them, a radically restructured society that generated its own problems with its own particular logics, conflicts, paradoxes, even absurdities – and they needed an internal, immanent critique. These social contradictions were historically specific and could not be reduced to a form of capitalism or seen as derivative of capitalism.

Lapin studied the category in a holistic way, taking into account its philosophical, economic, and political aspects. He argued that in the *1844 Manuscripts*, Marx quickly realized the limits of alienation as an explanatory concept for grasping capitalist relations in their concrete social forms. New and differentiated concepts were needed to capture the concrete social articulations of alienation, self-alienation, and their particular social expressions under capitalism, as well as the forms of social mediation that produced alienation as a subjective experience. It was a reading uncannily similar to the critique of the concept that Althusser developed in his later work. From there Lapin moved to questions about the division of labour as the source of social and class divisions, and the contradictions they bring about as they congeal into material forces.[48] These contradictions, running through the entire social order, created a split subject severed from the products of their own labour, a bourgeois subject divided into a private being and a citizen of the state, their own individual interest confronting their interest as a social being, their creativity negated rather than affirmed.[49]

To insist on a holistic reading and a continuity in Marx's work meant insisting once again that "human" alienation was specific to capitalist relations and that socialist countries had generated their own unique social problems that could not be understood by reducing them to "state capitalist societies." Teodor Oizerman, an influential Soviet philosopher who trained a diverse generation of post-Stalinist Marxists such as Lapin, Il'ienkov, Bagaturiia, and Mamardashvili, argued that, to divorce alienation from its particular historical conditions – that is, "private property, exploitation, and capitalism" – meant making it an absolute and ahistorical category that "obscures the real social content of this phenomenon, its historical beginnings, its foundation in [the capitalist] economy."[50] This was a "bourgeois" reading since it purposefully neglected the crucial connection between alienation and the private ownership of the means of production, and claimed instead that alienation emerged out of the contradictions between the private ownership of the means of production and the social character of labour under capitalism.[51] "Such universalization of the concept alienation obscures its actual historical meaning and serves idealist constructs," wrote Oizerman.[52]

But Oizerman's training was in the Stalinist tradition and his critique contained elements of economic determinism. Alienation had the power to capture the socialist experiences in multiple ways, others argued, and even if they could not be called "capitalist," socialist urbanization, industrialization, the division of labour, the bureaucratic and administrative orders of the state, and the multiple inadequacies and absurdities people encountered every day made them estranged and disengaged from the political system, from each other, and from their social contributions. These were the contradictory and unwelcome effects of a society that grew out of new and different political foundations.

Yugoslavian humanists found in alienation tremendous promises for a critique of socialist societies and their internal contradictions. Yugoslavian humanists were often in direct and continuous dialogue with Marcuse, Fromm, and other Marxist humanists from Western and Central Europe, and their interventions emerged in contact with the intellectual zones that shaped the Yugoslavian tradition from the period. For example, the Praxis group insisted on the direct relevance of alienation for opening what they called a "concrete criticism" of socialist reality – the loss of direct democracy through the formation of ruling elites and state bureaucracies, the formation of social and material inequalities of various sorts, the forms of labour that remained disconnected from the worker's sense of social and personal accomplishment, or the kinds of social estrangement that urban life creates. For some Praxis members, as Nikolay Karkov points out, alienation was a central political problem for socialist, not for capitalist, societies; under capitalism, alienation in fact served to structure social relations. Its critical power, then, could be tested not in capitalist societies but against "the stipulated goals of their counter-hegemonic project."[53]

If we stop thinking about alienation as a purely economic category, Yugoslavian philosopher Zagorka Golubović argued, and instead take it as an anthropological and philosophical one, we can account for multiple forms of alienation with broader existential, philosophical, and political meanings – one's estrangement from oneself, from other people or beings, one's alienation from "nature," from their surroundings, from society, from political governance, or one's loss of meaning and purpose in life, their disconnect from creativity and self-expression. Weaving together existentialism, phenomenology, and psychoanalysis, Golubović developed a socialist theory of personhood (*licnosti*), which involved the affirmation of one's "humanity" and the maximum possible expression of one's creative potentials through personal agency and the power to change one's own social conditions and surroundings, the power to act upon the world, to assert oneself as a social being. Stalinist social and historical determinism, the reified political hierarchies and systems it produced, could not account for or allow for ordinary people to grow into "persons" in the fullest sense. Stalinism was thus antithetical to socialism – and Golubović's was a kind of socialism that affirmed individualism as well as the universal validity of the "human" experience, with civilizational and human-centric biases.[54]

THE WORLD OF TSVETAN STOIANOV

In the 1980s, Bulgarian philosopher and essayist Tsvetan Stoianov published a stunning treatise on alienation. "Threads that Are Being Severed" takes up the theme and the concept in ways that make full use of its capaciousness and, as the title of the essay suggests, explores its far-reaching social consequences. Stoianov saw alienation as a problem of modern society and the modern subject, and explored the social conditions and the subjective experience of solitude, detachment, loneliness, indifference, emptiness, and void. The modern person had lost the worldly connection to the whole and the spiritual realms, where connections to nature, spiritual life, and various environments have been profoundly disrupted and reordered. Immediate, embodied bonds and social ties have been altered through various technologies and forms of mediation, while isolation, estrangement, suspicion, and fear have become the social norm.

Stoianov traces the myriad appearances of alienation in Western philosophy and literature, from Arthur Schopenhauer, Søren Kierkegaard, and Friedrich Nietzsche to Charles Baudelaire, Oscar Wilde, and José Ortega y Gasset – all translated and published in Bulgarian after 1956 – to offer a formidable critique of Western capitalist societies and their ideals of modernity. However, alienation was not just a problem of the Western world and its capitalist economies; Stoianov argued that "it is also a problem that pertains to us."[55] The theme had been present in the East since the era of Nikolai Gogol and Fyodor Dostoevsky, whose characters were caught in the contradictions that stemmed from the social transformation of Russian society in the nineteenth century. Stoianov reads the emergence of Russian nationalism, with its romanticized and nativist picture of the people, as an effect of alienation and a symptom of an emerging modernity. An attempt to recuperate the loss of immediate affective communal bonds, the nationalist quest for the Russian soul and all things vernacular was a deeply conservative, reactive, and nostalgic move, a turn toward the past – with no openings for a better future for the people.[56]

For Stoianov, alienation was a critical lens through which to study and reveal truths about his own contemporary time, socialist life during the post-Stalinist decades. Of course, it was first and foremost a problem of the capitalist city. "The capitalist industrial center, the modern macropolis, turned inward, is nothing other than an assembly of millions of miserable people with severed threads."[57] But he also critiqued socialist urbanization and modern life in the socialist city – "the city, that kingdom of alienation, with its dark street shadows, which we have inherited from the past and which we need to eradicate."[58] In this new world, people were no longer connected to their "home" as they used to be. The social and material practices that had once made up people's relationship to the "home" have changed dramatically. What was once the home with its historical aura, built by the ancestors, no longer exists. In the new home, furniture and objects could barely acquire history. They would get discarded without having had the chance to absorb the presence and the spirit of their inhabitants.[59] "Gone are the centuries-old kitchen cabinets and pantries and their squeaking doors, [gone are] the armchairs that have taken the shape of our elbows. Instead, there are light, bright-colored tables and chairs bringing joy to the eye – then they disappear … There is no time for them to acquire the resin of human touch and the warmth of the body."[60]

Modern homes were profoundly altered, Stoianov observes, to the extent that they were more like temporary habitats. In fact, people

> barely have a home even when they live in apartments with multiple bedrooms. First, they change [their homes] very often, from city to city, from neighbourhood to neighbourhood, and in one life they go through four, five, ten homes! The walls haven't yet absorbed their smells and haven't felt their presence, and they have to leave! And then they leave not only because of life necessities, jobs, or something like this, they leave out of their own will … Even when they have a permanent home, how much weaker is their connection? They leave in the morning to go to work, twenty kilometres away, then have lunch at the restaurant or cafeteria nearby, get dinner in their social club or with friends – and they go home just to sleep. And on Sundays, on weekends? Then they go away 120 kilometres away – this is where they like to rest and nurture their souls. How can you call this a home if you need to run away from it on Sundays?[61]

The *makhala*, the neighbourhood community, meant nothing any longer. Gone was the neighbour who would peek over the fence; there were no knocks on the door anymore – and everyone was blessed in their isolation. But then, Stoianov continues, you could faint, or die, and for weeks no one would know. Family and kinship ties had also fallen apart, and new friends were hard to find. You sat in the train car (*kupe*) hoping that nobody would talk to you, and there you were almost non-existent.[62] Only the "self" was left, "me together with myself," perhaps in some state of satisfaction. But then the most terrifying thing came – alienation of oneself from oneself.[63] For modern people, Stoianov laments, this is how "the world disappears as a living environment."[64] Places no longer gave us access to their history, and to our own, through collective social practices and their material, embodied continuities.

However, Stoianov falls in line with the dominant humanist traditions, which centred on the male experience and equated "man" with the "human." He imagines the unbroken continuity of material and social history through patrilineal kinship, and his critique leaves intact the patriarchal logics ordering the lost worlds that he laments. His "human" is presumed to be a man no longer capable of true love – for a female lover, that is. Homosexuality, in turn, appears as an effect of alienation, a psychological diversion, an estrangement from oneself and one's body. "Am I a man or a woman? If the body is replaceable, then maybe gender is as well?"[65] This possibility terrifies him as the ultimate expression of alienation and his dystopian critique of modern life becomes a mirror of a homophobic and transphobic mindset.

Stoianov refused easy comparisons between capitalist and socialist societies; to see them "as equally alienated," as mirroring each other, was to fall into an "extreme" view that failed to register their crucial differences.[66] The other extreme view, he continues, was to paint the realities of socialism in idyllic colours and to maintain that alienation "does not concern us in the present moment," to see it as an imported problem, an effect of "bourgeois" and Western influence, or a remnant of the past.[67]

Socialist societies faced their own social problems, all symptoms of the radical transformation of the social fabric. Bureaucracy was one of them; it was the plight of socialist societies: the political and administrative cadres of the state had morphed into a class of privileged elites. So disconnected had they become from reality, inhabiting their own separate world, that they had started hallucinating.[68] Seeing through their fraudulence, emptiness, and absurdity, the people reacted by disengaging and settling in their own apathy and disconnect.[69] Socialist societies were ridden with indifference and non-participation covered by fake political and social activity, "in which we only end up lying to ourselves."[70]

There were many other symptoms, some of which could be found among the socialist youth: careerism, rudeness, "hooliganism," disrespect, indifference, and lack of responsibility for others.[71] All these undermined the socialist ethos, which contained collective and personal tension that generated tremendous potentiating energy. Materialism and consumerism (*esnafshtina*) began to creep in as a social value as soon as people became overly focused on their possessions and domestic comforts and became too invested in acquiring and owning things. But Stoyanov agrees that the West played a subversive role in this process – its propaganda came in the form of affinity for commodities and things. "The West is not very good at infiltrating with ideas but it hopes to create *esnafs*, the ones who admire a pack of cigarettes or a nylon shirt ... Western-style ideology is commodified, literally presented to you in the form of commodities."[72] Money and commodities: market relations were haunting socialist societies like a ghost, "and as long as they remain present in latent form, they could become reality at any point."[73]

In Stoyanov's view, to overcome *esnafshtina* and other symptoms of alienation was not a matter of affirming scarcity as a collective social value, but on the contrary, increasing the abundance of goods and pleasures that expand the experience of joy and the sense of personal, creative, and social fulfillment.[74] His rather incomplete vision of communism imagines a strong socialist ethos combined with an abundance of creative, social, material, and spiritual life.

DIALECTICAL TURNS, MATTERS OF PRAXIS

Dialectical analysis held equal critical promise and power across these humanist traditions. By eliminating the dialectical understanding of history and "its key principle – the negation of the negation," Stalinism disabled the power of Marx's project of immanent critique, the possibility of engaging critically and self-reflexively with socialist realities on their own terms: "There is no reason to think that, however great the social progress, the foreseeable future will bring complete elimination of old forms of human deformation and degradation without introducing some new conflicts and contradictions."[75]

The return to dialectical analysis as critical method prompted some East European humanists, most notably the members of the

Yugoslavian Praxis group, to centre their work on the concept of praxis. "Matter" could no longer be seen ontologically, as an "objective reality" that determined social relations and forms of consciousness, but was a product of praxis, of historically specific social practices, and it should be seen as an effect and a medium of social relations. Praxis, then, was social activity or collective social energy understood to have concrete material and bodily effects – it was precisely this embodied material activity that altered the material worlds and practices that social relations were embedded in, it was the everyday practical activity that reshaped social relations, allowing for collective intervention on a larger historical scale.[76] "Man is the being that exists through and as praxis," Yugoslavian Praxis member Gajo Petrovic wrote, arguing that freedom is freedom only when asserted through the conscious material and creative activity of "men."

The concept of praxis also gave Yugoslavian humanists an opportunity to rethink freedom as direct material and social practice: freedom conceived as social practice in materialist terms, conceived as the dialectical metabolism of critical thought and action. How did freedom manifest itself through material activity, and vice versa? When and how did material activity become an expression of freedom? What did it mean to think of freedom in and as praxis? The goal of the praxis-oriented framework was to flee the determinism of the Stalinist system, the presumption that agency and consciousness are predetermined by the economic forces of society, which followed objective laws of development. "An action is free only when a man determines his deed by himself," when "what is human in him determines his actions, and when he, in his deeds, contributes to humanity," Petrović wrote. "Only that self-determined activity in which man acts as an integral many-sided personality, in which he is not a slave of one or another individual thought, feeling or aspiration, is truly free."[77]

But for these Yugoslavian humanists, praxis was the philosophical revolt of men against other men. Yugoslavian notions of praxis remained male-centric and therefore left patriarchal society intact. Its proponents never explored the feminist potentials in the concept to account for gendered social activities, to ask what counted as material and socially meaningful activity, or to probe which potentials the terrains of social practice opened for the reordering of patriarchal subjugation. The kinds of freedom, of social and creative agency imagined through the praxis framework was reserved for men of the dominant ethnos and religion, colluding with patriarchal domination and enabling the ethnic supremacist orders that re-emerged in the 1960s and unmade the fragile but radical social accomplishments of the multi-ethnic Yugoslavian socialist project.[78]

SOCIALIST SUBJECTIVITY AND THE HOLISTICALLY DEVELOPED PERSON

Anti- and post-Stalinist Soviet thinkers placed less emphasis on praxis and instead used the critique of Stalinist Marxism to move toward questions of socialist subjectivity and the importance of social and material practice in the formation of socialist subjects. Soviet Marxists likened Stalinist socialism to the crude versions of communism that Marx critiqued in his early works, where they found an implicit critique of Stalinism. These nascent, "incomplete" forms of communism privileged the "objective" conditions of alienation such as the abolition of private property, wage labour, and the unequal distribution of material wealth, while "tacitly accept[ing] the universal renunciation of human personhood."[79] Similarly, while abolishing the "objective" conditions of alienation, Stalinist socialism left unexamined the question of the subject's self-realization as a political, personal, and creative being. For Soviet Marxists, a communism-yet-to-be could open conditions for "human self-affirmation"; the task of this other, unrealized communism, was to refocus on the experiences of the socialist subject as they were mediated through social relations with political content oriented toward communal forms of social life.[80]

In post-Stalinist visions of communism in dialogue with the Soviet tradition, society's ability to deliver material equality "objectively" became irrelevant unless it successfully redefined social practices, brought into being new forms of sociality and collective experiences, made and remade persons, and encouraged their sense of integrity and power. Petur-Emil Mitev, the prominent Bulgarian sociologist and social theorist, refuted the "primitive notion" that "socialism consists of factories and assembly lines only. It is worth reminding ourselves of the 'ABC' of historical materialism: socialism – these are new social relations."[81] He continued:

> the social effect of the first brigade movements was much bigger and more important than the economic one. The slogan of the youth, "We build the passageway – the passageway builds us!" was genuine and meaningful. The first phase of the brigade

> movement was an example of true social creativity, creativity that proved immensely influential for the entire society, the entire social climate, for social relations in their totality. With the voluntary labour of youth the brigades were breaking down age-old barriers separating the person from society.[82]

These visions of communism established that socialist relations could no longer be considered outside of the subject's experience of autonomy and power, outside their sense of personhood and community – in short, outside the crucial dimension that takes into account the subject's agency and self-formation as it is embedded in networks of material support and mutual care. Communism no longer involved eradicating class divisions, delivering material equality "objectively," or bringing the state one step closer to the objective evolution of material relations through the next five-year plan. Instead, the specific organization of productive forces and material relations became a person-making and a relation-forming medium with the capacity to define the subject's sense of autonomy, self-expression, and togetherness, interpellate the self in relation to a collective order, and redefine social practices.

The "holistically developed person" (often translated in English as the "all-rounded individual") became a central concept in post-Stalinist East European thought. This was a new historical subject who personalized socialist values of freedom, social mobility, and the socialist community. "Reuniting humans with themselves" as social and creative beings,[83] the holistically developed person was imagined to embody a social micro-universe of sorts through their purposive self-activity. Abolishing dichotomies between the public and the private, the state and the social, work and leisure, production and social reproduction, the socialist-humanist person would become the living embodiment of the new society and eradicate all remnants of alienated life. The holistically and harmoniously developed person was contained as potentiality: the task of future communism was to take this structural potentiality to its actual articulation, where a humanized, socialized, and fully integrated subject would come into being – a marker of socialism positively realized. If given the conditions to develop fully their personal creative and intellectual capacities, this new socialist person would bring into existence the totality of social relations through their sense of accomplishment, their unique path to social and personal self-realization. As Svoboda Puteva, a Bulgarian Marxist-humanist sociologist and a feminist from the 1970s, wrote,

> the ideal of socialist humanism is the dialectical totality of the labouring, political, and exuberant human – in other words, the harmoniously developed person, who engages in creative activity in all aspects of human life – in labour, in public life, in science, culture, entertainment. Such dialectical totality is expressed both through the external products of social activity – the products of labour, public life, and relations with others – and through the subjective experience of the person themselves.[84]

In the socialist countries during the post-Stalinist period, the category of labour underwent tremendous revisions – another significant difference with Western humanist accounts of labour, which were still wedded to the social contexts within capitalist relations. Throughout the years, Western Marxists, such as those in the Frankfurt School, remained strong proponents of ideas of abolishing labour as the precondition for human freedom. They saw advanced technology as the most powerful means of reaching such abolition. Marcuse, for example, consistently endorsed technology as the solution to human freedom – he insisted that, if organized rationally and according to a political logic that liberates it from its capitalist content, technological progress opened up possibilities for the satisfaction of human needs and freedom from the "realm of necessity." In other words, if the prevailing logic of technological progress was subverted, the machine would liberate "man" from wage labour and become "the potential basis of a new freedom."[85] Following this line, some later Frankfurt School Marxists continued to believe that advanced technology had the potential to overcome scarcity and the need for labour; indeed, they called for the abolition of work and labour altogether.[86] But with no access to empirical research, they drew simplistic and reductive pictures of the realities of socialist life, critiquing their "productivist work ethic."[87]

But in the socialist countries during that time, "labour" was no longer a dominant category and no longer a primary focus of analysis. Giving way to more encompassing terms such as "social life" and "social activity," it was part of a new direction aiming to abolish distinctions between labour, reproduction, and leisure. "Labour" was

Figure 1.2 "Socialism and the Human," a 1974 article in the women's journal *Zhenata dnes* discussing socialism and the "care for the human" in the spheres of labour, social reproduction, child care, and the care of the elderly.

a form of creative, embodied activity that shaped the subjectivity of the labouring, but it also was a relation-forming medium, the site where social relations were expressed profoundly, the location where relations of domination and power could be transformed into practices of radical togetherness, community, and self-fulfillment.

Yet labour was only a fragment of one's life. In fact, as discussed in detail in chapter 2, labour contained no more social value than free time, leisure, and creative activity. The cumulative experience of the socialist person engaged in different spheres of creative, intellectual, cultural, and physical activity became the measure of freedom and social wealth.[88] Mitev argued that the socialist person, through their agency, "reunites separate spheres of human existence that have been historically fragmented, even juxtaposed or antagonized – the family, the professional sphere, and the public-political sphere. In this sense, the active life position means the multifaceted development of the person, and ... a moment will come when the holistic and harmonious human will enter the historical stage and become its main actor."[89]

Labour, therefore, was no longer tied to efficiency and productivity, but rather became a means of achieving the social and personal self-realization of the socialist person, subordinated to the needs of community, play, and the meanings of socialist personhood. These new approaches also gave socialist humanists the opportunity to refocus on the work of social reproduction in its myriad daily practices as well as the reproduction of social relations at large. The concept of social reproduction, the focus of the next chapter, acquired specific and expanded meanings in the post-Stalinist socialist contexts and became a central organizing principle of post-Stalinist governance.

In the work of socialist humanists across the board, "class" also nearly vanished from theoretical inquiry and political discourse in a move away from the Stalinist emphasis on class antagonism and class war. In the context of developed capitalist relations in the Western world, to abandon class as an analytical category was a troubling development – it meant the renunciation of class struggle, the erasure of class difference, a relapse into liberalism. As Althusser repeated, it needed ferocious critique. In the conditions of "developed socialism," however, shedding old categories made perfect sense: the Stalinist concepts of class antagonism, class war, and the class enemy were no longer relevant, not only because of their ahistorical uses but also because they were inadequate to the new social realities. Social thinkers and activists therefore faced the task of having to come up with a different language for social inequalities, injustices, oppression, freedom, and more. In the Bulgarian socialist-humanist tradition, "youth" became an important new collective subject. Consider, for example, Mitev's conclusion, when asked to elaborate on the relationship between youth and class: "We have a historical process that has more or less homogenized the generation and has transformed it into a separate social group. It is precisely this process that marks the beginning of the new phase of socialism. Overcoming class antagonism means that class differentiation decreases. At the same time, generational differentiation becomes more significant."[90]

Conceptually, the focus on youth helped Bulgarian sociologists to move beyond the category of class as the primary agent of history. Displacing class as an analytical framework and an agent of revolutionary change, the youth emerged as a new, heterogeneous collective subject that signified a rupture with the past and unsettled structures of understanding confined to class relations. As the first generation to grow up under socialism, they appeared on the historical horizon as a collective subject whose will and social power could no longer be ignored, but rather had to be taken into account and carefully studied. The socialist youth were powerful yet unknown, a puzzle that held both promise and fear because they bore the future to come. The socialist youth became a microcosm of the new society with all its problems, inequalities, injustices, paradoxes, and absurdities even, a subject profoundly unknown yet distinctly socialist.

In the post-Stalinist era, this new social conglomeration called "youth" – and by extension, the "holistically developed person," the subject who personalized the new social relations – became inseparable from a project of social normalization. As one essay from the early 1980s argues, the ultimate goal of socialist governance was the complete convergence between human self-realization and socialization, linking socialist meanings of freedom to the need for new regimes of normality and homogeneity.[91] In other words, the post-Stalinist concept of human freedom was imagined through a person's successful social integration into a governable, integral social fabric that was totalized yet differentiated, integrated yet diverse. Because it occupied the juncture where both social differentiation and social mobility occurred, the state saw the youth as a supple material for achieving the total social integration it had promised. Together with the holistically developed person, the concept of youth and other humanist frameworks played a central role in post-Stalinist experiments with social governance that, as subsequent chapters will show, led to troubling political developments.

While Marxist humanism was a defining political tendency of the East European (and also Western) Left in the 1960s and '70s, it has left us with a number of political developments that pose urgent questions: If "liberation," "freedom," and the "human" were central concepts around which the left political imaginary was organized, who was the subject of this freedom and the subject of political struggle? Who counted as a human? Who was rendered invisible in humanist accounts of domination and human liberation?

The humanist currents were too diverse to form a coherent political or theoretical tradition, but in the Western contexts they produced their own hegemonic discourses of the "human," which were male-centric, Eurocentric, and colonial.[92] The post-Stalinist humanist traditions from the socialist countries contain analogous tendencies, particular to their own socio-political and historical contexts. In the case of the Balkan socialist countries, they produced their own universalisms, progressivist discourses, and hegemonic notions of the "human," which participated in assimilationist and ethnonationalist visions of socialist modernity, socialist peoplehood, and socialist democracy. As subsequent chapters show, humanist visions of socialist modernity, social integration, and social mobility opened the conditions for the rise of ethnonationalism in the Balkan socialist countries and culminated in the ethnonationalist assimilation and ethnic cleansing projects of the 1970s and '80s.

Yet these humanisms held political promises and radical visions whose legacies are both ambivalent and contradictory. Social reproduction, the "holistically developed person," and other humanist ideas allowed social theorists and activists to initiate multiple reforms in the spheres of leisure and reproductive work, which collectivized reproductive, domestic, and care work and made available to ordinary people vast infrastructures of leisure, sports, and creative life. Through concepts such as "youth," the socialist countries forged global alliances and solidarities with the formerly colonized countries and imagined anti-colonial, anti-capitalist, anti-racist, and feminist forms of internationalism to challenge the imperialist ambitions of capitalist countries in Western Europe and North America.

The next chapter explores some of these moments in the writings and organizing activities of women in the sphere of gender and social reproduction in socialist Bulgaria from the post-Stalinist period. Through socialist visions of women's revolution and expanded notions of social reproduction, post-Stalinist feminists reorganized reproductive and care work on communal and collective grounds and managed to interrupt the structural reproduction of patriarchal relations in major ways. At the same time, by naturalizing motherhood and by binding women's reproductive capacities to nationalist visions of a socialist future, they placed women's bodies and social lives at the centre of the pro-nativist and ethnonationalist politics of the period.

2

Gender and Social Reproduction the Socialist Way

Social reproduction was a central concept in humanist thought in the socialist countries. While it is most often associated with the West European and North American Marxist-feminist literature of the 1970s, considerable work around the concept appeared in a range of places from the late 1960s to the 1980s in different parts of the world. In the West, Marxist feminists used the concept to develop feminist critiques of productivist Marxism and expose the blind spots in a largely male-dominated working-class struggle. Social reproduction also became an important concept in the work of Italian autonomists in Western Europe, in "anti-humanist" critics of orthodox Marxism such as Louis Althusser and Michel Foucault, in studies on slavery, race, and urban development in the United States, and in the work of post-colonial and Third World feminists.

In these bodies of work, social reproduction acquired a wide range of meanings and was put to many different uses. Some took the term to mean the material means of subsistence and survival, both immediate and infrastructural, from water and food to housing and health care. Others used the concept to underscore reproduction as a particular kind of labour involved in the regeneration and well-being of others, as in domestic, care, emotional, affective, and sex work, all of which have historically fallen mostly on women.[1] In addition, the body became an important focus of feminist work on social reproduction – the body seen as a site of biological reproduction, the regulation of sexuality, and the reproduction of the gender binary. In this work the reproductive and reproducible body figures as a kind of resource – a resource for labour but also for producing more bodies and lives, for workers. Scholars influenced by Foucault have showed how the body-as-resource was mobilized by population-control projects and by medical and administrative technologies of regulation toward the reproduction of heteronormativity, of racial and class control, and toward social-normalization projects.[2] Black feminist writers have showed how biological reproduction became central to the social and political reproduction of slavery, racism, and racial inequalities.[3] Further, some political organizers and theorists have taken social reproduction to mean the public and social institutions that reproduce social relations at large: the state, the school, the factory, and the family, the hospital and health institutions. And even further, work coming from critical urban studies has explored cities, urban environments, and infrastructures as sites for reproducing labour power and class and racial inequalities.[4]

In Eastern Europe, social reproduction appeared in the writings of socialist humanists as early as the mid-1960s. It is no coincidence that it became a focus of interest at that particular time, during the crisis and collapse of Stalinism. Humanist critics of Stalinist Marxism mobilized the concept to move away from an exclusive focus on industrial labour and to expose the limitations of Stalinist Marxism more generally. To a degree that has perhaps gone under-recognized, "reproduction," and "social reproduction" in particular, was a central concept of non-orthodox and anti-Stalinist Marxist work in the 1960s and '70s.

This chapter turns to the question of social reproduction to explore the rich contributions of humanist scholarship around gender, sexuality, care, and leisure – another under-studied topic in the history of East European socialism. In the context of the socialist countries, the concept acquired different and expanded meanings. While we can see some overlaps with Western Marxist-feminist and non-orthodox Marxist formulations, East European contributions extended it way beyond the focus on domestic and care work, biological reproduction, and regimes of population governance.

Here I trace the debates around social reproduction in socialist Bulgaria, which reveal a solid theoretical tradition with its own distinct formulations. Post-Stalinist meanings of social reproduction were organized around the humanist concept of the "holistically developed person" and the socialist person's self-realization in all spheres of social, public, and professional life. The hegemonic formulations of the "holistically developed person" and the "socialist human" contained unexamined ethnocentric and patriarchal elements, which lent themselves to the assimilationist agendas of ethnonationalist politics during the post-Stalinist period. But the concept of the "holistically developed person" was also embraced by women organizers in Bulgaria to elevate the social status of women in socialist society, to accomplish radical changes in the sphere of social reproduction, and to redefine the meaning of socialism by foregrounding social-reproductive needs. Feminist researchers and activists working in the humanist traditions made the social-reproductive domains central to the meaning of socialism and pushed the government to invest in vast infrastructures of social care and welfare. They also stressed the importance of free time, rest, leisure, health, recreation, and cultural and creative activity as a way of expanding the conditions that made possible the "holistically developed person." They prioritized the material infrastructures that made these activities possible and available for all and argued that these changes would benefit society at large. For them, it was not only about delivering social benefits to women; it was also a matter of breaking down deep historical structures of subjugation and reorganizing society as a whole. These reforms should be seen as radical experiments in socializing and communizing the social-reproductive sphere while at the same time expanding its material and conceptual parameters in ways that remain unparalleled in history.

At the same time, this work had ambivalent formulations and effects. Earlier, Stalinist discussions of gender were "productivist" in their logics – mostly focused on industrial labour, they made efforts to draw women into the workforce, provide equal conditions at the workplace, break down the gendered division of labour, and empower the leadership of women in professional and public spheres. They also unmoored women from normative and patriarchal forms of femininity and traditional gender roles. Post-Stalinist activists and researchers in the sphere of gender relations were a product of this first generation. To continue and deepen social transformation, they shifted their efforts away from labour and into the sphere of social reproduction. But they also returned to concepts of femininity and womanhood that reattached women to motherhood; they called on nature to bind women to child-bearing and child care and established the continuity between women's "nature" and the building of socialist society. Motherhood was made into a kind of calling that formed the core of women's gendered subjectivity, of socialist womanhood. Naturalized notions of motherhood became continuous with socialist notions of peoplehood and the public good. Most disturbingly, they converged with the rising politics of nationalist patriotism, when women found themselves at the centre of the pro-nativist reproductive politics characteristic of the ethnonationalist turn.

Through the social-reproductive regimes of the 1970s, women found their selves, their bodies, and their social and affective lives at the meeting point of the social contradictions characteristic of the later socialist decades. On the one hand, with their radical forms of collectivization, they rearranged the conditions of reproduction and care and thus opened terrains for communal and collective forms of social-reproductive life while also holding space for women's autonomy and leadership. On the other hand, with their naturalizing and imperative discourses, these regimes colluded with the biopolitical logics of the socialist state and its ethnonationalist agenda.

FEMINIST NARRATIVES TURNED SIDEWAYS

The feminist movements in the socialist countries follow a historical trajectory that confuses North American and West European periodizations of feminism, especially the familiar chronology of first-, second-, and third-wave feminism. They enacted reforms that not only historically preceded but also substantially exceeded the social and political achievements of Western feminist movements. Their history disrupts the linearity of dominant Western narratives of feminist movements and challenge Western feminists' normative frameworks and their self-perception as the global vanguard of the local movements.

This is one of the reasons why global comparative historiographies of the feminist movements can rarely make sense or register the developments that took place in the sphere of gender relations in the socialist countries. As Kristen Ghodsee has shown, global comparative accounts of women's organizing most often dismiss the social movements and reforms in the sphere of gender relations in the socialist countries as a product of "state feminism" delivered "from above" and used as evidence of the failures and flaws of the state-socialist projects. In her work on Bulgarian socialist women's organizations from the 1960s and '70s, Ghodsee critiques this sweeping and dismissive picture, which, she shows, does not account for women's organizing on the ground, the levels of administrative autonomy held by women's organizations, and the power and influence women were able to exert from leadership positions and from below on the administrative and political institutions of the state.[5] Women were able to enact radical reforms not only in the more familiar spheres of legal equality and labour, but, by centring on social reproduction, they built the conceptual, social, and material foundations for a profound reorganization of social relations that no Western capitalist country has been able to accomplish. Ghodsee shows that women from the "Second World" were leading voices in the global feminist movements of the 1970s and '80s. They transformed gender relations in the socialist countries and built social worlds unseen in the "developed" countries, the Western liberal-capitalist democracies. Globally, socialist women formed multiple alliances with the newly independent countries from the former colonized world, leading to powerful counterforces to Western hegemony, colonialism, and global capitalism. These contributions have been obscured, erased, or downplayed in the historiographies of the global feminist and women's movements due to the fall of the socialist governments in Eastern Europe and the anti-communist rhetoric that triumphed in the aftermath of 1989 and the subsequent rise of neo-liberal and right-wing politics globally. Cold War stereotypes, Ghodsee argues, continue to influence these historiographies, focusing predominantly on tensions between the global North and the global South, "disappearing" women activists from the former socialist East or downplaying their work through "the persistent stereotypes that they were dupes of male communist elites" and puppets of various ideological projects.[6]

In addition, Western liberal-feminist organizing in the international context from this era was steeped in discourses and frameworks of development. Post-colonial feminists have unpacked their Eurocentric, colonial, and evolutionary biases to show that they rested on universalizing notions of patriarchy and women's oppression and constructed the "Third World woman" as an imagined, singular subject, powerless, dependent, and uneducated, a product of the "backward" socio-economic conditions of which she was a part.[7] As Chandra Talpade Mohanty and Hazel Carby have shown, this developmentalism appeared not only in Western liberal feminism, but also in the work and organizing of Western Marxist feminists, who explored links between patriarchy and class exploitation in Western capitalist societies. Their concepts of "reproduction" and "unwaged labour" were extrapolated from the working-class experiences of Western capitalist societies, often from the experiences of the white working classes, but were framed as a universal experience. When applied to non-Western and non-capitalist contexts, they erased the kinds of culturally specific values and social meanings these activities assumed, as well as women's authority and social power, together with many historically and culturally specific forms of struggle, resistance, and collective agency.[8] Thus, paradoxically, Carby pointed out, Western Marxist feminists assumed capitalist relations as the gateway to emancipation and progress and implicitly embraced capitalist development as the vehicle for reforms in the "developing world."[9]

Frameworks of development dominated the international imaginary of Western liberal and Marxist-feminist writers and organizers. In contrast, women organizers in the socialist countries rooted their international visions and alliances in concepts of international solidarity with the people in struggle against imperialism, colonialism, racism, military aggression, capitalism, and class exploitation. The global dimensions of the feminist movements from the socialist countries always held together these intersections and sought to build conceptual and material links between these struggles, while foregrounding women's perspectives, needs, histories, and experiences. In this way they positioned themselves both against Western paradigms of feminist organizing and in alliance with countries from the global South in their struggles against colonialism and imperialism and against the global expansion of capitalism.

Black and women-of-colour feminists in the United States who worked hard to articulate the structural junctures between racism, patriarchal oppression, capitalism, and the carceral state also looked to the experiences of the socialist countries as a source of inspiration and power and joined their efforts. This is not surprising, because some of the most forceful international opposition against racism in the United States came from the socialist East, and a lot of radicalized women of colour from the United States as well as the post-colonial nations saw in socialism a promise to end structural racism and patriarchal forms of power.

In Eastern Europe and the Soviet Union, post-Stalinist discourses on gender used a set of terminology that acquired specific meanings in specific historical and social contexts. Even though their work was deeply and radically feminist, socialist women from Eastern Europe and the Soviet Union refused to the very end to self-identify as "feminists" and avoided the term "feminism" to describe their work; instead, as in the case of Bulgaria, they preferred terms such as "women's revolution." Insisting on writing a historiography of the feminist movements through their own pre- and post-revolutionary historical experience, they saw first- and second-wave West European and North American feminism as "diverting women towards the treacherous road of a struggle between the genders."[10] This narrow formulation of the struggle overlooked the ways in which capitalism, racism, imperialism, and colonial power played a role in women's subordination. According to Elena Lagadinova, a prominent feminist figure and chair of the Committee of the Bulgarian Women's Movement, "bourgeois historians continue to offer ... 'radical' ideas towards more and newer apolitical feminist theories. The goal is clear: to isolate women from access to Marxist influence, their participation in class struggle, and the proletariat."[11] Feminists in the socialist countries insisted on an alternative politics and genealogy of critique. According to Maria Dinkova, a sociologist, social theorist, and fierce organizer, this genealogy included, among others, Belgian advocate for women's equality Louis Frank, British feminist activist Beatrice Webb, German democratic socialist Lily Braun, Russian "cosmopolitans" active in the international communist movement, such as Aleksandra Kollontai and Angelika Balabanova: all were part of the feminist, social-democratic, and communist movements from the late nineteenth and early twentieth centuries.[12]

In short, in the East European context, feminism was reductively associated with its Western bourgeois-liberal tendencies, with all the problems of racism and class privilege that this entailed, and complicit with the colonial and imperialist politics of their countries. As Dinkova explains, "feminism was a deadly word in the discursive system of our society because of old disagreements between the bourgeois and socialist women's movement."[13] When they began to negotiate their proposals with the leadership, women faced strong reactionary push-back from men who used the term pejoratively to accuse them of having "consumerist demands" and bringing in "bourgeois diversions." Women ultimately used strategic manoeuvring to navigate these traps.[14]

But we should also remember that in the 1970s and '80s, many women of colour in the West as well as women from the formerly colonized spaces questioned the term on similar grounds. Black feminists in the United States have repeatedly pointed out the exclusion and erasure of Black women, women of colour, and working-class women from dominant feminist frameworks and critiques.[15] Chandra Talpade Mohanty recalls that women of colour in the United States and the United Kingdom associated the term with cultural imperialism, white liberal feminism, and the expansionist politics of the Western capitalist countries, and many women of colour in the United States and women from the post-colonial nations who were critical of the hegemonic tendencies of white Western feminism were reluctant to identify themselves as feminist.[16]

East European women's refusal of the term should be taken precisely in this context. They faced discursive and political impasses similar to their counterparts in the Middle East and other non-Western contexts, where women's struggles were often subsumed within Western imperial frameworks and discounted on those grounds. Yet the reductive historicizations in East European feminist thought cannot be exempted from critique. By contrast, women of colour from the United States, the United Kingdom, and the post-colonial countries did not give up the term altogether, but instead reconfigured its histories and meanings – namely, by foregrounding the radical traditions within the feminist struggles.[17] I read this tendency as a symptom of the 1970s and the '80s, informed by the narrow and oppositional genealogy that prevailed in the East European contexts. There, feminists emphasized their commitments to social-democratic and communist political visions, and yet, due to the peculiar structures of the Cold War, they could not respond to the dynamism of feminist thought internationally as it was being radically reshaped by post-colonial, women-of-colour, and queer critiques. To call East European women's and feminist movements "feminist," then, as I do here and throughout this narrative, is not to disregard their adherents' agency and self-definition, but to recognize their work as deeply feminist while honouring their affinities with radical Black and post-colonial feminist traditions, as well as the profound work the latter did to redraw the political horizons of feminist consciousness and feminist struggles.

At the same time, it is a common misconception that East European feminism was steeped in class and economic determinism, which held that the end of patriarchal oppression and gender equality would somehow follow effortlessly if class relations were abolished. On the contrary, East European feminists were deeply committed to intersectional approaches in their own ways, at least in a global political context, because they always remained attentive to the structural links between class and patriarchal subjugation, and between capitalist expansion, colonial domination, racism, and women's social and economic conditions. They argued for women's multi-faceted involvement and leadership "in struggles against imperialism and capitalist domination, in struggles for freedom of the peoples, for the right of working people to govern their own lives and interests."[18] This, they believed, would not only "empower" women, but would radically transform these struggles themselves.

However, we can hardly speak of intersectional analysis with respect to local racial, ethnic, cultural, and religious minorities. In fact, the work on gender and social reproduction from the post-Stalinist period converged with the assimilationist politics of the ethnonationalist turn in unfortunate ways. At a time when the ethnic, religious, and cultural identity of minorities was under attack, and when minority categories were officially removed from censuses and from political speech, the experiences and histories of Muslim women and women of Turkish, Pomak, Roma, and other minority ethnicities and religions were similarly erased. In fact, national patriotism was one of the main driving forces of the pro-nativist turn in the 1970s, and Bulgarian feminists embraced it. The feminist imaginaries at the time were steeped in orientalizing and colonial tropes about the Ottoman period and they tended to see women's liberation under socialism as a victory over patriarchal cultural "traditionalism" from the Ottoman past.

SOCIAL REPRODUCTION AS A FOUNDING PRINCIPLE

"The social liberation of the woman is one of the greatest accomplishments of the socialist revolution" – thus opens *On Raising the Role of Women in Developed Socialist Society*. Drafted by a team of women activists and researchers between 1969 and 1972 after years of research, this resolution ultimately passed into law in Bulgaria in 1973.[19] The socialist revolution, the document states, "provided the conditions for her to develop and establish herself as an equal member of society and as a creator in all spheres of human activity."[20] On 14 September 1944, just days after the revolution, Bulgarian men and women were declared legally equal, a condition then affirmed as a constitutional principle in the 1947 and 1971 constitutions. In the first decades of socialist government, according to the resolution, women "overwhelmingly entered the labour force as well as the social and political governance of the country ... They are state representatives, council members on national and local levels, tens of thousands of women participate in party leadership, professional unions, youth organizations, and other public and political organizations."[21] Maria Dinkova, who as one of the driving forces behind the resolution, writes that in the first few decades of "building socialism,"

> [we] transformed women's occupational duties by transferring women's labour from agriculture and crafts to social and public institutions; we gave independent income and independent legal status to all working women, liberating them from economic dependence on their family [and men]; we created conditions for building a new social structure for working women ...; we removed all legal obstacles to the professional and social realization of the woman; we created the conditions for women to acquire education so that they can participate in all spheres of social production, receive equal wage for equal labour, combine professional labour with motherhood, and pursue their social interests in all spheres of public life and social governance.[22]

These were the decades of socialist development under Stalinism, which in Bulgaria continued up until the late 1950s and early 1960s. Gender-specific reforms under Stalinism incorporated women into education and the workforce by introducing affirmative quota systems and equal pay, removing legal obstacles to social mobility and gender equality, and opening conditions for women's economic independence.[23]

Seen through a global comparative lens, these were remarkable accomplishments, especially when we consider what women's struggles had achieved in the ostensibly "developed" capitalist world. Ghodsee shows that this historical and social experience placed socialist women at the forefront of international women's movements.[24] Penka Dukhteva's report from the 1971 United Nations conference in Moscow captured precisely these asymmetries. She observes "a remarkably rich and contradictory picture of the rise and hardship of the working woman around the world, at the juncture of radically different or similar social problems, according to the dominant social order."[25] For women in the capitalist world, the 1967 UN Declaration on the Elimination of Discrimination against Women provided effective support for their struggle for social emancipation, economic independence, and political empowerment. But to socialist women, the demands set forth in that document had long been realized. This is why for socialist women, many of whom also actively contributed to international women's organizing, the struggles of Western women could sometimes seem "anachronistic." Women in the "developed" capitalist world, Dukhteva reported, worked predominantly in traditional women's sectors such as the textile, garment, and service industries, low-level administrative jobs, and domestic and care work, where wages tended to be much lower. Her research showed that in the United States, for example, the average salary for women was still only 48 per cent of what men received. Only 7 per cent of doctors, 3 per cent of lawyers, and 1 per cent of engineers were women. Dukhteva also wrote about the inadequate legislation and the political opposition that North American women faced in trying to pass anti-discrimination laws, and she showed that after fifty years of having the right to vote, the United States had only one woman in the Senate.[26]

These realities presented a stark contrast to the situation in the socialist countries. By the early 1970s, women in socialist Bulgaria comprised 68.5 per cent of those in post-secondary professional education and 51.6 per cent of those in higher education; at the same time, 36.2 per cent working women already held university degrees and 53.8 per cent held degrees in specialized post-secondary training. Women also made up about 59.3 per cent of teachers, 58 per cent of economists, 41.7 per cent of doctors, 25.4 per cent of engineers, 36 per cent of agronomists, and 28.1 per cent of all technicians.[27] In their first decades, the socialist countries had taken active efforts to break down the gendered division of labour and to encourage women's interest in intellectual labour and in what were traditionally considered male professions in the belief that "gender balance in the workforce positively reflects on the social climate and the results of labour."[28] These realities made it apparent that the "social liberation of women" during the first decades of socialist government were, in Maria Dinkova's words, "among the most significant contributions of state socialism and that this extended far beyond the limits of the country. With our education, our professional placement, and our position in family we have come to the forefront of the global women's revolution."[29]

But the new social realities presented new social challenges. In a retrospective account of what she called the "passions around the women's revolution," Dinkova describes the first decades of development as a kind of accumulation of socialist resources that laid the public infrastructure for a modern economy and a modern state: "One of the most important leaders of the nation had once said that 'now the entire country is a construction site.'" This was true, she conceded, as "they were building at the same time industrial enterprises, irrigation systems, roads, housing, resort towns, hospitals, schools, buildings for cultural institutions ... We were observing this growth in amazement, a growth unseen on our lands before ... We had no [such] traditions."[30]

However, early socialist development allocated most of the state's resources to the expansion of infrastructure while "sacrificing" areas related to workplace conditions, appropriate housing, and social services for workers. As Dinkova notes, "the state's governing bodies were confronted with the following dilemma: we can build public infrastructure ... faster but with more casualties, or allow small comforts and slow our country's liberation from misery. Which was better?"[31] And also, who bore the "sacrifices" necessary to build the socialist future for all? Like every similar beginning, Dinkova recounts, "much of the accomplishments were at the expense of the human component,"[32] but more to the point, they disproportionately affected women workers, who absorbed the political dilemmas and social contradictions of their time and ended up paying "the highest price for the sake of the future."[33] Dinkova's humble conclusion was that "the success we've achieved in our society in the past in the direction of the social liberation of women has opened new problems."[34]

In the mid- to late 1960s, the women's journal *Zhenata dnes* and the Committee of the Bulgarian Women's Movement conducted and published sociological and ethnographic research on the experiences of women workers in different sectors of heavy industry, including at the largest oil processing and metallurgy plants in the country, Neftokhimicheski Kombinat, near Burgas, and Kremikovtsi, near Sofia.[35] This was one among many sociological studies published in the 1960s and '70s on the experiences of women working in heavy industries, on housework and care work, on young women's "time budgets" (this important concept is addressed later in this chapter), on women in leadership roles, on women involved in intellectual labour, and more. The journal reported that inadequate material conditions enabled sexual harassment and reinforced misogyny and prejudice toward women who chose these professions; men subjected women workers to ridicule and pressured them to give up their positions or expected them to serve their male colleagues at the workplace. Women who challenged normative femininity, patriarchal roles, and the gendered division of labour faced various forms of backlash.

Inadequate conditions around safety and personal space encouraged a culture of sexual harassment and the shaming of women's masculine gender expressions. Men often resented women for their expertise and professional growth.[36] In 1967 Penka Dukhteva and Maria Dinkova interviewed women in construction – general workers as well as specialists such as crane operators, concrete mixing specialists, welding and rebar specialists, among others, who made up about 11 per cent of the industry's workforce. The women shared that they loved their professions and found great satisfaction in the work but complained about unsanitary bathrooms, lack of changing rooms and spaces for rest, and ill-fitting work clothes and oversized shoes. They were exposed to relentless catcalling and cursing. Men treated them like servants and ordered them to bring them cigarettes or water, regularly expecting or asking women to bring lunches from the cafeteria for the entire brigade. They rarely occupied leadership positions. Even as specialists, they faced disrespect from the men and wouldn't get promoted even when they were the most experienced members of their brigades.[37] The journal publicized realistic descriptions of the unsightly conditions in the temporary housing for the women. Women with families and children had better housing but complained about the negative effects of their frequent relocations on their children's lives and progress in school.[38]

At the same time, the first publications about the infamous "second shift" appeared as early as 1967 – five years before *The Power of Women and the Subversion of Community* by Selma James and Mariarosa Dalla Costa. Considered a groundbreaking feminist intervention in the West, *The Power of Women* insisted on recognizing domestic and care work as labour. It showed that women's work in the home was an invisible and unrecognized yet structurally necessary part of the organization of wage labour, value, production, and exploitation under capitalism. "Let's Abolish the Second Shift!," a short and sharp article that reads more like an urgent manifesto, appeared in the June 1967 issue of *Zhenata dnes*. It presented a variety of facts pertaining to socialist society in the 1960s: on average, women spent between three and eight hours per day during workdays and six and a half hours on weekends performing domestic work, and together with their time spent at the workplace, women ended up working for eighty to ninety hours a week. This and a series of similar articles that followed in the journal attacked perceptions of domestic work as women's "duty" and argued that women's disproportionate workload negatively affected not only individual women but society at large. Women no longer had time to spend with their children, go to the library, or participate in cultural activities; they had no opportunities to earn higher professional degrees or continue their postgraduate specializations; this created conflicts in the family. Most importantly, however, women did not have the time to develop fully their creative and intellectual capacities and thereby to contribute fully to their communities and to socialist society at large.[39]

To women organizers in the late 1960s and '70s, one thing was clear: socialist governance neglected the many challenges that stemmed from women's increased role in socialist society. It became apparent that approaches to gender equality under Stalinism, while accomplishing a great deal, remained productivist and male-centric. As in other contexts, women, their bodies, and their reproductive capacities and social lives absorbed the contradictions arising from early socialist development. In addition, early socialist attempts to "build socialist relations" called for forms of collective sacrifice, which inevitably unfolded along gender lines and disproportionately affected women.

"A socialist society cannot allow half of its population to suffer insurmountable difficulties in their effort to access general education, higher professional qualification, to attend to family and pedagogical duties. It cannot allow its members to acquire these while making personal sacrifices," proclaimed "Let's Abolish the Second Shift!"[40] The new challenges opened new horizons for political organizing and for radical visions that pushed social imagination to the very edges. Dinkova describes these times as a kind of social dreaming, a collective social imaginary, or a "social fantasy let loose."[41] She writes,

> Considering that in society women are [legally and economically] equal to men; that when in this society women have, with their own means and efforts, achieved a higher level of education, professional qualifications, and social-political activity; considering that the revolutionary changes in the social conditions of women have led to changes in all spheres of social life; and since these changes inevitably come into contradiction with certain established social practices, conditions of labour, everyday customs, cultural values, and stereotypes in social and individual consciousness – society will be up against huge losses if it allows only for women to adjust to the contradictory moments in the new reality.[42]

In other words, it was not enough to include women in education and in all spheres of labour, not enough to empower them to take leadership roles in all spheres of administrative and political governance, not enough for them to take up intellectual work and other privileged domains formerly accessible only to men. Rather, "society as a whole," the entire material and social organization of life, needed to be adapted to "women's new positions and new social functions."[43]

SOCIALIST TIME, LEISURE TIME

In Bulgaria as in other parts of the socialist world, the 1970s marked a pronounced shift toward issues of social reproduction in multiple spheres of life. The social-reproductive sphere became an organizing principle of "developed" socialist society and a terrain for the shaping and reshaping of social relations and subjectivities. Post-Stalinist notions of social reproduction included, importantly, social-reproductive needs in the sphere of biological reproduction and domestic and care work. But this was only one of the many aspects of the socialist framework of social reproduction.

Unlike concepts of social reproduction that emerged in capitalist contexts, which focused on relationships between the invisibility of unwaged labour and exploitation, socialist notions of social reproduction centred around questions of leisure and free time. Post-Stalinist humanists saw an integral relationship between the question of women's social emancipation and the centrality of free time in socialist society. Svoboda Puteva, a social thinker whose writings explored intersections between leisure and socialist personhood from the perspective of women, writes that "the solution to society's strategic problems is to a great extent related to the solution of the problems of free time and the conditions that allow for the development and realization of the free person in terms of their interests, needs, relationship to their free time and their life attitude."[44] Puteva juxtaposes her vision of socialist free and leisure time with the way it functioned in capitalist societies, which she called "the civilization of leisure." The approach to leisure within a framework of capitalist relations was organized around "the search for means of mitigating the social conflict, of adapting to the so-called leisure industry, entertainment, and propaganda industry," so that it preserved the existing social structure and existing social relations. She continues, "the theoretical basis of this approach is the presupposed antagonism between work time and leisure time."[45] By contrast, post-Stalinist socialist concepts of leisure and work dissolved these antagonisms; instead, leisure and work were configured around and in service of personal, social, and community self-realization and the full expression of the capacities of every member of society. After all, socialist labour was an intrinsic part of personal, social, and collective self-realization, not just a method of extraction. Labour was "a form of realization for the person, of their potentials, of their talents, and their moral responsibility. The labouring person cannot and should not be reduced simply to a 'means of production' … This labourer is an acting person with interests, needs, and demands."[46]

Further, leisure was a measure of social wealth: free time, in the words of Puteva, represented the "true wealth" of a socialist society, a "horizon for the development of our capacity" and "the focal point of all problems of the relationship personhood-society."[47] In his early works, Marx wrote that free time was the expression of freedom in a society; under communism, society's wealth was to be measured not in terms of labour but in free time. While post-Stalinist social thinkers continued this line, they maintained that such a measure would only be effective if it "served as the realization of social values, which is as important, if not more important, than those values created during work time."[48] They insisted, then, on "humanizing" the structure of time as multiple activities outside the traditional wage labour form acquired social visibility and social value. The category of the "time budget" appeared as early as 1968 and became a normative analytical framework for social reforms in the future. In the 1970s, a large volume of research on the socialist person's time budget was conducted. The concept sought to account for diverse, loosely defined activities, including social labour and public work; simple reproduction, family, and domestic needs; culture and the arts; self-education; the reading of books, magazines, and newspapers; sports and recreation; trips to the mountains and other parts of the country; rest and entertainment, including the working person's need for doing "nothing in particular"; and importantly, socializing.[49] The socialist person's time had to be harmoniously distributed so that they could experience social life in its diversity. This way a host of activities acquired social value – they became available to the socialist person and opened up more terrains for their experience of autonomy, social and creative self-realization, community, togetherness, and play.

And yet, as Svoboda Puteva argued, the socialist system didn't give women the adequate material conditions to become holistically developed persons: "Free and leisure time represents the degree of freedom in society and for the person. The cultural and physical development of the working woman depends on access to free time. The broad inclusion of women in social production presupposes the creation of necessary social-economic conditions that would allow women to combine work with motherhood and child care and to develop their personhood."[50]

After studying the structure of young women's time, researchers pointed out a number of injustices and made recommendations: because they spent too much time on domestic work, young women had disproportionately less time to explore their interests and talents, and as a result their interests were not "as balanced as they could be"; a significant minority of women saw free time not as time for the exploration of their interests and but as time for rest and simple reproduction.[51] Women found this unacceptable, considering that "these were specialists who needed constant development by way of self-education; they needed to improve their qualifications and to meet their cultural needs."[52] In addition, researchers conducted interviews and revealed that women needed to enrich their cultural and social lives and found the number and quality of cultural venues and events – such as film screenings, theatre productions, art exhibitions, and music concerts – unsatisfactory.[53]

Thus the concepts of "free time" and "the socialist person's time budget" served as analytical tools in the larger argument over gender inequalities, particularly with respect to reproductive labour and the unequal opportunities faced by women who sought to live according to the ideals of socialist personhood. These concepts were also behind the vast infrastructures of cultural life, leisure, sports, recreation, and extracurricular learning that were built during the last three decades of socialism.

SOCIALIST MOTHERHOOD, HETEROSEXUAL DICTATES, AND THE INFRASTRUCTURES OF CARE

In 1970, the journal *Zhenata dnes* published a questionnaire addressed to Bulgarian women and their social, professional, and family needs.[54] Dinkova recalls that over five thousand anonymous responses came to the office by mail, "like white birds."[55] These anonymous reports dispelled "fears" that the emancipated working woman in a modern socialist society would abandon her family values in pursuit of her carrier. "It became clear for the first time that most women would like to combine motherhood and family duties with their professional labour and the intention to build a solid professional career ... Bulgarian women in their majority were seeking to harmonize different values, and they remained mothers and wives as much as they loved their work."[56]

The main problem was identified in "the contradictions arising from the social function of motherhood and the function of women in other spheres of social realization, most importantly in the system of professional labour."[57] To resolve these social contradictions, society would have to recognize the social function of motherhood, to see it as a social responsibility at large. Dinkova writes,

> The traditional argument is that because of motherhood, the woman is unable to realize her professional and social capacities and aspirations. But this is not the case. In fact, the opposite is actually true: by itself, motherhood does not impoverish but enriches the structure of social activity ... Motherhood by itself does not exclude the possibility for the full participation of women in social life, but on the contrary requires that social organization itself needs to be adapted to accommodate every new instance of the relationship between the production of the means of subsistence and the reproduction of humans, between immediate production and social reproduction – a relation that changes with every change in the forces of production.[58]

The recognition of motherhood as a social function meant that "society is responsible for providing mothers with multi-faceted support, including financial support from public funds, during the time of pregnancy, and during birth, and during recovery after birth, and when she gives indispensable care [for the newborn]."[59] Activities in the sphere of family life belonged to the reproduction of the human, and so did those activities related to "the creation of conditions for her birth, upbringing and education, the organization of the material conditions for her physical needs and life, for her health, and for her recreational needs when she is not capable of [what is commonly considered] productive labour."[60]

While foregrounding issues of social reproduction, these projects lent themselves to the biopolitical agendas of the post-Stalinist state. Socialist political imaginaries and practices from the 1970s contained radical elements that deeply unsettled older patriarchal social patterns, wrenching women's lives out of patriarchal regimes of subjugation. However, they also bound women to nature, introducing normative regimes that ushered women into heterosexuality, family life, and motherhood according to a linear script. They linked "women's nature" to visions of developed socialist society and made women's reproductive labour central to the reproduction of socialist relations at large. Similar to dominant feminist intellectual frameworks in Western capitalist societies during the 1970s, discussions among socialist women were steeped in unexamined biological determinism, which understood gender equality not in an "abstract sense" but rather as a "biological specificity of women's bodies and their purpose of carrying a womb, giving birth and feeding the future human being."[61] In this sense, they share some of the contradictory aspects of Western socialist feminisms from the 1970s, which Donna Haraway has called both denaturing and naturalizing.[62] They denaturalized gender as a social relation tied to a regime of property relations, a mode of production, and the extraction of surplus value. But their ideas about women's bodies were steeped in biological essentialism. They enforced reproductive heterosexuality as a social norm and privileged biological notions of motherhood as a primary parental bond and social role.

These frameworks organized the material infrastructures of social reproduction developed during the post-Stalinist period. In the following years, the state made it a priority to invest in infrastructures of care and social reproduction to enable socialist women to combine motherhood with their professional and public lives and to open the conditions for their social self-realization more broadly. "Social governance made it imperative to regulate the totality of factors that form the optimal conditions for the realization of the woman as a mother," continues Dinkova, describing the robust work that followed in multiple areas. This included the passing of legal reforms; the protection of women's labour; the allocation of public resources for financial support for motherhood and child care; the development of public institutions for child care and early childhood education; the development of cafeterias and after-school programs in schools. They also worked to provide services for women's reproductive health and preventive care; to prepare women and men to become parents; to maintain and increase the professional training of mothers; to raise the social prestige of motherhood; to reorganize family life

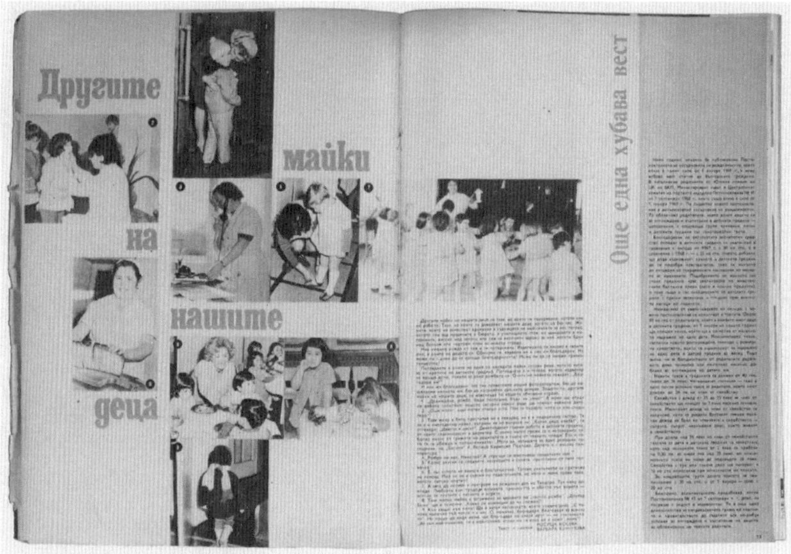

Figure 2.1 "The Other Mothers of Our Children," a 1968 article in *Zhenata dnes* by Rositsa Boseva and Varvara Kirilova honouring teachers, kitchen staff, and medical personnel working in daycare centres.

according to these newly available social services; to encourage the equal distribution of domestic work and child care between the spouses, and more.[63]

These principles were outlined in the 1973 resolution *On Raising the Role of Women in Developed Socialist Society.* The document emphasized the centrality of women to socialist society in three major spheres, which were often referred to as the "the tripartite role of women in socialist society" – the birth and care of the human, participation in social labour, and participation in social and political governance. It pledged material and political support for women's leadership in all spheres of social and public life, to "care for her own spiritual growth and physical well-being," "to strengthen her sense of dignity and confidence in her own powers," and "to encourage her social activity" – all without abandoning motherhood.[64]

In this sense, in contrast to the logics that organized capitalist societies, socialist societies did not *reduce* but *elevated* women to the status of child-bearers and mothers while simultaneously providing the conditions for freedom from the toils of child care. With an addendum to the labour code in 1973, the state dramatically increased paid parental leave, which up to that moment included three months for the first child, four months for the second, six months for the third, and six months for each subsequent child. Previously covered at 80 per cent of the parent's salary (usually the mother's), the new reforms extended parental leave benefits to 100 per cent and expanded them by up to six months for the first child, seven for the second, eight for the third, and six for subsequent children. Women could also receive up to three years of unpaid leave after the child's birth, which counted toward their retirement time even if they were unemployed. The state also passed additional rights and regulations providing financial support for mothers engaged in university education, and gave special protection to single mothers (students, including doctoral students, were given twenty-four months of allowance equal to the minimum salary). The budget for child support and child care was drastically increased, and, as Dinkova reports, by the 1980s full-day child-care centres were able to accommodate up to 80 per cent of children in each age group.[65]

These were the concrete provisions based on principles that had already been guaranteed by the constitutional reform of 1971. Preserving the right to labour, fair pay, and safe working conditions granted by the 1947 constitution, the new constitution additionally guaranteed the freedom to choose a profession (Article 40, 1971) and made "socially useful work" (*obshtestveno-polezen trud*) a social duty (Article 59, 1971). It expanded the rights to leisure and rest (Article 42, 1971); the rights to welfare in the case of unemployment, inability to work (*netrudosposobnost*), illness, accident, pregnancy, child care, disability, old age, or death (Article 43, 1971); and the rights to free education and health care (Articles 45 and 47, 1971). Reflecting the humanist spirit of the era, it protected "the freedom and inviolability of personhood" (Articles 48 and 50, 1971) and expanded privileges for the socialist youth (Article 39, 1971). It added "special protections" for "minors, juniors, the disabled, and the elderly who have been left without care" (Article 44, 1971). It expanded the protection of "women-mothers" by guaranteeing paid parental leave, access to free reproductive health, and relief from reproductive labour through the institutions of social reproduction. Like the 1947 constitution, the new document vowed to protect the development of science, culture, and the arts, this time including film, radio, and television (Article 46, 1971).

But women did not stop there; instead, they continued to pressure the government by pointing out low incomes, housing problems, and the continued difficulties women had in combining work, motherhood, social and professional life, and participation in the public sphere. They also envisioned a gradual transition toward the full support and care of children by society and its collective micro-units. After another ten years of work and organizing, in 1984, activists were able to gain some of these demands through a resolution on the further development and increase of living standards. Once again, this centred on the needs of women and the necessity of addressing outstanding social-reproductive concerns. The order made available new and much more effective material support for non-working mothers, single mothers, and families in financial hardship. It increased budgets for child-care centres and kindergartens, as well as for free medications for children. It called for socializing the household and organizing parts of domestic work and consumption by expanding cafeterias, public services for household repairs, dry cleaning, and other services that tailor to household needs. It also began to restructure social services and food cafeterias at every workplace and institution to help its workers and their communities. It launched a public credit system, making available special housing loans for young families.[66]

The same legal reform also extended all these rights and benefits to either parent by turning "maternity" benefits into "parental" benefits – "because men develop into better citizens if they are more closely engaged in parenthood."[67] In fact, films and published materials began to circulate as early as the 1960s to aid in the social normalization of men in parental and caretaking roles, while fighting social prejudice and stigmatization in public space. The film *Siromashko liato* (1973), featuring renowned actor Georgi Partsalev, centres on a newly retired, sixty-year-old man who had a successful career in the mid- to upper levels of the state administration. In the first months of his retirement, he is experiencing a crisis of purpose while trying to adjust to his new free time. His younger family members have a lot going on so they toss him the baby, his grandchild. At first he is reluctant to walk the streets with a stroller, yet in the process he bonds with the child, and his male embarrassment disappears and gives way to social pride as he embraces his new purpose in life as a grandfather and primary caretaker.

In fact, the 1971 reforms turned "maternal" benefits not only into "parental" supports but into partial "kinship" benefits as well. In addition to the legal father, they were applicable to a grandparent who could claim primary responsibility for the care of a child.

Figure 2.2. *Family* (1981), a sculptural composition by Nikolina Parikian, near the Wedding Ritual Hall, Plovdiv.

However, these benefits could only be claimed by the father or the grandparent six months after birth or adoption and with the explicit agreement of the mother. This was an ambivalent formulation as it still posited the mother as the primary parent and conferred upon her the primary responsibility of care, at least for the first six months. At the same time, it was an interesting development, not only because it recognized the responsibility of the "father," but also because it granted a material and social recognition, albeit a limited one, of the kinds of kinship and community care networks involved in raising children and the multiple forms of parenthood already present in the local cultures that defied modern Western models of the nuclear family. It is unclear to what extent it had any tangible influence over patriarchal perceptions that see parenthood and child care as women's "obligation." However, they at least opened the material and legal conditions in some intriguing directions.[68]

Through their organizing, feminists were able to bring social visibility and social value to reproductive and care work, and socialist society had to acknowledge these activities, politically and socially, in multiple forms. In her retrospective account of feminist work and organizing in the post-Stalinist decades, Dinkova explains that all of these reforms were not necessarily aimed at delivering rights or social gains that benefit women. But because women historically carried the responsibility and the burden of social-reproductive and care work, their bodies and their social lives contained the social contradictions at the centre of modern socialist society. By focusing on women's collective and historical burdens, she continues, feminists had the opportunity to accomplish a deep and profound transformation of society as a whole. In this sense, their goal was not only to bring visibility to social-reproductive work, but, in the process, to make this work central to the idea of what a socialist society is – to underscore the fact that, first and foremost, a socialist society is socialist because it recognizes the function of social-reproductive work in society at large, its social un-disposability, its material inevitability. These were radical visions that not only redistributed resources but also collectivized social-reproductive and care work in unprecedented ways. In some sense we should look at these traditions as some of the most radical contributions to the larger movement toward the communization of the social-reproductive sphere, of its material and social forms.

PRO-NATIVISM IN SERVICE OF ETHNONATIONALISM

With all their positive moments, these ideas and practices rested on a host of premises that naturalized reproductive heterosexuality and motherhood and deployed them in the service of population-management projects with ethnonationalist agendas. They also went hand in hand with the feminization of women. Post-Stalinist constructions of femininity both called on women's social power and independence and summoned them into normative orders of heterosexuality and femininity, redesigned in the context of post-Stalinist material and social life. The social indispensability of the woman-mother was enforced through the double imperative of naturalized motherhood and motherhood as social obligation, and was positively rewarded as social labour and as a political contribution. In this sense, the woman-mother acquired a tripartite obligatory meaning: once posited as nature, once as social obligation, and once again affirmed as social labour, which in socialist society held great political value.

With motherhood as a dictate of nature and a duty to socialist society at large, women found themselves in the grip of unforgiving social expectations, normative regimes of sexuality and social life, and biopolitical strategies of population reproduction and growth. Socialist women's subjectivities and social lives thus carried the pressures of prescriptive post-Stalinist visions of socialist peoplehood, socialist nationhood, equality, public access, and collective material prosperity – their bodies were to literally carry these ideals to reality. Further, because child-bearing and child care were seen as an important form of socialist labour, and because labour in socialist society constituted political activity in a very material sense, mothers who gave birth to a third child also received political recognition as "heroes of socialist labour" (*geroi na sotsialisticheskiia trud*), a title that gave them political and social status.

Through state-supported motherhood policies, women acquired functionality according to the rational governance of resources, productive forces, and bodies, in which women's reproductive powers were reconciled with their new social and leadership roles within a framework of gender equality and the democratization of gender relations. They were also at the heart of the pro-nativist turn of the 1970s. The 1973 resolution – the same order that outlined policies to improve the material and social conditions for women in political and professional leadership, and dramatically expanded the public infrastructures and means of addressing social-reproductive needs – also committed to pro-nativism and prescribed a path of womanhood that stretched from girlhood to motherhood. It promised all material resources, including free reproductive health care, for women to take this path, and sought to assure the woman-mother that her career and her political participation would be equally rewarding and rewarded.

Existing research places the demographic crisis of the 1960s at the heart of this pro-nativist turn, which also set the grounds for the emergence of the fields of social governance and population management. Ghodsee and others have argued that by the 1960s, birth rates had plunged dramatically as a result of women's integration into production and other spheres of social labour and public life, and that this was one of the reasons why the reproduction of socialist relations became an urgent concern.[69] But the general trend was relatively stable birth numbers up until the end of the 1980s. Abortions, by contrast, were on the rise since 1956, when a legal reform made them free and legal, and in the period between 1957 and 1989, the annual number of abortions was often higher than the number of births. The pro-nativist politics of the 1970s were certainly informed by these numbers and were embraced by some of the most conservative demographers. However, many women organizers were also on board and thus did not mount significant opposition to the legal changes limiting access to abortions in the early 1970s. "Our politics of social governance is taking a pro-nativist approach," Dinkova writes. "A number of party and government documents established a norm for Bulgarian families to give birth to and raise between two and three children. But today our young couples give birth to about two children, and the tendency is for this average number to decrease. Our citizens have been oriented toward a low number of births."[70]

The social value of the mother was henceforth directly linked to the demographic politics of the state and the larger goal of increasing the population "according to the development of the productive forces of society."[71] Atanas Totev, a leading Bulgarian demographer, argued that a "two children norm" would lead to a systemic decrease in population numbers, and to this end proposed a strategy for population growth that articulated the biopolitical logics of the late-socialist states:

> Socialism creates the necessary conditions for the right use of natural resources and care for the environment, which, together with the achievements of science and technology, guarantees the systemic development of the means of production and the possibility of creating favourable conditions for the material and cultural life of a larger population. Further, these possibilities are based not only on the natural resources of each country, but on the entire integrated system of socialist countries. This is why the demographic politics of the socialist countries, including that of Bulgaria, is to reproduce the population according to

the development of the productive forces of society. The strategy of this politics is "a family of three children."[72]

In 1972, the Bulgarian Ministry of Health signed a decree partially restricting access to abortions; these would now be available only to single, divorced, and widowed women and to married women with two or more children. This partial ban remained in place until 1990. In addition, the "family of three children" strategy proposed in the late 1960s offered various economic incentives to all mothers, and, as changes in the laws from 1968 to 1972 show, it gave the most political reward and economic incentives to mothers with three children. Awarded according to three income categories, the allowances for three children in the lower-income categories would match or exceed the monthly income of the parent. The changes also criminalized abortions performed in alternative settings and instituted a tax on the income of all single, divorced, and widowed working citizens (between the ages of twenty-one and forty-five for women and twenty-one and fifty for men).[73] During the early 1970s, the journal *Zhenata dnes* supported these policies by encouraging single women to keep their babies and publishing articles on the risks to health and fertility posed by abortions, on alternative birth control methods, and on the social virtues of motherhood.[74]

Looking at developments in other socialist countries such as Romania, which banned abortions completely in a similar attempt to increase its population, Ghodsee interprets these measures generally in a positive light, stressing the fact that even with limited access, abortion services in Bulgaria remained free, safe, and legal.[75] But these measures should instead be seen as a reactionary move that folded women's bodies into the reproductive and biopolitical regimes of the post-Stalinist state. With their pro-nativist approach and normative visions of motherhood, with no radical critique of heterosexuality and the heteronormative family, and with no critique of their relation to state power, the visions of socialist women who worked with the state structurally converged with the biopolitical agendas of post-Stalinist state governance. The "socialist woman" thereby became a central political resource for building socialist relations and became deeply embedded in the biopolitical logics of developed socialist society.

The pro-nativist turn of the late 1960s should also be seen in the context of the rise of ethnonationalism in the post-Stalinist decades.

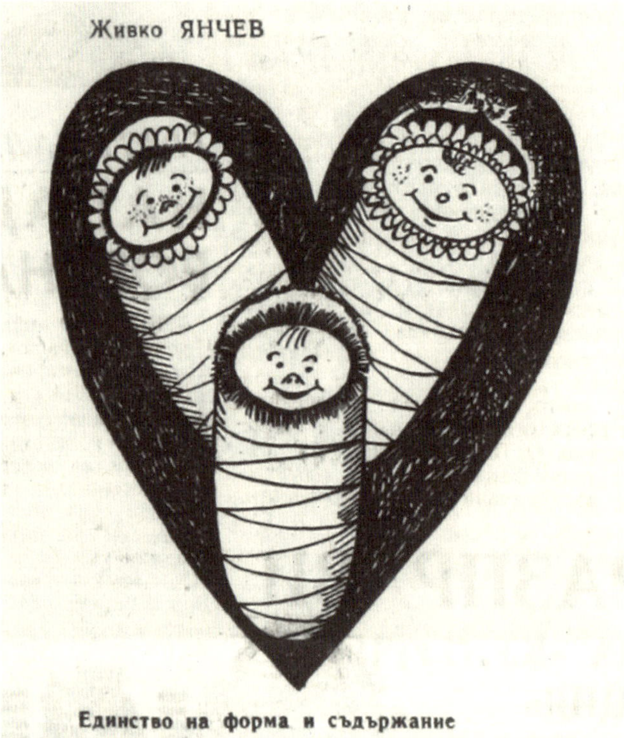

Figure 2.3 Zhivko Ianchev, "Unity of form and content," *Narodna mladezh* (10 March 1968). A friendly if satirical comment on the three-child policy introduced in the late 1960s to encourage population growth.

Women found themselves not only entangled in biopolitical regimes of population management during this period, but also became the foundation of the reproductive politics of the post-Stalinist ideologies of ethnonationalism. Discourses on gender embraced modernization and development frameworks that saw in the social emancipation of women under socialism an effort to overcome the patriarchal legacy of pre-modern Bulgaria, especially the "backward traditionalism" of the Ottoman period. Sociologist Savina Sharkova, in her work on gender during the socialist era, points out that the 1973 resolution, the same decree calling for support for women's leadership in all spheres of public and social life, also introduced a nationalist agenda.[76] Bulgarian women, the resolution stated, were central to "the survival of our people for thirteen centuries, its liberation from foreign occupiers, from capitalism and fascism, and for building a national spiritual and material culture."[77] Grounded in post-Stalinist constructions of nationhood as a singular, unified peoplehood, it also made Bulgarian women central to the linear narrative of Bulgarian nationhood: "Our call is: more children in every Bulgarian family, more young forces for the Motherland! … For the realization of this national task – the birthing and raising of children, for developing and strengthening the family – the woman plays a major role."[78]

Appeals to such national patriotism were not simply an attempt to legitimate women's demands in the dominant ideological framework of the 1970s; they were first and foremost a structural element of socialist gender politics of the period. These tendencies are apparent in the developmentalist and orientalizing discourses deployed by theorists such as Dinkova and Puteva, which rendered Bulgarian family culture during the pre-socialist, pre-modern, and Ottoman times backward and frozen in the past. Dinkova, in her study of the history of Bulgarian family relations, deployed a quasi-colonial gaze to construct a static, ahistorical picture of the pre-modern, pre-capitalist Bulgarian family: according to this view, change begins only with the development of capitalist relations, the market, and the commodification of labour.[79] Similarly, Puteva depicted pre-modern Bulgaria as an underdeveloped and backward country characterized by unchanging patriarchal relations, which the socialist order turned into a developed industrial-agrarian society capable of overcoming patriarchal relations and a culture of traditionalism.[80]

According to Dinkova, pre-modern Bulgarian kinship was characterized by single, self-sustained economic micro-units or micro-communities of up to two hundred people organized along patriarchal and patrilineal lines. While relying on a gendered division of labour, this form of economic organization contained a great deal of collectivism and equality, with its systems of communal of labour and egalitarian distribution from which any notion of individual labour was absent. The family contained historically resilient elements of autonomy and egalitarianism, which neither "forced Islamization" during the Ottoman period nor capitalist development were able to break down. Bulgarian socialist family relations, in their communal and egalitarian forms, drew on these vernacular forms, but socialist modernization liberated them from the dominant patriarchal models of the Ottoman period.[81]

These orientalizing notions were deployed in more popular accounts of contemporary womanhood, manhood, and the revolutionary transformation of gender relations. "Bulgaria has been through the Turkish yoke," Dinkova wrote in a widely popular article from 1966, a critique of contemporary men and the patriarchal values they held onto when it came to household work. "We all know how the oriental mores have influenced our people … The man from the past treated his woman mainly as a means toward settling down with his material life … In many families, the man would beat, curse, and cuss his wife, he rudely commanded her and denied her rest and personal life, used her labour without acknowledgment, and got irritated when she was sick or tired."[82] The men of the revolutionary generation, by contrast, joined in the radical transformation of gender relations, often confronting their parents and their patriarchal values, Dinkova explains. And yet, when they themselves entered family life, "tradition crept back in." "It is not pleasant to come back from your day job in your factory or institution only to start working again for more hours. It is more appealing to seek rest and sink into the world of books. And then tradition comes to aid, according to which household work belongs to women."[83] The Ottoman past became a depository of a backward, traditional, and tyrannical patriarchy, and post-revolutionary social change was to overcome its remnants.

These connections appear even more clearly when we look at their practical applications. By 1979, the government had revisited the country's new demographic politics in the context of the Revival Process, the campaign targeting Turkish, Roma, and Pomak minorities for ethnic assimilation. In her history of the Revival Process, Evgeniia Ivanova discusses the new demographic politics in light of birth statistics among ethnic minorities. Indirectly targeting non-Bulgarian ethnic minorities, the government highlighted the need for "limiting spontaneous births" (*ogranichavane na stikhiinata razhdaemost*). In the case of Roma and Turkish minorities in particular, statistics showed birth rates close to three times higher than those of ethnic Bulgarians, figures that triggered the ethnophobic anxieties of the nationalist leadership.[84] This is why, while working to establish three children as the national norm, the pro-nativist policies actively discouraged families from having subsequent children, thereby decreasing the need for additional child-care support.

From the 1970s on, feminist movements in the socialist countries made social reproduction a central focus of their work in a way that extended far beyond any similar concerns in Marxist and left-feminist traditions in the West. As this chapter has shown, the socialist meanings of social reproduction included more familiar notions such as biological reproduction, domestic and care work, housing, food, and health care, as well as such institutions as the school and the "family." Yet they also included leisure, rest, culture, creative activity, social life, and a range of other social activities. In some ways, these displaced the dominant role of "labour" as an organizing social principle, or rather positioned it as just one aspect of a more expansive picture of social and creative life. In this way, post-Stalinist feminists managed to make social reproduction central to the meaning of socialism. They pressed the question: What kind of society is this if it doesn't take collective responsibility for social-reproductive needs and activities, if it doesn't make them a shared social responsibility at large? By pursuing these questions, activists in the movement eventually made the government allocate resources for and build vast infrastructures of care, leisure, culture, and creative activity. These material conditions opened possibilities for women to have more social autonomy and mobility, and they had the potential to break down gendered divisions of labour and the material structures of class and patriarchal subjugation.

Yet the designs of these socializations carry the mark of their times and had uneven effects. In line with a good deal of feminist work in the West as well as other places in the 1970s, they adopted binary and heterosexual notions of gender and sexuality and essentialized women's bodies. They privileged the biological mother as the primary caregiver, turning "motherhood" into both a dictate of nature and a social duty. Because these and other patriarchal notions were left intact, this kind of labour remained largely feminized, even if it was more socialized. It is also not surprising that these policies became entangled in the most disturbing ways in population-management projects and ethnonationalist visions of nationhood. History has shown that women's bodies and social lives often serve as the terrain on which these biopolitical projects are enacted, and the restrictions on abortion in the early 1970s should be seen in the context of this pro-nativist turn.

The nationalist elements were present not only in the work of socialist feminists from the period; they were embedded in their humanist frameworks as well. The chapters that follow explore in detail the convergence between socialist humanism and ethnonationalism in Bulgarian political thought and Bulgarian politics during the post-Stalinist period. The turn to ethnonationalism at that particular time was not accidental: it was a possibility contained within the epistemic logics of socialist-humanist thought and its concepts of modernization, progress, and socialist development. Combined with a singular, monistic understanding of nationhood and a linear, progressive narrative of national history, humanist visions of democracy, human freedom, social mobility, and social integration became a vehicle for the state's erasure and assimilation of ethnic minorities during the last three decades of socialism.

3

In the Darkness of Humanism

The monument known as 1,300 Years Bulgaria (*1300 godini Bulgariia*), built in the centre of Sofia in 1981, was a cultural landmark of the socialist-humanist tradition. It was part of an ambitious vision of cultural and urban renewal in the capital and throughout the country in the 1970s and '80s, a period that eventually came to be known as the "Zhivkova era." These renewal efforts aimed to forge a new chapter in the life of the nation by using culture to emancipate the country from Soviet hegemony and to construct a "unique" national cultural heritage that could gain world-historical recognition and circulation. It also aimed to reimagine the nation's identity and history through a kind of humanist universalism and to signal its belonging to a wider international or "world" culture.

The 1,300 Years Bulgaria monument was designed by a collective of architects, urban planners, engineers, sculptors, and artists as part of a larger effort to energize an area of the city destroyed during World War II and abandoned in the following decades. Selected through a design competition, the winning monument was chosen for its formal radicality, its conceptual novelty, and its ambition to engage the viewer in communication with the surrounding space. One of the most radical works of public monumental sculpture during the late socialist period, it belonged to the finest and boldest examples of socialist modernism. The monument was adjacent to a cultural centre and was embedded in a large recreational area in the city centre. The entire ensemble achieved a remarkable synthesis of architecture, monumental sculpture, and urban planning.

The monument offered a visual interpretation of the abstract theme of "Past, Present, and Future" by combining narrative and

Figure 3.1 1,300 Years Bulgaria in its original condition, Sofia, 1981. The monument is viewed here from the north, with the National Palace of Culture in the background.

symbolism, abstraction and figurative detail. It consisted of several large, multi-faceted geometrical bodies that spiraled upwards and converged into the structure's highest component, signalling a forward, upward movement. The dynamic and abstract but somewhat austere architectural body anchored a series of four large sculptural scenes cast in metal and created by the famous sculptor Valentin Starchev. They loosely represent four key historical moments in the nation's epic narrative: the lowest scene, "The Golden Age of Simeon," pictured the glory of the First Bulgarian Kingdom. A little further up was "Baptizing the Community," which emphasized the centrality of Christianity to the formation of Bulgarian national consciousness – despite the country's sizable Muslim, Jewish, and other non–Orthodox Christian populations. Right above was "Pieta," a composition that referenced national self-determination movements during the late Ottoman period and symbolized the suffering of the Bulgarian people throughout the ages more generally. Finally, "The Builder" represented the socialist worker as well as ordinary toiling people throughout the ages.

The monument embodied the contradictions of its era. It celebrated socialist humanism's political values of democracy, peoplehood, progress, and liberation, as well as the idea that "humans are the creators of their own environment." However, while highlighting ordinary people's struggles for liberation, it also endorsed the ethnonationalist politics of the post-Stalinist period. It rewrote the socialist present of the early 1980s by forging a historical continuity and conceptual symbiosis between the socialist-humanist and nationalist projects.[1]

Post-Stalinist socialist humanism came into being to celebrate ordinary people's struggles for liberation throughout history as they culminated in the socialist present. At the same time, it imagined the triumph of universal humanism as a convergence of the socialist and national projects, inviting ethnonationalism into its world. It gave expression to a notion of peoplehood and a sense of national unity that excluded hundreds of thousands of people by imagining a linear, progressive national history and by erasing the historical presence and cultural contributions of multiple faith, language, and ethnic communities that had cohabited the region for centuries.

The central thesis of this chapter posits that socialist-humanist philosophy and culture in Bulgaria opened the conditions for the rise of ethnonationalism, and that it welcomed the construction of an ethnically homogenous nation. How did this become possible and why at this particular historical juncture? What is the link between humanism, ethnonationalism, and "developed socialist relations"? What is the relationship between the nationalism of the 1960s, '70s, and '80s and the nationalisms before the socialist period? What were the specific constituent elements of the ethnonationalism of the post-Stalinist period?

Figure 3.2 The sculptural compositions that comprise the 1,300 Years Bulgaria monument by Valentin Starchev, pictured here in May 2008. Originally built in 1981 in the centre of Sofia, the monument was neglected after 1989. Over the next three decades its condition progressively deteriorated, until the municipal government demolished it in 2017.

This chapter looks at the formation and political logic of the ethnonationalist doctrine in post-Stalinist socialist Bulgaria, tracing the continuities and discontinuities with earlier, pre-existing historical articulations of national consciousness and ethnonationalist projects. It places the developments of the so-called Revival Process (*Vuzroditelen protses*), a campaign of forced assimilation among ethnic and religious minorities in the 1980s, in the context of post-Stalinist socio-political life and shows how the politics of ethnocentrism emerged from within the specific logics of Marxist humanism. An anti-Stalinist but also partly an anti-Soviet discourse, the doctrine of Bulgarian ethnonationalism was developed on Marxist-humanist foundations, where ethnonational monism became embedded in humanist visions of socialist freedom and peoplehood, of social totality, mobility, and social integration. All these ideas, part of the socialist vision of social progress, rendered ethnic and religious minorities backward, underdeveloped, and "traditional." This was in keeping a quasi-colonial discourse deployed in the assimilation and historical erasure of ethnic and religious minorities.

ETHNONATIONALISM, BUT ANEW

The Revival Process marks a violent political turn in the history of late Bulgarian socialism, one of the most disturbing chapters in the country's modern history. An escalation of the ethnic and religious assimilation campaigns begun as early as 1958, it forcibly renamed hundreds of thousands of people with Turkish and Muslim names and took a wide range of measures toward the erasure of their culture, faith, ritual, language, and history. By the summer of 1989, after a decade of demonstrations and unrest, the Revival Process had escalated to the expulsion of several hundred thousand Turkish people into neighbouring Turkey. Having lived in Bulgaria for generations, they were uprooted from their homes and the lands of their ancestors and forced to seek political asylum from what was in effect the biggest ethnic cleansing campaign in Bulgarian history. Countless stories of mass departure, displacement, and exile, of broken communities and families, of abandoned homes, of lost or stolen land and cattle, of dispossession, trauma, loss, and grief, continue to emerge as uprooted communities maintain their efforts to rebuild their lives and recover their obliterated histories.

While the history of the Revival Process is still being written, the majority of existing research has underscored various continuities with earlier waves of ethnic assimilation, expulsion, and population exchange conducted as part of the nation-building process in the Balkans during the late nineteenth and early twentieth centuries. For example, historian Mary Neuburger places the minority policies of both early and late socialist governments on a continuum with previous efforts to modernize society and build a secular communist state by eliminating the remnants of the Ottoman past.[2] The vast majority of Bulgarian-language research shares this reading – in fact, according to Rumen Avramov, this continuity is one of the only points of consensus in the vast Bulgarian-language scholarship on the Revival Process.[3]

While this reading is beyond dispute, it captures only part of the logic. The Revival Process is indeed part of a continuous history of ethnic, linguistic, and religious homogenization in the Balkans dating back to the formation of national consciousness in the nineteenth century. It built on the practices and the experience of earlier governments, on earlier campaigns of assimilation, migration, and population exchange, and on a sequence of policies and bilateral agreements. Further, the ethnonationalist doctrine of the Revival Process adopted earlier uses of language, ethnicity, and national identity in a return to the pre-socialist period of national independence, to order national identities rather simplistically along the continuous axis of ethnicity–language–religion. Even as it insisted on the freedom of religious consciousness, it triumphantly collapsed religion, language, and ethnic origin into a singular line. This singularity was incorporated into the vision of socialist society and became a central vehicle in the effort to accomplish the social integration and mobility that socialist humanism had imagined. Further, in congruence with earlier ideas of national consciousness, the doctrine reinforced a pre-existing, and already antagonized, Christianity-Islam dichotomy, and continued to marginalize ethnic and religious communities that did not fit neatly within the binary logics of this order.

But further inquiry into the historical developments of the 1970s and '80s reveals a kind of specificity shaped by the unique social and political conditions of the post-Stalinist period, a specificity that needs closer analysis. In fact, post-Stalinist nationalism presented a radical shift from the early Stalinist period, which emphasized the right to national self-determination, guaranteed religious, linguistic, and cultural equality, and granted cultural and educational autonomy to ethnic, national, and linguistic minorities.[4] During the early years of socialism, the government experimented with Muslim populations in harmful ways, relocating people from entire villages along the southern border to other parts of the country. These campaigns followed a geopolitical logic concerning matters of national security in the new post–World War II international border regime, when the Bulgarian-Turkish border became one of the frontiers of the Cold War. But after 1958, the shift in direction was so sweeping that we can speak of a regime change with a nationalist agenda. In some ways the post-Stalinist government embraced ethnonationalist humanism as a form of resistance or an alternative to the Stalinist model of national diversity. However, while enjoying a kind of revival during the post-Stalinist era, ethnonationalism did not simply import right-wing, pro-fascist nationalism from the pre-socialist era, but instead gave it anti-capitalist and anti-fascist foundations and rearticulated it within a socialist-humanist framework.

In the post-Stalinist context, ethnonationalism was also mobilized to enact a kind of cultural emancipation from Soviet hegemony. The post-Stalinist ethnonationalist doctrine constructed a continuity of

Bulgarian sovereign statehood with independent territories that predated the Russian and even some of the oldest European states. Bulgaria had to be ancient and socialist at once.[5] This new historical imaginary rewrote the narrative of liberation and universal freedom, anchoring the world-historical revolutionary coordinates not in the February and October Revolutions, but in the local histories of national independence movements and struggles for autonomy, as well as in pre-socialist cultures of communal egalitarianism. Further, it had to be a kind of nationalism thoroughly imbued with socialist content. National history had to be simultaneously a socialist history, a people's history, and a revolutionary history, one rooted in the stories of ordinary people's oppression and collective struggle throughout the ages.

A discourse of socialist modernization, progress, and development became a central element in the emerging doctrine of socialist ethnonationalism. As historians Maria Todorova and Mary Neuburger have shown in different ways, the Ottoman period became deeply entangled with the notions of underdevelopment and backwardness as they relate to discourses of modern nation-state formation.[6] Ideas of modernization and development projected social and material backwardness onto the Ottoman period and its material culture, and continued the cultural and material erasure of the Ottoman legacy. The Ottoman past was imagined as backward and frozen in time, the historical agent of patriarchal relations, of "cultural traditionalism" and "religious fanaticism." Seen through this lens, ethnic Turkish and Muslim communities and their culture were treated as a remnant of the past, a kind of social and cultural anachronism that only socialist modernization could overcome.

Post-Stalinist discourses around social mobility and democratic access played a tremendous role in the establishment of ethnonationalism, and in fact, as this chapter shows in detail, socialist-humanist ideas of democracy and social integration became almost entirely identical with ethnic homogeneity and were imagined in terms of it. Ethnic assimilation became the dark side of the humanist values of social mobility and universal access to education and culture and the fulfillment of material needs.

In this sense, post-Stalinist ideas of ethnic monism and ethnic homogeneity were structurally tied to socialist-humanist notions of state governance and its totalizing ambitions. In fact, as the next chapter develops in detail, the renaming of all people with Turkish and Muslim names and the expulsion of the Turkish population in the 1980s were carried out mainly through the use of the modern state apparatuses of welfare, population management, health care, the administrative bureaucracy of the state, and the socialist employment system. The deliberate use of the apparatuses of the modern state as a primary instrument in the assimilation and expulsion projects establishes with certainty that the campaign was a premeditated and state-organized project of ethnic cleansing, the result of what I call post-Stalinist "ethno-statism."

PROGRESS AND ONENESS, THE PATH TO ETHNIC ASSIMILATION

The zeitgeist of the 1970s is well-captured in the work and vision of Liudmila Zhivkova, chair of the Bulgarian Committee for Culture and the Arts for most of that decade and the main architect of the country's cultural politics during the period.[7] In her voluminous writings she developed a cultural philosophy that combined universal humanism, nationalism, and spiritualism. This was an eclectic assemblage containing social teleologies and universals, but also subaltern and decolonial elements. Zhivkova's cultural vision and scholarship was decidedly anti-Stalinist and people who knew her would often suggest that she wasn't even a Marxist. It would be more accurate to say that she took East European Marxist-humanist ideas in some unique directions. Influenced by non-Western cultural and spiritual traditions, she pushed strongly for these in the context of Bulgarian culture and supported numerous alternative political, cultural, spiritual, and quasi-religious communities in the country influenced by local and Eastern religious, philosophical, and spiritual currents. Zhivkova's idiosyncratic influences and her resistance to categorization disrupted the established vectors of cultural exchange, and in particular the Soviet and largely Stalinist orientation of the political establishment.[8] Her public work and scholarship made her a rather odd and uncomfortable figure in the eyes of many, but also a beloved and widely supported cultural leader among communities of diverse political and cultural orientation. Thanks to her influence, during the 1970s a number of previously marginalized or repressed radical social movements enjoyed a robust revival. Some of these included the Dunovists, a social and spiritual movement inspired by the work and life of local spiritual philosopher Petur Dunov, and the Tolstoyists, the social movements influenced by the Russian writer and social thinker Lev Tolstoy, which were particularly strong in Bulgaria. Along with anarchists, Tolstoyists and Dunovists often formed shared communities based on radical communalism and egalitarianism. The Tolstoyists were known for forming dozens of vegetarian communities and land communes in the early twentieth century, one of which lasted up to several decades.

Yet Zhivkova's multiple and seemingly disconnected passions were unified in a kind of universalist humanism, and the socialist concept of the holistically developed person was central to her work. In each person, she saw creative potential with universal meaning. The holistically developed person was a subject whose creative self-realization depended on social opportunity because "the principles of general universality will act according to the unique specificity of every human being."[9] Each individual was a micro-universe of social relations, and by realizing their full social and creative potentials, they contributed to "social progress" and the development of socialist relations, and also to a kind of universal human "development."

In Zhivkova's philosophical system, culture occupied a privileged position in that it was indispensable to the realization of the holistic universal spiritualism for which she advocated. About the arts and culture, she said, "It is time to overcome the limited perception that these concepts and activities are part of unrelated spheres, isolated from the larger social practice, insulated within themselves. The universal unity of life, the dialectical interdependency and mutual determination of all spheres of social life, the need of interconnectivity in social development – all these could be achieved only through human activity and human consciousness."[10]

It was the mission of culture and the arts to create cohesion and integration among the spheres of social life and to express the progressive historical continuity of her evolutionary vision of spiritual and cultural progress. "Regardless of which side we look at this historical development from," she wrote, "it is unthinkable without culture."[11] The "end goal" of aesthetic education, then, was "the holistic and harmonious formation of the human individual and society according to the laws of beauty, and the transformation of reality by humans according to these laws."[12] Through their aesthetic and cultural development, every labouring human being would become a creator and all social activity would become creative activity, socially and personally fulfilling. In conditions generously open to the creative

Figure 3.3 Detail from the mural *The Fire* (1981), with a portrait of Liudmila Zhivkova, at Auditorium No. 7, National Palace of Culture, Sofia. The artist, Khristo Stefanov, was famous for his work in the public monumental arts in the 1970s and '80s.

potentials of every human being, "labour would turn into creative need and a major factor in the perfection of the person that concerns not just the separate individual but relates to all social spheres."[13]

From Mahatma Gandhi and Rabindranath Tagore, to Nikolai Konstantinovich Rerikh (Nicholas Roerich) and Vladimir Lenin, to Leonardo da Vinci and Goethe, to Patriarch Evtimii and Konstantin

Kiril the Philosopher, every nation and every people, she claimed, gave birth to countless named and nameless humans who struggled for universal truth, whose creative work contains universal human values – and they belong to humanity as a whole.[14]

Every nation, every national history that had survived through the ages, contained universal aspirations because its culture had preserved and communicated timeless, universal human values in harmony with "the universal laws of truth and beauty." Testament to these universal truths were "thousands of monuments of culture in stone and metal, written and spoken, in revolutionary documents and upheavals." They embodied "the spirit of the national genius" and the "rich spirituality and strength of our people," which had endured centuries of challenges on the road to "worldly social renewal."[15]

The national idea came to provide a core element in the post-Stalinist vision of socialist humanism and its universalist aspirations. Post-Stalinist socialist humanism aspired to create a socialist community rooted in the idea of the nation, to bring into being a national culture that is distinctly socialist. National culture was the main historical expression of the "people" as part of a universal socialist humanity, to the extent that socialism became inalienable from nationalism. In her report for the Third Congress of Bulgarian Culture in 1977, Zhivkova wrote that "socialism and Bulgarian national culture are inseparable,"[16] and that Bulgarian "patriots" and Bulgarian communists stood hand in hand as the heroes of Bulgarian socialist history.

Because of Zhivkova's heterodox vision and her eclectic and defiant contributions to Bulgarian culture, many saw the "Zhivkova era" as a kind of cultural renaissance that opened spaces for great cultural, intellectual, and political plurality. Ivan Elenkov, an author of a detailed empirical history of the cultural policies of the socialist period in Bulgaria, saw in the Revival Process a break with Zhivkova's cultural legacy, a move away from the universalism of her vision and a "narrowing" of the ideological and thematic field of cultural production toward a nationalist agenda.[17]

While it is certainly true that after Zhivkova's death in 1981, the government deliberately revised the political directions of the nation's cultural development, a process that Elenkov traces convincingly, positing a break between the Revival Process and the Zhivkova era would fail to register crucial conceptual continuities. The reality is that national monism and its progressivist historical linearity were core elements in Zhivkova's spiritualism and cosmopolitan aspirations.

Further, the ideology of ethnonationalism should not be seen as a return to Marxist-Leninist principles.[18] On the contrary, it wasn't Marxism-Leninism but humanism, its resistant alternative, that remained foundational to the ethnonationalist doctrine to the very end and that opened favourable conditions for the establishment of ideas of ethnic homogeneity. These enabling conditions could certainly be found in Zhivkova's eclectic humanism – which was neither properly "Marxist" nor expressly ethnonationalist. The Revival Process did not emerge but rather culminated in the 1980s, and it cannot be divorced from the context of anti-Stalinist humanism that began to take shape in the late 1950s and early 1960s. Even with some lip service to Marxist-Leninist vocabulary, it was still a break from the Stalinist doctrine of Marxist-Leninism, both in a historical and philosophical sense, and a break from the ways Marxism-Leninism organized questions of national and ethnic identity, as well as linguistic and cultural plurality.

It is important to point out, however, that Zhivkova was not a theorist or a conscious agent of the ethnonationalism that emerged during her time. In fact, as I explore in chapter 6, her nationalism and even her universalism contained strong decolonial and subaltern elements that made possible Bulgaria's global realignment with anti-colonial liberation movements and with newly independent post-colonial nations. She was crucial in shaping the international imaginaries of the seventies, rooted as they were in global anti-racism, anti-imperialism, egalitarianism, and anti-war politics, and she made serious contributions to the reshaping of the political geographies of the era in favour of the politics of non-alignment and the building of global socialist solidarities with the people in struggle against social injustice, racism, against colonial and imperial projects, and against military intervention.

The revival of the national idea within a socialist and humanist framework provided favourable conditions for an ethnonationalist agenda and emboldened proponents of ethnic homogeneity and ethnic assimilation.[19] Historian Georgi Iankov, among the main architects of the ethnonationalist turn, argued for a "thickening of national relations and an increase of the ethno-cultural monism and homogeneity of the Bulgarian socialist nation," which, he argued, should encompass the country's community and social life in its entirety.[20] For him, the ethnonational idea was necessary for society to function as a unified social organism and community. Total social integrity "gives birth to a spirit of commonality, shared national culture, a shared way of life, and shared characteristics found in every person."[21]

The call for "unity" was a core element in the emerging discourse of ethnonationalism. On one level, unity, cohesion, and integration appeared as the dialectical unity between individual and universal, the overcoming of their oppositions, and it was part of the social imaginary that promised social integration and social mobility. To be fully realized, the holistically developed person had to be part of and an expression of the social whole. The builders of the modern nation-state promised material well-being, social integration, social mobility, and spatial connectivity for every corner of the nation. As society strove toward oneness and perpetual integration (*priobshtavane*), discourses of mobility and democratic access became synonymous with ethnic homogeneity and assimilation.

Two related theories formed the ideological core of the campaign and were adopted in its language: first, the "shared kinship roots" (*obshti rodovi koreni*) between Bulgarian- and Turkish-identifying people, which inferred an ancestral affinity and an "ethnic" sameness, and second, the "Islamized Bulgarians" thesis, which saw the identity of present-day Turkish people as the historical result of forced mass conversions to Islam during the fifteenth and the sixteenth centuries. Here is some of Iankov's reasoning:

> Having grown with and participated in Bulgarian public life, having lived with the grief, hardship, and joy of our people, the descendants of Islamized Bulgarians have no roots or national interests other than the interests of the Bulgarian socialist nation. They live in a Bulgarian environment, develop their culture, and are therefore fully justified to feel part of our people and should not be separated from the overall national flow. They are children born on Bulgarian land, their ethno-genesis and historical fate is tied to the fate of Bulgarian people, with the fate of the People's Republic of Bulgaria, with the fate of socialism.[22]

The "strategic line" and "main tasks" of the Revival Process were, according to its ideological proponents, "the holistic development of the socio-economic, cultural, ideological, and everyday life of citizens; more active inclusion in a developed socialist society; relentless struggle against Turkish bourgeois nationalism, Islamic fanaticism, and cultural conservatism; the formation of a class-based, Bulgarian patriotic socialist consciousness; and the creation of the material and cultural preconditions for their full integration into the socialist nation."[23]

National oneness and ethnic homogeneity, the nation's "monolithic ethnic unity," became the foundation of a developed socialist society and an expression of the social totality and the full social mobility it had promised.[24] From this perspective, non-Bulgarian ethnic consciousness and identity were seen as dividing the "unity" of the Bulgarian people, and the Revival Process an attempt to integrate the population into a unified whole, to restore its broken integrity.[25]

The principle of unity projected a sense of historical togetherness and reinforced the historical linearity of the ethnonationalist narrative. The identity of the socialist nation required a new historical consciousness, which expressed the people's unity in thought and deed (*edinomislie* and *edinodeistvie*) "in their struggle for freedom, independence, and democracy, for socialism and communism, and for the consolidation of the spiritual unity [*dukhovno edinstvo*] of the Bulgarian socialist nation."[26] These are the words of Orlin Zagorov, another outspoken ideologue of the Revival Process. He saw unitary historical consciousness (*edinno istorichesko suznanie*) as a central element of national consciousness, a sort of collective awareness and knowledge of the common historical fate of the Bulgarian people.[27]

Formerly named Shukri Takhirov, Zagorov was himself of Turkish descent. A party member and established philosopher who held various prestigious academic positions, he changed his name of his own volition, embraced his new Bulgarian identity, and became an outspoken advocate for and a model of the renaming campaign. In his words, "the historical consciousness of the Bulgarian people, its specific forms and manifestations throughout the ages, reflect the knowledge about the common historical fate in all Bulgarians regardless of their religion."[28] Further, Zagorov saw in the unity of historical memory one of the most important pillars of every "ethno-social community."[29] Unitary historical consciousness, in other words, was by definition hostile to the possibility of multiple, competing, and alternative historical narratives of national memory, origin, suffering, or struggle, and a singular historical continuity was crucial for the integrity of the national whole.

NATIONAL HISTORY SHALL BE A REVOLUTIONARY HISTORY

The nationalist imaginaries of the era embarked on an ambitious project of historical revisionism. According to Zhivkova's vision, the formation of a socialist society required the formation of a national consciousness that is "qualitatively different."[30] "Following the unity between past, present, and future," Zhivkova wrote, "the Bulgarian people had the historical occasion to examine the depth of its own revolutionary past."[31] Turning back to the past and reinventing the history of socialist struggle through the idea of the nation also meant rewriting the world-historical revolutionary narrative outside and independently of the February and October Revolutions. National discourse gave Bulgarian socialist humanists the opportunity to trace an internal genealogy of revolutionary traditions in the struggles of its own people and to displace Soviet-centred histories of the socialist revolution as a world-historical phenomenon: "Our times, heirs of ancient cultures and civilizations, of countless material and spiritual values, of heroic historical events, today, at the gates of our 1,300-year anniversary, the Bulgarian people proudly turns toward the past, carrying the responsibility toward the present, with the faith in the inevitable communist future."[32]

In other words, national history had to be socialist history as well, a history rooted in the struggle of the ordinary people against the oppression of feudalism, the "yoke" of the Ottomans and the emerging bourgeoisie, against an escalating right-wing nationalism that became a breeding ground for fascism, and against an authoritarian monarchic regime with elements of military rule. Put differently, to be socialist, national history had to be a people's history, a revolutionary history, one grounded in the stories of oppression and collective struggle. This was "because a creator of history is not the separate person, but the people," claimed First Secretary of State Todor Zhikov. "The people spill blood, they carry the struggle ... If we let the genesis of Marxism slip out of sight for us, nothing will be achieved. The people's masses are the creators of history."[33] The national narrative had to be rewritten to convey a socialist meaning in its every chapter, to highlight "everything progressive, humanist, and democratic," to construct a continuity of endurance, suffering, and struggle leading to the socialist present – a present that had no precedent in history because it brought liberation, democracy, and material and cultural wealth to the ordinary people.[34]

National history also had to be rethought and rewritten through a kind of materialist social analysis that took into account class and social inequalities and foregrounded the struggle of the people. "We approach history through class consciousness to rethink the historical road to the heights that we have reached in the socialist present," wrote Zhivkova.[35] The national project and its history was no longer the hegemonic project of the economic elites and their intellectual and literary cultures. Purged of "exploiters, murderers, and [national] traitors," cleared of feudal lords, tsars, monarchs, and bourgeois exploiters, and cleared of bourgeois individualism, socialist humanism reinvented a national past steeped in the heroism of the ordinary people and their collective struggle. It celebrated "the democratic and revolutionary traditions of the people, their heroism and audaciousness, the revolts of the Bogomils and the peasants, the *khaiduks* and the heroes of national liberation struggles, the partisans and fighters for social justice, the great patriots and internationalists."[36]

Some of these were treated as milestone historical events. Such was the case with the Bogomils, a mass religious movement with anti-feudal foundations from the early Middle Ages that spread both eastward and westward from the Balkans and called for the spiritual transformation of society on egalitarian principles; the Ivailo uprising, a victorious peasant revolt in the northeastern part of the Second Bulgarian Kingdom against Tsar Konstantin and his feudal aristocracy in the late thirteenth century; struggles for national self-determination and autonomy against the Ottoman Empire in the nineteenth century, in which post-Stalinist Marxists saw strong anti-feudal elements; and the communist guerilla insurrections of the early twentieth century, epitomized by the uprising of September 1923 and the 1944 socialist revolution. The narrative also highlighted links between national independence movements in the nineteenth century and later socialist ideas and movements, foregrounding the national heroes whose politics connected these struggles. These and other historical events, together with figures, symbols, and cultural traditions, formed the linear historical and cultural canon of socialist nationalism.

Emphasizing the role of historical interpretation in the local historiographies of the Ottoman era in the Balkans, historian Maria Todorova examines the political stakes behind readings that see the legacy of the period in singular terms. She traces conceptual and narrative frameworks privileging continuity, discontinuity, or outright negation of the Ottoman past to lend legitimacy to various political struggles, projects, and claims in the region's modern nation-states.[37] It is not surprising that during the 1970s and '80s, heated debates were reignited around a number of issues concerning the Ottoman period. This included a re-examination of what Todorova called the "conversion trope" in Bulgarian national historiography – a consistently present yet radically unstable and contested element of the historical narrative grappling with the increasing Muslim population in the Balkans during the Ottoman period, mostly between the fifteenth and seventeenth centuries. Todorova's work shows how this narrative has been chronically revisited in Bulgarian national historiography, often invented through "literary mystifications" and dubious reconstructions of historical documents, to establish an account of coerced and often violent mass conversions of Christian populations to Islam. In the Turkish-language historiography of the period, Todorova finds an emphasis on territorial mobility, mass migration, and resettlement in the context of *Pax Ottomana* (referred to as "colonization" in the specialized literature), while in the national historiographies in the Balkans, especially research into Muslim minorities and Orthodox Christian-Muslim relations, she observes an emphasis on conversion.

As Todorova points out, scholarly debates from the period produced some invaluable contributions. Many scholars were critical of nationalist reconstructions of the past, raising multiple questions, including on such issues as voluntary conversions and the socio-economic incentives and privileges that came with the acceptance of Islam.[38] Regardless of serious scholarly research and debate, however, the state unyieldingly supported and promoted scholarship with a nationalist agenda. Mobilizing empirical research and a discourse of historical objectivity, the state sponsored large amounts of research across such disciplines as linguistics, ethnography, anthropology, archaeology, musicology, history, and the fields of *kraevedie* or *kraeznanie* (the study of local regions), to "prove" the Bulgarian ethnic origin of Bulgarian-born Turkish people, their shared roots with ethnic Bulgarian people, and to establish a generally accepted narrative of forced conversions.[39]

Nationalist historians of the 1970s constructed Turkish-identifying communities as descendants of ethnic Bulgarians: they were, according to this reading, Orthodox Christians who were forcibly converted to Islam and thereafter assumed a Turkish identity. Ali Eminov's history shows that this thesis appeared as early as 1958 with respect to the Pomaks, and by the 1970s it became the state's official historical account of the past, at which point it enveloped Turkish and other Muslim minorities.[40] In the words of Georgi Atanasov, member of the Politburo of the Central Committee of the Bulgarian Communist Party,

> the historical truth is that these are Bulgarians who have been assimilated after they accepted Islam during the "Turkish yoke" [Ottoman rule] ... We were able to establish as a matter of fact that in many regions, the so-called "Bulgarian Turks" are in reality descendants of Bulgarians converted to Islam in the past, who, in different periods, in one way or another, got turkified [*turtsizirani*] ... This research ... confirmed the Bulgarian origin of entire villages and regions. It has been established as historical fact that in the regions of Krumovgrad, Momchilgrad, Dzhebel, and others, the population is Bulgarian in its ethnic origin and belonging. Icons and Christian burials were found, and elements in the toponymy, culture, dress, and other evidence showed the Bulgarian origin of this population.[41]

These were highly speculative narratives that were also imagined through Marxist and socialist principles. The work of Ilko Tatarliev from 1959 to 1960, along with the work of Orlin Zagorov, Khristo Khristov, Georgi Iankov, and Nikolai Mizov in the 1970s and '80s, shaped the scholarly parameters of this doctrine. Most importantly, they gave Marxist foundations to the theory of forced conversion and developed a critique of pan-Turkism as a "weapon" of imperialism and anti-communism, an instrument of "bourgeois chauvinism."[42]

In this sense, ethnonationalist historians saw the Revival Process as a concept that referred to and was continuous with the historical developments of the period of national independence from the eighteenth and nineteenth centuries. It is not a coincidence that the term "revival" (*vuzroditelen*), sometimes translated as "resurrection" or "rebirth," tautologically plays on the terminology of the nineteenth-century National Revival period (*Natsionalno vuzrazhdane*). This was a well-calculated move that aimed to invoke precisely such associations and continuities. Historian Nikolai Mizov articulates these embedded links in the following way: "Our National Revival (from the first quarter of eighteenth century to the 1870s) first reaches full maturity and realization among Bulgarian Christians, whereas during the Islamized Bulgarians the Revival is realized in full only under the conditions of socialist development. This means that our [socialist] phase of the Revival Process is not just a quantitative continuation of our National Revival, but a relatively new qualitative phenomenon in our national and social history."[43]

For ethnonationalist historians of the 1970s, then, the new phase of "national revival," the Revival Process, was qualitatively different, first, because it had been freed of the "bourgeois ideology" of the nineteenth-century national independence movements, and second, because the people's liberation was formulated not against a feudal-religious system and its elites but against what looked like patriarchal and socially anachronistic practices among part of the "Bulgarian" population.[44] It was a "process" because it captured the continuous and "progressive" aspects of the project and conveyed a sense of an unfinished historical task. Mizov found in it not only a "retrospective" and "corrective" significance, but an important "forward-looking" social dimension that takes into account equality, social mobility, and access to the means for addressing one's material and cultural needs as an essential element of the liberation of the (Bulgarian) people.

The official historical narrative aimed to justify the Revival Process as an act of historical redress by "restoring" a national and an ethnic identity to Turkish minorities according to their "true" Bulgarian origin. The narrative established a historical account that saw the present-day name conversions as a continuation of the unfinished liberation of the Bulgarian people from Ottoman rule. According to its defenders, it was "a historical act, which heals the last remaining scars from the Turkish yoke on the body of our people and creates the conditions for the strengthening of our national unity, our moral and political togetherness [*splotenost*]."[45] State discourse therefore insisted on seeing the erasure of ethnic difference as a continuation of the national independence project, which restored the national to a condition of wholeness and thereby completed the unity of the people. It was seen as a progressive, revolutionary historical movement, part of building developed socialist relations and a socialist national-patriotic consciousness. According to Atanasov, the Revival Process

> will achieve full consolidation of the Bulgarian socialist patriotic consciousness among those citizens who, in some periods of our

> past, by different means and motivations, have been separated and distanced from the wellspring of the Bulgarian national spirit. [The Revival Process] is a revolutionary deed, which strikes hard at Turkish bourgeois nationalism and its perpetual attempts to divide and spoil the consciousness of part of our Bulgarian citizens. We are accelerating the process of liberating them from their religious, conservative, and nationalist anachronisms.[46]

Mirroring its own political move, this ethnonationalist historical interpretation denied contemporary Turkish communities their ethnicity and instead viewed their modern Turkish identity as a product of coercion, violence, and historical injustice. The state declared that "there are no Turks in Bulgaria" and ordered that all official documents and discourses begin referring to Bulgarian-born Turkish people as "Islamized Bulgarians" (*isliamizirani bulgari*).[47]

The official historical narrative also contained a moralizing discourse that projected historical guilt and responsibility onto Turkish and Pomak communities and turned their identity, religious practices, and culture into a source of national betrayal. Pomaks became a primary object of this shaming discourse: they were often called "traitors" of the nation and the people, were made to bear responsibility for the conversions of their ancestors, and endured a culture of shame and disdain. But the state went even further: the unity of the Bulgarian people was the responsibility of every citizen of the country and it became a matter of patriotic duty for Bulgarians, Pomaks, Roma, and Turks, for Muslims, Jews, and Orthodox Christians alike, to comply or collaborate with the state's ethnonationalist offensive. Anyone opposing it, regardless of their identity, was condemned as anti-patriotic and divisive.

SOCIALIST MODERNITY FROM THE OTHER SIDE

Socialist humanism contained a strong discourse of progress, and of social, cultural, and historical evolution, and these were put to the service of ethnonationalism. With respect to social relations, progress meant "the democratization of cultural life." But to post-Stalinist socialists, democracy meant not its liberal forms, practised through political membership, political rights, freedom of speech, and representative institutions, but rather mass access to cultural life and education, to the means of cultural expression, and to the creation, distribution, and the use of cultural goods. This democratization was to be achieved through culture and creative self-activity.

Zhivkova wrote proudly that by the early 1980s, socialist Bulgaria, a country of about 9 million people, had 10,305 public libraries with close to 70 million titles, 209 state museums and galleries, 53 state theatres, 4,254 local cultural centres (*chitalishta*), 265 youth, union, neighbourhood, and other cultural and social spaces (*kulturni domove*), and over 22,000 autonomous creative arts collectives (*samodeini khudozhestveni kolektivi*). Each year the country held 15,000 concerts from professional musicians and 353 art exhibitions by professional artists and published a total of 52 million copies of 4,337 different books.[48] The autonomous, self-organized collectives in the spheres of arts and culture, specific to post-Stalinist social and cultural life, organized 120,266 shows, performances, and exhibitions per year.[49]

In short, by 1981, in less than four decades of socialism, the country had developed a vast material infrastructure to support the creative, cultural, and leisure activities of the population outside their educational, professional, and domestic lives. In so doing, it provided a tremendous number of flexible spaces for autonomous organizing and local initiative in all spheres of cultural and creative life.

On a historical level, this progress appeared in the service of constructing a linear historical narrative of liberation, one that drew a continuous line between national oppression, suffering, and endurance, as well as an evolutionary progression of struggle throughout history that posited socialism as the liberation of the people. As Zhivkova wrote in her work on the role of culture in developed socialist societies,

> During the different eras of centuries-old historical development, the Bulgarian people have created significant material and spiritual culture; they have created remarkable and lasting works of art and culture. Mature national, democratic, humanist, and revolutionary traditions reveal the depth, substance, and the specificity of Bulgarian spiritual culture, which was selflessly developed by named and nameless heroes and creators – tireless builders of beauty and truth. But in the entire history of the country, there is no equal to that which was created under the conditions of socialism. As heirs to everything valuable and progressive in a thousand-year-old heritage, our contemporary

socialist culture is historically and qualitatively higher in the cultural progress of our country and our people.[50]

As part of its evolutionary narrative, post-Stalinist socialist humanism constructed the historical trajectory toward communism as an endless, forward-spiralling progression that, in Zhivkova's words, "moves higher and higher in the unceasing chain of development in its different aspects – cosmic, natural, historical, social, universal-human [*obshtochoveshki*], individual human, and so on."[51] Humanity, she professed with a pathos that defines the era, "has climbed and continues to climb the steep road of progress. The people have carved mountains of heroic deeds on the infinite spiral … Historical memory has preserved the highlights of human spirit, highlights that shine light on humanity's steep journey on the endless stairway of evolution."[52]

With respect to material conditions, progress meant modernization. This included developing industry, collectivizing land and privately owned enterprises, reorganizing and mechanizing rural agriculture, eliminating illiteracy, providing access to education, supporting the growth of science and technology, developing a social infrastructure of health and child care, improving housing conditions, and satisfying "the material and cultural needs of the population."[53] Progress was still measured in terms that emphasized industrial labour and production, increased monetary income, and the productivity of land and the industries according to traditional Marxist notions of labour and productivity. But it went far beyond such traditional labour- and industry-centric understanding, which was more characteristic of the Stalinist era. Instead, as I explored in chapter 2, it prioritized access to the means of social reproduction, leisure, community, and creative life as the most important measure of social wealth. All of these laid the foundations of a modern social infrastructure whose form, content, and meaning were meant to be distinctly socialist.

Yet socialist discourse embraced the developmentalist framework of existing modernization paradigms and subscribed to notions of socio-economic backwardness (*izostanalost*) and underdevelopment (*nedorazvitie*). Poverty, the "primitive" instruments and organization of labour, and the lack of public infrastructure and education were explicitly embedded in the socialist meanings of backwardness and underdevelopment and the related concept of modernity. While socialist modernity projects were quite distinct from and resistant to capitalist and Western modernity projects – which scholars have called "alternative" and "competing" modernities – they contained strong teleological moments.

The internal structure of socialist modernization discourse also contained a self-orientalizing element that structured historical interpretations of socialist development as well as the fabric of contemporary socialist societies. In her book on Muslim minorities in Bulgaria, Neuburger has shown how the very concept of national modernization in the Balkans was tied to the idea of overcoming the "Oriental" traditions of the past.[54] The Ottoman period became deeply entangled with meanings of underdevelopment in both nationalist and socialist discourses of modernization. As the socio-economic features and cultural practices of the Ottoman period were perceived as provincial, backward, and frozen in the past, their remnants were seen as a historical anachronism that prevented the building of a new social order and therefore had to be overcome in a revolutionary movement. In the words of nationalist historian Iankov, "The contemporary process of 'Revival' in its character solidifies internally the development of the Bulgarian nation, a process of casting away traces and differences that had remained from the assimilationist politics of the Ottoman conquest. These [traces] had turned into an anachronism and for one reason or another, they were contained in this part of our people, holding back the consolidation of the Bulgarian socialist nation."[55]

These perceptions were not unique to the socialist era. Todorova observes that national historiographies of the Balkan region, while marred by "mutual enmity," nationalist claims of a common cultural heritage, and "passionate polemical traditions against each other," nevertheless share the negative historical renditions of the Ottoman period. Todorova shows how the Ottoman period was perceived as interrupting "the natural development" of pre-existing societies, sending them into "deep cultural regression."[56] This was in great part due to the civilizationist and colonial elements in Western Enlightenment knowledge adopted in national discourse after independence, which had demonized and orientalized the Balkans.[57] Portrayed as the barbaric invaders of the region's autonomous and mostly Orthodox Christian populations, the Ottomans became the agents of a less-developed civilization that had imposed an alien cultural, social, and political order on local societies.

The socialist era adopted this colonial narrative of the Ottoman period, reproducing and continuing much of its renunciation, stigmatization, and erasure. Via socialist development, the Bulgarian people were to emerge from the darkness, social underdevelopment, cultural backwardness, and patriarchal traditionalism of the Ottoman period. According to post-Stalinist discourse, the Revival Process was an enormous "historical leap" in the forward progression of revolutionary development – a leap from "medieval darkness toward socialist civilization." To this end, society was to "shed the heavy, dark remnants of the past, the elements of cultural conservatism and religious fanaticism."[58]

Turkish, Pomak, and Roma populations, who represented the remaining legacy of this "backwardness," therefore had to be uplifted and modernized. For post-Stalinist proponents of forced assimilation, the Revival Process was to bring "deep, revolutionary changes" in their consciousness, "in their life, culture, world views, and education, strengthening their Bulgarian and socialist self-consciousness and their national pride." It was to "emancipate" and "strengthen the self-confidence" of minorities, to help them "participate more actively in the building of socialism."[59]

"Isn't it true that thanks to the victory of our socialist revolution and our socialist government, the Muslim population was brought out of the darkness, misery, and lawlessness to which it was abandoned under Ottoman rule?" So asked First Secretary Zhikov in his infamous "Unity" speech of 29 May 1989.[60] The speech was publicly aired during a political crisis of tremendous proportions set off by the mass exodus of the Turkish people from the country. I will return to the historical details of the speech in chapter 5. Here, I bring up its content because it makes explicit the link between ethnic assimilation and the colonial underpinnings of socialist modernization. "Capitalist Bulgaria could not achieve this," Zhikov continued, citing the accomplishments of the socialist period in minority population areas – industrial development, economic growth, increased income, increased literacy and access to higher education, improved housing, transportation, plumbing and water supply, access to the means of social-reproduction, roads, and electricity, as well as drastically reduced child mortality rates and increased average life expectancy, the allocation of doctors, dentists, and teachers in regions populated by majority Turkish and Bulgarian Muslim communities. Of Razgradski region in northeastern Bulgaria, which was around 50 percent Turkish and 53 percent Muslim, Zhivkov boasted that "in the last 30 years, the main branches of our industry grew by 32 times, and net industrial production – by 30 times. Income growth – by four times; productivity of land

– by three or four times. Illiteracy in the region is completely eliminated, and more than 95 percent of the kids attend socialized child care and kindergartens. Each year 500 young men and women enter higher education. In the villages, housing funds have been replenished 100 percent, and transportation systems, water, and plumbing problems have been resolved."[61]

Speaking of the Kurdzhaliiski region, located in the Rhodope Mountains in central Bulgaria, whose residents were about 66 percent Turkish and 76 percent Muslim, Zhikov claimed:

> Before the revolution, every third child died at birth; the region had one doctor for 22,000 people and one dentist for every 54,000. [It had] a total of seven teachers and roughly only 7 percent of the population could read. Only 2.4 percent of the inhabited areas were connected to plumbing and roads, and 0.9 percent electrified. People and animals lived together and the average life span was 40–45 years.
>
> Today, the number of teachers is higher than the number of students before the revolution. The average life span in the region is 70 years for men and 75 years for women – higher than the average life expectancy for the entire country. This region has the lowest child mortality. People's savings are among the highest in the country. In Ludogorie, Kurdzhali, and other areas with Muslim populations, miracles have been created, new ways of life, new towns, new people. This is because under socialism, for the first time in history, humans, freed from the chains of their yoke, exploitation, and unemployment, became free to actually create their own fate and their future. Guaranteed were equal rights to labour and its rewards; guaranteed was the care for every person from birth to deep old age; guaranteed was wide access to culture and working people's participation in social governance ... All these values are inalienable characteristics of the socialist way of life and of this population.[62]

Capitalism had a short history in the region, and due to this historical fact, modernization was for the most part a socialist project, which meant that from the very start Bulgaria's modern social infrastructure rested on social principles. Yet modern socialist development projects delivered these material and social improvements with a patronizing force. Not only were "they" pulled out of darkness and the "mud," lifted up from "the bottom" and "the lowest step," but "this was all given to them on the back of the Bulgarian people."[63] Thus, the social well-being of ethnic and religious minorities came at a great price: in return for electricity, roads, hospitals, and jobs, minorities were expected to perform patriotic loyalty and have their identity and history defined for them. As Atanasov put it, "The main activity should be their patriotic and class-party education, to form in them the conviction that they are part of the socialist nation, that the People's Republic of Bulgaria is their country, that the national consciousness and communist education is the main measure of their loyalty to the socialist project."[64]

In addition to its patronizing mode, this was a xenophobic discourse that rendered minority cultures and communities inferior and powerless while taking for granted their social contributions and levying obligation, indebtedness, and gratefulness from them. By speaking on their behalf, the post-Stalinist government took away minorities' power of self-determination, their power to define their own collective identity and history, to name themselves and their children, to speak their own language and practise their own culture.

The very infrastructures that gave the government access to the social well-being and integration of minorities became the primary instruments of cultural assimilation and historical erasure. The traditional means of political propaganda – mass media, party organizations, and educational institutions – were fully mobilized toward ethnonationalist propaganda and the re-education of the general population, as were professional and labour organizations, co-operative collectives, and various women's organizations and committees. School programs focused on national patriotism introduced curriculum reforms, including "subjects related to questions of socialist patriotism," in an effort to "fuel the fire of patriotism and the unity of our people."[65] All these were tasked with "confirm[ing] the historical truth about the Bulgarian ethnic origin of this population, of their forceful *turkizatsiia* [turkification], of their reactionary role in Turkish bourgeois nationalism, [and revealing that] the true reactionary forces behind this process [were] Turkey, the US, and NATO."[66]

RELIGION AND ETHNOS PARTING WAYS?

To the very end, the state denied that the campaign was a matter of religious membership and religious practice and insisted that it was about settling historical accounts of ethnic belonging. The ethnonationalist doctrine professed the freedom of religious expression and continued to maintain that, according to the Bulgarian socialist constitution and socialist law, "there is full freedom of practice of all faiths and religions, including Islam."[67] It was not a matter of religion but of national consciousness and national identity – which was exclusively defined in terms of origin and language. In fact, the doctrine defined the process as an "internal national consolidation" that would undo the fusion between faith and "ethnic" identity in national consciousness. The formation of a unified Bulgarian consciousness required a "process of separating national belonging and religious affiliation." Iankov argued that "the nation is not a religious community. Religion is not a national holiday"; instead, he emphasized "factors of national determination" (*natsionalnoopredeliashti faktori*) as the main integrating force.[68] "The Bulgarian socialist nation unifies Bulgarians independently of whether they are atheists, whether they are under the influence of Christianity, Islam, or other religions," he continued. "This process leads to the overcoming of the selfsameness of religion and ethnos."[69]

It was, on the contrary, through the distinct and autonomous articulations of religion and national consciousness that internal social consolidation could be achieved while leaving the constitutional foundations of socialism intact: "The separation between nation and religion, between national consciousness and religious affiliation does not lead to curtailing of religious freedom and religious conscience."[70] Zagorov argued that even when they practised different religions, the "Bulgarian" people were united in their historical destiny and memory, as evidenced by their shared customs and cultural rituals, community life, traditions, and material culture, which was unmistakably Bulgarian in content.[71] Muslims and Christians thus shared a common historical consciousness through the ages, and despite their differences in religion, they managed to preserve "the consciousness of their unity through labour and everyday culture, in customs and habits, in their way of life ... This way, they have preserved not only their dignity and their property but the signs of their Bulgarianness, their Bulgarian character and sensibility, their love for labour, their ancient traditions."[72]

Indeed, when party leaders declared publicly, time and again, that, "as it is the case in all other countries around the world, religious membership at home does not determine national consciousness and nationality," they meant it, at least in part.[73] Following political doctrine, the first secretary insisted that "we do not tear down mosques, they are there, the *hodjas* are there, the rituals continue to be practised. We do not deal with these questions. Every Bulgarian citizen according to the constitution has the right to practise whatever religion they want. So when it comes to religion, we are not concerned, only the names."[74]

But these distinctions remained theoretical because of a persistent dichotomous association of Turks with Islam and Bulgarians with Christianity in the shared perceptions and collective consciousness of the larger community.[75] Those who executed the campaigns – lower-level party administrators, the military, the labour bureaucracy and management – often failed to perceive subtleties and thought the best way to eliminate one's "Turkishness" was to persecute the practice of Islam. But it is beyond question that despite the reigning political doctrine, the upper-level party leadership was Islamophobic and Turkophobic and often deferred responsibility for the worst crimes onto the lower ranks. In declassified documents revealing the internal logistics of the campaign, the first secretary himself expressed strongly Islamophobic views: "Fifteen to twenty years will pass and this will be forgotten. Then we will go after their religion. Gradually all *hodjas* that are ours will become the leaders of their religious organizations. In a few years we have to go strongly against Islam. In the schools this has to be taught as a subject. There are some features grounded very strongly in the family among the Turks ... We should not destroy these features, but rather gradually purge them from Islam."[76]

What is then distinct about the nationalist paradigm during the post-Stalinist era was not only that it anchored the national narrative in the struggles of the common people and brought out egalitarian and anti-feudal class elements. Socialist concepts of the nation attempted, at least in theory, to undo the convergence between religion and ethnos – a radical departure from earlier, pre-socialist formulations of the nation. This separation served a crucial function in the formulation of a secular socialist state inclusive of religious difference, and was also used in service of ethnic homogenization.

But the ideas of a secular socialist state inclusive of religious difference did not take hold. This project for the most part remained on paper. As it tried to undo the unquestioned equation of religion with ethnos, it subsumed religion under cultural ritual (*religiozno-obredni praktiki*) and opened the door to the persecution and erasure of Islam through arguments for cultural assimilation. As a result, popular national consciousness from the post-Stalinist era reproduced the complete convergence between ethnos, language, and religion and ordered them, rather simplistically, along a continuous axis. This monstrously monistic vision emerged not only as a path to fulfill the promises of social integration but also to bring about the full liberation of the socialist people from the remnants of oppression in the past.

Further, ethnonationalist discourse during the post-Stalinist era operated well within a long-ingrained dichotomy between Christianity and Islam, which marginalized and rendered invisible those who did not fit neatly within the binary logics of this order. Todorova has argued that whereas in Western Europe, the formation of nation-states resulted rather effortlessly in ethnic and religious homogeneity, the historical conditions in the Balkans and the complex demographic context of the newly established independent nations made such a project politically untenable, thereby bringing societies into tremendous convulsion.[77] Continuously drawn and redrawn, borders tore into the social fabric, cutting violently through communities and kinship ties, through commonly shared pastures, land, and material resources, while the identity and religious categories introduced by the states caused confusion, disorientation, and quite a lot of protest.

In this context, such a reductive, one-dimensional structure of national identity not only produced and intensified social antagonisms; it also failed to provide legibility to those who belonged to multiple registers of the ethnic, religious, linguistic, and cultural traditions, or those who did not fall into the dichotomous divisions between Islam and Christianity. Gagauzes, Pomaks, Jews, the Roma, Armenians, Macedonians, Greeks, Shops, Vlahks, Tatars, Sarakatsani, and other ethnic, religious, and linguistic groups, in addition to families and persons of mixed ethnic and religious backgrounds, all of which have historically been part of the region for centuries, were subject to multiple forms of marginalization and erasure. Some of these populations were thrown into confusion and discord, and, often subject to the most intense forms of assimilation, they bore the cultural stigmas of being othered in multiple ways, or, in the absence of available categories, of being completely erased.[78] But through their rather persistent ambiguity, they continue to refuse, unsettle, and disrupt the one-dimensional and dichotomous identity modalities characteristic of the ethnonationalist turn that culminated in the Revival Process.

ETHNOCENTRIC STATISM

In the socialist narrative of Bulgarian national history, the year 1981 was celebrated as a particularly significant anniversary: it marked thirteen hundred years since 681 AD, the founding of the earliest Bulgarian state and the beginning of the First Bulgarian Kingdom. The government launched a massive, ambitious campaign celebrating the anniversary, for which the ruling elites spared no material or creative resources, time, or labour power. In its grandeur and ambition, the commemoration was to be unsurpassed in history. To this end, the country was immersed in an abundance of cultural activity throughout the year. Gigantic monuments were built, parades and demonstrations were organized, speeches were given, and festivals were held to celebrate national culture and tradition as the bearer of world peace, internationalism, and universal humanity.[79]

The monument in Sofia built that year, 1,300 Years Bulgaria, was conceived precisely in this context. As its official name suggests, it was dedicated to thirteen hundred years of Bulgarian statehood and it was part of the ambitious programs commemorating the anniversary. In this sense, the monument was above all a manifestation of socialism's state-centrism, according to which the state was foundational to the nation's birth and its continuity throughout history. The beginning of the First Bulgarian Kingdom (*tsarstvo*) came to mark the foundation of Bulgarian statehood (*durzhava* or *durzhavnost*), and for this reason 681 AD became the legitimate historical beginning of the Bulgarian nation. This perspective emphasized the historical depth of Bulgarian independence as a succession of sovereign states throughout the centuries, a continuity which rendered the Byzantine and Ottoman periods as a time of foreign domination over the Bulgarian people, an interruption of Bulgaria's political autonomy. In the name of a continuous history of statehood, post-Stalinist socialists, who professed the abolition of monarchic and bourgeois forms of government and championed the self-rule of the common people, endorsed and celebrated the succession of monarchies, as long as they were "Bulgarian" and sovereign.

While paradoxical on many levels, the construction of a history of continuous Bulgarian statehood had important political implications for the 1980s. It resulted in a re-examination of Bulgarian national history through the lens of state sovereignty and solidified in Bulgarian

Figure 3.4 1,300 Years Bulgaria in its original condition, Sofia, 1981, seen from the west.

national consciousness a link between land, statehood, and Bulgarian national identity. It reinforced a sense of historically legitimate territory, which was claimed as inalienable because it was seen as ancient.

In the context of Bulgaria and other East European socialist countries, this historical reading contained anti-Soviet tendencies and became an important political weapon. By insisting on their ancient statehood, the young socialist nation-states affirmed their political autonomy and sought to allay anxieties about the Soviet Union's overarching influence and the related fear of a weakened Bulgarian sovereignty. To insist on a thirteen-century-old history of statehood was to affirm the will to sovereignty against a powerful state that was both an ally and a menace. In the end, the logic went, Bulgarians had an autonomous state long before the Russians – who could argue with that?

Thus, even as an anti-Soviet and anti-Stalinist tendency, post-Stalinist humanism reinforced statism as a dominant ideology of political autonomy and self-rule and continued the state-centrism of the Stalinist period nearly uninterrupted, although significantly revised and redesigned. It foreclosed, as it had from its foundation, possibilities for imagining forms of communism beyond the state and its regimes of social and territorial control, suppressing further social movements with anti-statist elements – whose ideas, material exchanges, and notions of self-governance extended beyond the forms of the modern nation-state.

On another front, state and territorial sovereignty became the privileged point of departure for the narrative of socialist ethnonationalism and also served as a justification for the government's ethnic-assimilationist offensive. This was by no means Bulgaria's first assimilationist project toward its ethnic, linguistic, and religious minorities. Yet it was not until the post-Stalinist period that all elements of the modern state apparatus were fully deployed in the service of such campaigns of ethnic assimilation, erasure, and expulsion. In addition to the instruments of violence and warfare, of education and political propaganda, the state mobilized, perhaps most crucially, the apparatuses of population management and social welfare. In other words, ethnonationalism emerged as a central organizing principle of post-Stalinist state governance, bringing forth a sort of ethnocentric statism that I call "ethno-statism."

Ethno-statism was also fuelled by the assumption that an ethnically and religiously diverse population is not only an obstacle to forging national and socialist community but also a threat to state sovereignty. Because it posited a natural and legitimate link between ethnicity and land, the philosophy of ethno-statism saw ethnic difference as a threat to territorial integrity. Ethnic difference contained by definition a claim to territory and political autonomy and was a potential instigator of secessionism and territorial separatism.

Forging a linear, ethno-lingual (and by assumption religious) community became not only a major element of national consciousness but a primary weapon against what was seen as a threat to territorial sovereignty. In a return to pre-socialist nationalism, post-Stalinist socialism continued this tendency. This is why the leadership automatically interpreted the resilient and unyielding protests against the Revival Process, and some eventual clashes with the state, as movements for territorial autonomy or secession and threats to national sovereignty. This also explains the heavy-handed military suppression of the enduring demonstrations that took place in the 1970s and '80s, and the way the government welcomed, encouraged, and facilitated the mass exodus of Turkish-Bulgarians in 1989. The next chapter recounts these events in detail.

4

Stalinism to Post-Stalinism: Shifting Histories, Shifting Readings

A handwritten letter from April 1960, addressed to the highest order of government – one of many letters of complaint, support, appeal, or demand regularly sent to the authorities by ordinary residents – raises objections to the recently launched reform of the Turkish school system in Bulgaria.[1] The writer, who identifies as a man of Turkish descent, opens by stating that he would like to keep his anonymity so he can "express himself more freely" and apologizing for his imperfect use of the Bulgarian language.[2] Yet the letter is crafted in marvelous language and a respectful voice and is composed with great thought and political insight. The man was travelling on the train to Sofia from the town of Kolarovgrad (today Shumen), when two young men, Turkish teachers, came into the cabin and started a conversation. The men spoke freely in Turkish, as they did not suspect that their co-traveller would understand them. One of them began to despair: "Sali, Sali, there is no bread for us in our country. Why did they have to open the Turkish teachers' institutes and train thousands of young people for teachers, when they are now closing the Turkish schools? We would be better off if we were uneducated."

"It's not true, Osman," the other passenger replied. "Educated or not, we all grieve the closure of our schools. I cannot understand why the politics, the course of the Party toward the Turkish population, changed so abruptly. Up until last year, we were treated one way, and now it's different."[3]

The letter captures the turmoil that Turkish and other Muslim communities experienced in 1958–59, when the politics toward national and religious minorities took an abrupt turn. Few studies on the minority politics of the socialist period in Bulgaria offer a nuanced

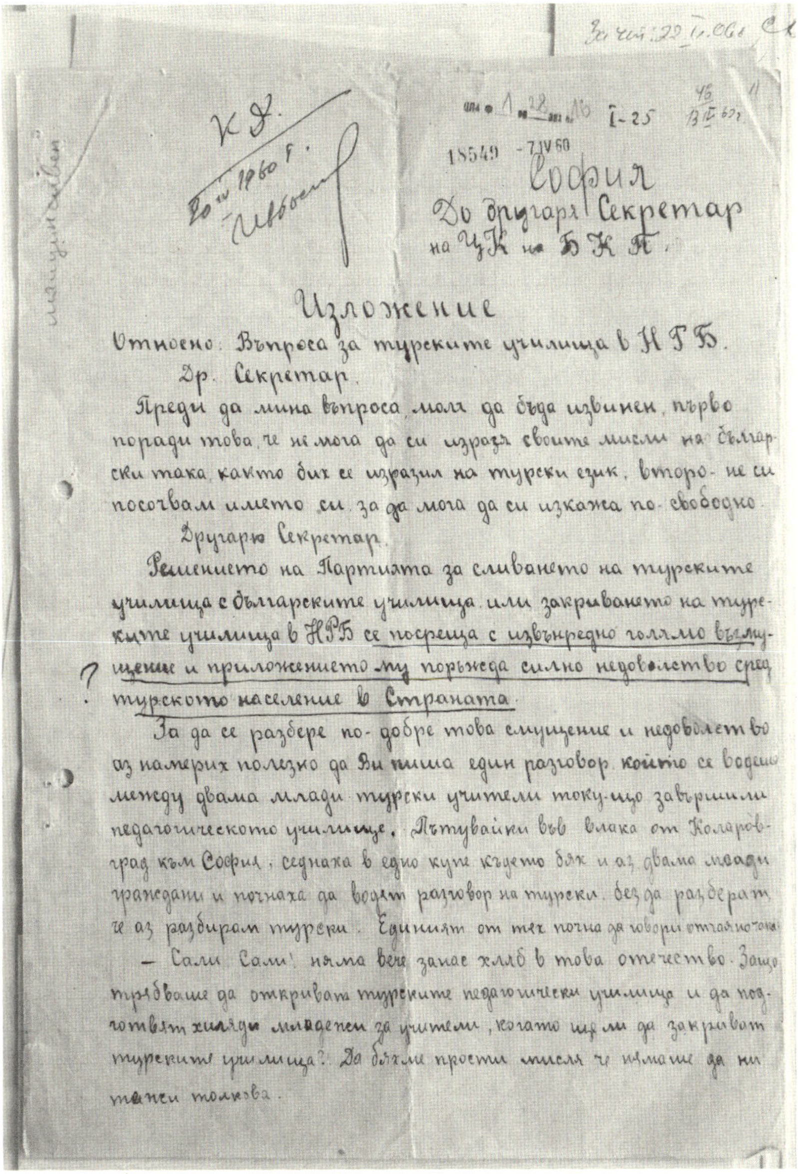

18549 - 7.IV.60

София

До другаря Секретар на ЦК на БКП.

Изложение

Относно: Въпроса за турските училища в НРБ.

Др. Секретар.

Преди да мина въпроса, моля да бъда извинен, първо поради това, че не мога да си изразя своите мисли на български така, както бих се изразил на турски език, второ - не си посочвам името си, за да мога да си изкажа по-свободно.

Другарю Секретар.

Решението на Партията за сливането на турските училища с българските училища, или закриването на турските училища в НРБ се посреща с извънредно голямо възмущение и приложението му поражда силно недоволство сред турското население в страната.

За да се разбере по-добре това смущение и недоволство аз намерих полезно да Ви пиша един разговор, който се водеше между двама млади турски учители току-що завършили педагогическото училище. Пътувайки във влака от Коларовград към София, седнаха в едно купе където бях и аз двама млади граждани и почнаха да водят разговор на турски, без да разберат че аз разбирам турски. Единият от тях почна да говори отчаяно:

— Сали, Сали! няма вече запас хляб в това отечество. Защо трябваше да откриват турските педагогически училища и да подготвят хиляди младежи за учители, когато щяли да закриват турските училища? Да бяхме прости мисля че нямаше да ни тъпчи толкова.

Figure 4.1 The first page of a letter of complaint sent to the government in April 1960 by an anonymous citizen about the decision in 1959 to eliminate the educational and cultural autonomy of Turkish-speaking minorities in Bulgaria.

reading of the transition from Stalinism to post-Stalinism that registers the change of direction after 1956. There is a great deal of Bulgarian-language work on the history of the ethnic assimilation campaigns during the communist period, which have been researched, documented, and chronicled in great detail. Much of it views the Stalinist and post-Stalinist periods through the same political lens – that is, as part of a progressive development that continues and escalates projects of religious and ethnic homogenization undertaken during the post-Ottoman period of nation-state formation. The communist regimes continued and intensified this practice in the most repressive form, culminating in the so-called Revival Process and the mass exodus of Bulgarian-born Turkish people at the end of the 1980s.[4]

But drawing too straight a line between these different political campaigns erases a lot of complexity, such as the differing political orientations of the governments that undertook such campaigns, and the different political shades of nationalism – their communist, liberal, or fascist leanings, their pro- or anti-Western (or Soviet) alliances, their complex intersections with other political forces, and their relationship to national self-determination movements and the nationalist politics of neighbouring Balkan countries. Historian Mary Neuburger, in her study on the minority politics of twentieth-century Bulgaria, treats the modernizing efforts of the communist state as monolithic. Unlike the Soviet multinational federal model, she argues, the Bulgarian Communist Party "since the inception of its bid for power and influence" pursued a nationalist agenda cloaked in the language of Marxism-Leninism.[5] "In the communist period," she continues, "the state targeted the same kinds of everyday markers of Turco-Ottoman occupation, but with new ideological and practical tools of implementation ... Although all minorities were sucked into the current of integration to some degree, the Party viewed Muslims in particular as obstacles to communist progress."[6] Anti-communist historians of Bulgarian socialism often overlook what are sometimes drastic turns in political orientation and the different political logics of ethnic homogenization campaigns. Rumen Avramov or Mikhail Gruev and Aleksei Kal'onski, for example, see the same approach to minorities in the right-wing, pro-fascist, Nazi-allied government of 1941–44 as the anti-fascist socialist government that replaced it.[7]

If we narrow in on these political complexities, we can see the different directions that nationalist ideas have taken throughout the twentieth century and register the shift toward minorities within the socialist period itself. Documents from the early years of socialism in Bulgaria reveal a distinct picture. The period between 1944 and 1956 marks a radical shift from the politics of the earlier right-wing government, which envisioned a state founded on ethnic supremacy, territorial expansionism, and the primacy of the Bulgarian people and Orthodox Christianity over other ethnicities and religions.

The early socialist period also differs from the ethnonationalist turn of the later post-Stalinist socialist government. Chavdar Marinov, Ali Eminov, and Evgeniia Ivanova are among the scholars who note of these developments. Their work registers a general shift from "internationalism" to nationalism, from "class to nation," and unlike others who see this change as no more than a shift in political rhetoric, some of them trace the radical changes in the material, social, and political conditions of religious and ethnic minorities on the ground.[8] Eminov describes the early socialist period as a brief opening for minorities that was obliterated during the post-Stalinist years. In fact, as I argued in chapter 3, ethnonationalist humanism in the context of Eastern Europe was mounted as a resistance to the early socialist model of the national question and framed as its alternative. While enjoying a kind of revival during the post-Stalinist era, ethnonationalism did not simply import right-wing, pro-fascist nationalist ideologies from the interwar period; rather, it gave the ethnonational idea anti-capitalist and anti-fascist foundations and rearticulated it within a socialist-humanist framework.

On the national question, socialist Bulgaria departed quite a lot from the Soviet Union, even though it drew on some of its principles. There is already a voluminous literature on the nationality policies of the Soviet Union during the Stalinist period. Because of its progressive politics and affirmative action programs for national minorities, Terry Martin called the Stalinist Soviet Union the "affirmative action empire," although recent scholarship has stressed the difficulty of applying frameworks of empire and imperialism to the Soviet and socialist contexts, considering their anti-imperialist foundations.[9] In his political analysis of national self-determination movements in the context of the Russian Empire, Lenin showed that national movements on the empire's periphery were developed against Russian nationalist and ethnic supremacy and the extractivist and colonial logics of the feudal state. The right to national self-determination and national autonomy thus contained anti-imperialist, anti-feudal, decolonial, and democratic content. The Soviet Union's constitutional model guaranteed the equality of its nationalities, their right to national culture and political representation, and it gave its republics administrative autonomy and the right to secession. Martin writes about Soviet *korenizatsia*, usually translated as "indigenization," which consisted of supporting the formation and development of minority languages and cultures. The early Soviet federal model also ensured the political participation of national minorities within a constitutionally organized state that emphasized national, ethnic, and religious diversity and the equality of all peoples.[10] It also granted national autonomy through the self-governance of administrative territories, which, as Yuri Slezkine has shown, often invented nationalities and constructed their national cultures within the context of the newly formed "ethno-territorial units."[11] As Rogers Brubaker has pointed out, there were major "incongruities" between the territorial, legal, and political definitions of recognized nationalities, which created a host of confusing and paradoxical situations.[12]

Colonial imaginaries, however, asserted themselves through logics of social progress, development, revolutionary telos, and the historical vanguard contained in certain kinds of Marxism, creating orders of geographies and knowledge according to notions of social and historical backwardness.[13] Even though they had anti-imperialist content, Bolshevik approaches to the non-Russian peoples of the "East" and the "North" were designed with "civilizing" goals in mind, and as Ali Iğmen has discussed in the case of Kyrgystan, local revolutionaries were "torn between the constructive and destructive effects of the revolution" and "conflicted about its contradictory results."[14] Yet as he shows, the Kyrgyz people fashioned novel ways of life that escaped the dichotomy thought to exist between traditional and modern life, forging alternative modernities that reimagined and reshaped older cultural practices as part of Soviet culture.

In addition, efforts to reassert the hegemony of Russian culture over non-Russian peoples had already appeared under Stalinism and had become pronounced after World War II, undermining socialist principles concerning religious, national, and cultural minorities. Stalin himself exhibited ethnic-supremacist tendencies, stressing the greatness of the Russian people and its culture above all other Soviet peoples. As post–World War II Stalinism increasingly recognized itself as a Sovietized version of the Russian Empire, imperial continuities and legacies persisted. The post-Stalinist context in the USSR, especially in the sphere of language and education, affirmed the Russian nationalist direction, eliminating policies on national diversity, autonomy, and self-determination so as to consciously deepen Russian hegemony through language and education reforms.[15] These conflicting principles, tensions, and evolving political realities made the Soviet experience an ambivalent one, and its internal tensions continue to be a source of contradictions and a plurality of narratives.

Even though it provides a useful comparison, Bulgarian socialism developed in a very different demographic, historical, and geopolitical context. The turn to ethnonationalism was not only a move away from Stalinism as a doctrine; it was also an expression, albeit indirect, of political autonomy from the Soviet Union. In fact, the way the Bulgarian government directed its politics toward the Turkish minority involved perpetual negotiations and tensions with Moscow, and it fielded the directives and disagreements of the Soviet government by insisting that these issues are are a matter of "internal affairs" and political sovereignty.

THE NEW TIMES (1944–56)

In 1950–51, only six years after the Bulgarian socialist government gained power, over 155,000 Turkish people, along with some Pomaks and Muslim Romas, left en masse for Turkey. This organized mass exodus is one of the most tumultuous moments in the early socialist period. The "new times" (*novoto vreme*) brought hope and promise to ethnic and religious minorities in the country, but also fear and disappointment. It intensified the mobilization among Turkish communities, many of whom permanently left the country as a result of their widespread mistrust toward the new government. Anti-communist historians attribute this discontent to the first wave of land collectivization, or the formation of land co-operatives (*kooperativni stopanstva*). According to this rather dominant reading, Turkish people experienced the land co-operatives as an oppressive reform imposed from above, and the resulting exodus is generally seen as an expression of Turkish people's opposition to the communist regime.[16] Most histories of this period also reconstruct these events primarily through the political rationality of the state in the context of the emerging frontiers of the global Cold War, where the logic of state sovereignty, national security, spheres of influence, and foreign relations dominates: the new socialist government remained suspicious of and hostile to the Turkish minority because it saw them as a threat to national security and the territorial integrity of the state, and as a population that generally undermined the sovereignty of the state and the socialist project. The Turkish government, in turn, saw Bulgaria's Turkish minority as a fertile terrain for Turkish nationalism and anti-communist propaganda, and encouraged secessionist tendencies.[17] In the years prior to the mass exodus, the Bulgarian state relocated Turkish people living near the Turkish border to other parts of the country for national security concerns. Declassified documents show the government strategizing behind the scenes to support and facilitate the exodus.[18] In 1949 Bulgaria and Turkey signed a bilateral agreement over the legal transfer of Turkish-descended people and during the next two years scores left the country until the Turkish government, overwhelmed by the flood of migrants, closed its border.

While the new government remained suspicious toward the Turkish population from a national security standpoint, it worked to create a better political environment for minorities and to improve their material lives. The new constitution gave national minorities the right to cultural expression and education and to have a press in their languages. It banned all fascist and right-wing nationalist organizations, which believed in the ethnic supremacy of the Bulgarian people and terrorized Muslim communities. Among them was the infamous Druzhba Rodina organization, a nationalist group founded in the late 1930s with right-wing and fascist elements; it was supported by the right-wing nationalist government in the lead-up to World War II, and it engaged in various campaigns of cultural assimilation among the Pomak minority, including a campaign to exchange their Turkish and Muslim names for Bulgarian ones.[19] The organization worked toward the social and ethnic integration of Pomaks by fostering Bulgarian national consciousness, introducing Bulgarian-language worship in mosques, translating the Qur'an into Bulgarian, and promoting education among young Bulgarian Muslims. As the histories of this period show, the organization generally advocated for "Bulgarianization without Christianization," while separating the consciousness and the community of Bulgarian-speaking Muslims from Turkish Muslims.[20] After the socialist revolution, Druzhba Rodina was condemned for its pro-fascist political orientation and its aggressive nationalist assimilation. The new socialist government restored the original names of the Pomaks and took urgent measures to stop the repression and coerced assimilation of religious and national minorities.

Ideas about a multinational Balkan federation occupied an important place in the political imaginary of the local Left during the interwar period – not only for geopolitical reasons but also because the federal model centred on questions of national and religious diversity and many therefore found it to be more relevant to the unique historical, demographic, and cultural context of the Balkans. A strong supporter of the idea of building political autonomy in the Balkans, Georgi Dimitrov had begun preliminary discussions with the leaders of socialist Yugoslavia about forming a Balkan socialist federation, a project which eventually fell apart and soured his relationship with Stalin.[21] Yet Dimitrov himself exhibited Turkophobic tendencies, which fuelled his anxieties around national security and national sovereignty, and he supported the internal relocation of Turkish people living near the border.

The constitution of 1947, Bulgaria's first socialist constitution, declared equal rights to all people, abolished "privileges" based on "nationality, origin, faith, and material status," and banned "the spread of racial, national, or religious hate" (Article 71). It established gender equality "in all spheres of state, civil [*chastnopraven*], administrative [*stopanski*], public, cultural, and political life" (Article 72). Pledging to end unemployment and material deprivation, it guaranteed the right to labour, rest, and social welfare for the elderly and in the case of illness, accident, disability, and unemployment, a right "guaranteed by a public social security system and affordable health care" (Articles 73–5). In addition, the new constitution recognized religious pluralism and secular conscience – a radical change from the past – by granting the "freedom of conscience and faith" (*svoboda na suvestta i izpodevaniiata*), as well as "the freedom to practice religious ritual." Article 78 separated religion from state and practically ended the state-sanctioned dominance of the Orthodox Church. It also guaranteed the freedom to establish temples and religious organizations and gave religious communities the right to "internal administration and self-governance." It banned "the abuse of Church and religion for political purposes, and the formation of political organizations on religious foundations."

Article 79 established the right to education for all citizens. It stated that "education is secular and bears a democratic and progressive spirit." It also ensured that "national minorities have a right to education in their mother language [*maichin ezik*] and to develop their national cultures, and [made sure that] the study of the Bulgarian language is compulsory." Additional legislation guaranteed minorities the freedom of press and media in their native languages and the right to national and cultural self-determination, which included the freedom to wear traditional clothing and other public expressions of culture.[22]

As one communist writer explained in 1949, the new constitution meant to establish the foundations of a "new, just socialist state." From now on, he observed,

> all people regardless of nationality, origin, faith, or material status have equal rights and equal duties. Bulgarians, Turks, Jews, Romanians, Greeks, Armenians, Gypsies [Roma], and others – we are all people. We all have the right to a place and happiness in life and the Constitution guarantees full equality before the law. In Bulgaria there are Orthodox Christians, Muslims, Jews, Catholics, Protestants, Armenian-Gregorians, and others. They all have their rituals, temples, their gods and their saints. Besides those who believe in gods and saints, there are also those who believe in science ... The old constitution, because it recognized only one religion – Orthodox Christianity – forced people to do things they didn't believe in ... It turned religion into profanity and made people duplicitous. The new constitution guaranteed its citizens the freedom of conscience, of faith, of religious ritual.[23]

But even when the new coalitional socialist government had made the political empowerment of minorities, their social freedom, and the improvement of their economic conditions one of its central goals, the vast majority of the Turkish population did not support the Otechestven Front in the elections of 1946, but instead voted for the opposition. An extensive report prepared by the new government on the situation of Turkish minorities in the early years after the revolution, particularly from 1946 to 1947, found that the political attitudes of the Turkish communities almost fully "aligned with that of the Turkish and the Bulgarian bourgeoisie." They shared a mistrust of any calls to abolish the monarchy and democratize economic power and remained suspicious of a government that "wants to make the poor rich and the rich poor."[24] The vast number of Turkish people, the report continues, followed the lead of those who held authority in their communities – these were mostly the religious, cultural, and economic elites who maintained primary ties, interests, and alliances with Turkey.[25] Further, mobilizations by the Communist Party and the Otechestven Front coalition in majority Turkish regions were largely unsuccessful because, according to the report, the Turkish people in Bulgaria were influenced by the Turkish government's propaganda and its influence in the country. Indeed, the report complains that the Turkish government conducted "its own minority politics" among people of Turkish descent in Bulgaria.[26]

The document captures the formation of a Cold War political logic in the immediate postwar years, one that was framed around concerns about spheres of influence, military intervention, and the balance of powers. Turkey saw in the Bulgarian socialist government the threatening influence of the Soviet Union in the Balkans and a possible ally in the Soviets' covert efforts to establish political control over the Bosporus and the Dardanelles. Renewed negotiations about the construction of a bridge over the Danube River was seen as a threat to the national security of the Turkish state since it might facilitate a future Soviet military invasion. The document reports that, in line with these kinds of calculations, many Turkish people were turned against the Communist Party because it was believed that it wanted to lead a war against Turkey. Many also thought that the Americans and the British would come and kill all the communists, and that all Turkish people who have become communists should therefore give up before the communist government falls.[27]

From the perspective of the rationality of the Bulgarian socialist state, which after two world wars and two Balkan wars was overly focused on its territorial integrity and its sovereignty, the secession of Turkish-majority territories was its greatest fear. Turkey was called an "enemy" state, an ally of the "Americans" and their imperialist and pro-capitalist agenda. It had instrumentalized the Turkish ethnic minorities in Bulgaria for its own political interests and territorial ambitions. National security anxieties rendered Muslim and Turkish populations along the border with Turkey an "anomaly" and an "enemy population" that needed to be "cut off with a surgical knife."[28] The report recommended the relocation of Turkish and Muslim populations to regions inside the country, which the government was quick to implement in the next couple of years. "It is absolutely necessary," the report claimed, "to populate this region along the border with Turkey and Greece with Bulgarian people. The Bulgarian people would serve as a barrier or a shelter against every incidental attack, and will interrupt the flow of all these suspicious elements."[29] Following the logic of national security in this emerging Cold War context, the socialist government relocated about ten thousand Pomaks (and some Turkish residents) from the southern border to other parts of the country, causing mass displacement.[30]

The report identifies Turkish nationalism as one of the main reasons for the government's failure to bring Bulgarian-born Turkish people to its side. According to official government documents, Kemalism, pan-Turkism, and a pronounced Turkish nationalism was widespread among Bulgaria's Turkish minority, and nationalist ideas travelled across the border through political literature, pamphlets, books, newspapers, calendars, and popular songs.[31] Turkish nationalism manifested in ideas ranging from the territorial secession of regions with majority Turkish populations to the mass migration of all people of Turkish descent into Turkey's current territories. In fact, the possibility of a mass exile into Turkey had been part of the political imaginary of Turkish people in Bulgaria for decades. After the Otechestven Front came to power, mobilizations for mass migrations increased. Turkish people were convinced, the report details, that "there is no life for them here, that the communists will tear down the mosques, that they will burn the religious books, that the women will become communal, and that if you become a communist, you will not be able to see the 'sacred Turkish land.'"[32] It was also believed that the women would be forced to take down their head scarves and that Turkish peoples' land, houses, and cattle will be taken away – much of which indeed became the terrifying reality of Turkish and Muslim minorities two decades later, when the support for the cultural autonomy and self-expression of minorities during the early socialist period gave way to the politics of ethnonationalist assimilation.

The strongest opposition to the new government came from the wealthier urban populations, and in particular from those whose economic activity and capital was threatened. They were also the most pronounced proponents of the exodus because they owned convertible or mobile capital such as factories and real estate, or held occupations in which it was easier to relocate – as opposed to those in the villages whose means of subsistence and material wealth was tied to the land and its resources, mostly in agriculture. The Turkish government welcomed the transfer of capital and helped factory and workshop owners relocate to the country, as was the case with a textile factory owner from Razgrad, who sold everything and moved her sewing machines to Turkey.[33] The Turkish government also encouraged particular categories of Turkish people to migrate, including owners of factories and other kinds of wealth that could be converted and transferred over the border; people with education or those skilled in various crafts; and people whose material support was guaranteed by their relatives in Turkey.[34] According to the testimony of Bekir Reshet, a merchant from Nikopol who travelled through different towns, cities, and villages in the northern part of Bulgaria to conduct his business, at first it was mostly people in the towns and the cities who were considering migration, and almost no one in the villages. But ideas of migration began spreading to the villages through the authority and political influence that the economic, religious, and cultural elites in the urban areas held among the Turkish communities.[35] As a result, the politics of mass migration was dramatically activated and became a topic of discussion in every village and every household.[36] The wealthier families promised to take care of their relatives of lesser means; some members of the community renowned for their wealth even pledged responsibility to entire families or kinship groups – for example, according to Reshet, a wealthy person from Svishtov promised to take with him fifteen families who couldn't afford to emigrate; another one from Ruse took responsibility for thirty poor families.[37] There were already multiple known channels, the report explains, where animals and cattle could be transferred over the border, as well as many others, unknown to the authorities, by which people crossed the border in both directions on a daily basis.[38]

This wave of migration was the first major challenge to the new government, which had pledged to improve the material and social lives of minorities, to put an end to their marginalization, harassment, discrimination, and forceful assimilation. It revealed inconsistencies and failures that turned into a first crisis of legitimacy for the new Bulgarian socialist government. Even with an anti-fascist government, there were the "wounds of fascism, [which] had not healed."[39] During the years preceding the revolution, a number of discriminatory laws established the political and social supremacy of ethnic Bulgarians and the Orthodox Church, and Muslim and Turkish people were subjected to daily terror and harassment by a combination of escalating nationalist and fascist grassroots forces and governments with various pro-fascist and nationalist leanings. In such conditions, "[Turkish people] had all the reasons to flee."[40] But both before and after the revolution, Turkish people felt that they lived under the

"Bulgarian yoke," as one teacher put it – they felt like orphans, the most cursed and wretched children on earth.[41] A minority national and religious consciousness had already been formed in the context of a dominant Orthodox Christian and ethnically Bulgarian nation-state order. The new government made no difference – it declared equality and freedom, but the Turkish people were still marginalized or completely excluded from public and political life, and they weren't willing to give it a chance. "[Bulgarians] are trying to take care of their own people, and we are struggling to live around them": this was a common attitude among the Turkish people in Bulgaria during this period.[42] Above all, the new government had failed to forge a kind of social consciousness that did not see communism as incompatible with Turkish identity and the Islamic faith.

NÂZIM HIKMET, POET OF THE PEOPLE

In an attempt to address this crisis, the government invited Nâzim Hikmet, the Turkish revolutionary poet, writer, and activist, to visit the country and speak to the Turkish communities. Hikmet arrived in Bulgaria in September 1951 from the Soviet Union, where only a few months earlier he had found political refuge from Turkish state persecution. This was in the immediate aftermath of the Turkish exodus from Bulgaria. Though Turkey was quick to close its border to the refugees, about 150,000 people, mostly of Turkish descent, had nonetheless already left the country.

Hikmet visited twenty-six villages, towns, and larger cities with concentrated Turkish residents in order to talk to the people, identify the reasons for their political discontent, and persuade them to remain in the country and keep their land, animals, and homes. He was warmly welcomed by the Turkish communities, who gathered in the hundreds and thousands to hear the renowned poet and revolutionary – a beloved hero of the people – speak, and also to make their stories heard. Thousands of Bulgarians and people of other ethnic backgrounds also joined these meetings. Throughout his journey, Hikmet held twenty rallies, twelve public discussions with ordinary residents, and nine meetings with different local party leaders. According to his own estimates, he managed to reach about 130,000 people.[43] Among those who accompanied Hikmet on this trip was Bulgarian communist writer Blaga Dimitrova. In her travelogue about the journey, she described his warm and personable engagement with the ordinary people. He spoke to smaller and larger gatherings with galvanizing energy, and talked to numerous women, men, and children without rest. His resilience and energy never ceased to bewilder Dimitrova, who accompanied him for the long journey across dusty roads to festive villages and captivating mountain folds.[44]

Dimitrova herself was deeply influenced by the Turkish communist poet. In her reflections published in 2004, she wrote that it was because of her encounters with poets such as Nâzim Hikmet, Pablo Neruda, and Nicolás Guillén, along with some contemporary Polish poets, that she was able to break out of the strict forms of classical rhyme and begin to experiment with free verse.[45] A prolific writer, she became a colossal figure in Bulgarian literature and one of the mothers of the Bulgarian literary avant-garde, but her travelogue is written in the socialist realist tradition. Back then, she was still early in her career as a writer, and she was able to join Hikmet's tour through the help of a Turkish comrade in the youth organization.[46]

The group began their journey from Ruse, a major city on the Danube River, and for several days travelled through the smaller towns and villages of northeastern Bulgaria, eventually making their way to the cities of Stalin (now Varna) and Tolbukhin (now Dobrich). In the northeast, they visited the town of Kubrat. There, Dimitrova writes, Hikmet addressed a crowd of five thousand people, standing on the same square where, a year earlier, Turkish and Bulgarian people had organized rallies in support of his hunger strike while serving a sentence in a Turkish prison for his political work.[47] Then Hikmet went to the Rhodope Mountains and visited seven more towns and villages, from Kurdzhali to Plovdiv, including the village of Nâzım Hikmet (formerly and currently Chiflik), which the people had just renamed in his honour.[48] As news spread about Hikmet's tour, people flocked to the train station or the side of the the road to greet him before filling squares, cinema halls, schoolyards, or open fields – wherever the poet was about to speak. All the while festive drums and *zurnas* echoed everywhere and celebratory dances were woven. Dimitrova writes that the women in the village of Ostrovets staged something of a revolt because the men wanted to leave them behind; eventually, all came to the city to hear Hikmet speak.[49] In Kurdzhali, thirty thousand people came out to meet him; in Momchilgrad, then thousand. The squares and the streets in Krumovgrad were filled to the brim, and of course the guest did not miss Dimitrovgrad, the youngest city in the country, an ambitious child of socialist planning founded in 1948 that was practically a construction site at the time. His voice got coarse from exertion but he kept going. Along the way he helped found two co-operatives and gave moral strength to those who were skeptical of the changes, and according to Dimitrova, the people spontaneously named a newly founded land co-operative in his honour, as well as a street in Kurdzhali, and a school, a mosque, a brigade, and a village in other places he visited. Dimitrova saw that the kind of respect and open recognition Hikmet received affected him deeply; it was a jarring contrast to the repression and persecution he faced in his own country.

Hikmet was tasked with studying the reasons that compelled Bulgarian-born Turkish people to want to leave their country, to find out about their experiences, concerns, and demands, and to recommend ways of redressing the situation. He surveyed Bulgarian- and Turkish-language periodicals from the past two years to see how the exodus was covered in the press. He then prepared a report in Russian that outlined the main reasons why Turkish people were leaving their homes and drafted recommendations for the government.[50]

His report presented a curious picture of the situation, an alternative to the government report from 1946–47, which had placed a heavy emphasis on the political rationality of the state and blamed the exodus exclusively on the spread of Turkish nationalism and its "agents," the Turkish bourgeoisie and community and religious leaders. Hikmet's report turned the tables on the socialist government itself with an analysis of the social life of Turkish people in the context of a dramatic social transformation as well as a systematic critique of the socialist government from the social and historical perspective of Turkish and Muslim people.

The new government's work among the Turkish minority had failed on several points, Hikmet observed, because the party did not undertake a careful social analysis and cultural understanding of the Turkish population. Moreover, it did not have sufficient political representation among the minority population, and where such representation existed, it was not according to a "class approach." Most of the new political and administrative positions had been taken by the wealthy and socially privileged members of the Turkish minority, such as spiritual leaders, big landowners and affluent peasants (*kulaki* and *zazhitochnye sredniaki*), the urban intelligentsia, and other influential members of the population. As a result, he reports, the conditions of poor peasants and working people had remained nearly the same as

Figure 4.2 The cover of Nâzim Hikmet's selected poems, translated by Nikolai Tsonev and published in Bulgarian after Hikmet's visit to the country in 1951. Cover design and illustrations by the renowned illustrator Boris Angelushev.

it was before the revolution since the government did nothing to empower them. The lack of ordinary peasants and working class people in the governance of social, material, and political life, he reports, had kept them dependent on the socially and economically privileged. Under the socialist government, the same class and social power structures had been replicated and older social and material privileges had been reproduced. In many villages, as it turned out, peasants with minimal land and only the barest means of subsistence were excluded from the first wave of collectivization by the bigger Turkish landowners; they were also marginalized in political representation. Hikmet gives an example from the village of Izgrev, where the formation of the village land co-operative was controlled by an alliance between the Muftis and the wealthy landowners, who joined the co-op with their large land possessions but excluded the peasants with small plots of land. The co-op became very successful – it paid its dues to the state and exceeded the assigned quotas, so the national leadership was quite pleased and gave it a truck as an award. The vast majority of the peasants with small plots of land in the Turkish communities had been pushed out of the formation of land co-operatives in similar ways, and they had remained as private landowners with no access to technology, efficient irrigation, or other means of production available to the co-ops. State taxes were a much higher burden for them, and when their crops failed, they did not possess the means to survive such losses.

In addition, Hikmet continues, Turkish people were not properly represented in local government and local social administrations, thereby undermining their autonomy and participation in the larger governing process. For example, in the village councils of majority-Turkish villages, the council chair was Bulgarian and the vice-chair was Turkish. "This could be done the other way around," he advised. The co-operative stores, where mostly Turkish women went to do their shopping, were run by Bulgarians. There was also a case where a Bulgarian man, who was known for raping Turkish women, was removed from his post thanks only to the news about Hikmet's visit, and only three days before the high-profile guest arrived.[51] Furthermore, where representation existed, it was mostly from the privileged strata of the Turkish community, and working-class people and poor peasants were nowhere to be seen. The state representatives Hikmet met were intellectuals, teachers, or craftsmen, but among them he did not see members of the lower peasantry or even industrial workers.[52] There were not enough poor peasants even among the rank-and-file members of the party. This was an effect of the party's labour-centrism – it was heavily focused on mobilizing the working classes in the urban areas, while most Turkish people resided in the villages using their small plots of land as a means of subsistence.[53]

All these realities fuelled resentment among the poor peasants, who felt abandoned and further marginalized, disappointed by the perpetuation of pre-existing class and social inequalities.[54] The new political and economic structures were appropriated by those with more economic power and social influence, and as a result, they reproduced older social hierarchies and social dependencies, and the socialist *stroi* (order), which meant to empower precisely the most socially and economically marginalized, failed to carry out its politics among the minorities. These structural continuities in material and social life, carried over from the past, suggest that the early forms of collective opposition among minorities did not target the political principles of socialism, but rather the government's failures to turn them into reality, as well as the co-optation of the new political and economic structures by the socially and economically privileged.

A TURN TO ETHNONATIONALISM

The first decade of socialism revealed contradictions between political principles with progressive content and the crude rationality of *realpolitik*. By contrast, the post-Stalinist leadership represented an explicit shift toward the erasure of national autonomy and the beginning of a series of assimilationist measures informed by an ethnonationalist logic. The new leadership empowered supporters of the nationalist cause and enacted a sweeping nationalist agenda. Todor Zhivkov, the new first secretary, found Dimitrov's stance on national and ethnic diversity and self-determination completely unsustainable in the Bulgarian context. For Zhivkov, it was not only untenable from a historical perspective but also a danger to the country's national and territorial integrity. One of his first tasks, then, was to dismantle national self-determination and administrative autonomy statutes and to introduce a number of decrees and resolutions that targeted the educational, cultural, and religious autonomy of minorities. Zhivkov was particularly concerned about the former government's recognition of Turks as a national minority population and the Turkish language as an official minority language. In his memoirs, he reiterated his understanding that this political line "deepened the process of disintegration of the Bulgarian people and resulted in the encouragement of pan-Turkism and the artificial formation and isolation of minority groups."[55] This was written in the 1990s, when the tragic aftermath of the Revival Process was still unfolding and the full proportions of the campaign and its effects on people were still coming to light. In his reflections, the former head of state concedes nothing and instead reinforces his firm nationalist positions with respect to Muslim minorities, Turkish national and ethnic identity, and the Macedonian identity and language, which drove the politics of assimilation, erasure, and expulsion during his time in power.[56]

Some of the first state documents to come available in the archives signifying a shift in direction to a coherent ethnonationalist logic date from 1957 and 1958. These are minutes from meetings of the highest orders of the party that build up to a resolution titled "Theses on the Work of the Party among the Turkish Population." This document was difficult to locate due to a buildup of secondary citations and inaccuracies in referencing.[57] Like many state and public archives, the National State Archive, with its headquarters in Sofia, is a vast maze holding an astounding volume of diverse materials. It spans multiple storage locations across the city and the country, which often requires days or weeks of travel to get to the reading rooms. Many layers of classification, cataloguing, reference volumes, and indexing systems have been designed in an attempt to introduce some order to the ocean of documents filed erratically or according to different logics, but instead these have created webs of intertwined historiographies and systems of knowledge that make the archives an endless puzzle. Access to its content is also inevitably marked by its various states of circulation, citation, and stagnation, while what may be missing, damaged, lost, or stolen always informs what is currently "there," making it the open, disjointed, and boundless environment it is. This environment always turns ironically on those who try to privilege some types of historical material over others, or to master its contents in some totalizing way. Yet this instability, at once epistemological, material, and discursive, offers the researcher many journeys with an open end.

The discussions in the higher ranks leading up to the "Theses" are revealing – while outlining the future directions of the state's politics toward the Turkish minorities, the document speaks of the Turkish population as backward, undeveloped, and undereducated, gripped by "fanaticism," "prejudice," and cultural traditionalism; they are seen as easily susceptible to manipulation and swayed by hearsay, a condition "inherited from the past."[58] "Enemy elements" in the communities take advantage of the people's "religious fanaticism" and their "national-cultural characteristics" to increase religious and nationalist sentiments, to agitate the people against the land co-operatives, and to influence people to emigrate.[59]

The "Theses" stresses that the socialist country has made a commitment to its minorities and it highlights the material and social improvements in the Turkish communities during the years of socialism in the spheres of education, cultural and public life, health care, electrification, infrastructure, housing, and inclusion in leadership. The document and the discussions preceding it recognize Turkish and other people as ethnic and national minorities because of a "common origin, language, and faith" with Turkish people in Turkey and elsewhere, yet a striking discourse of unity already emerges that becomes the foundation for monistic theories of ethnogenesis and nationhood developed in later visions of socialist development and integration.[60] For the last twenty years the Turkish minority has been developing as a "socialist national minority," the "Theses" states in a nutshell, and because Turkish people share socio-economic and cultural conditions with Bulgarian and other people in the socialist countries, they were a national minority in a socialist sense. In fact, it was precisely the project of building a socialist society that set the Turkish population in Bulgaria apart from Turkish people in Turkey and provided a unifying fabric with the Bulgarian and other people living in the country. "We believe that the actual life, production, economic and cultural development of our country require the communication and constant mobility of thousands of people from one side of the country to the other, the formation of new construction sites and economic centres. This inevitably leads to the coming together of all working people. Socialist life requires that Turkish people learn the Bulgarian language and that the Bulgarian people who live in Turkish-populated areas learn the Turkish language."[61] Later in the 1980s, through the work of nationalist historians, which took historical revisionism to extreme ends, the leadership would give up the claim that Turkish people in Bulgaria share a common origin with Turkish people in Turkey in favour of the "shared kinship roots" thesis. This core element in the ethnonationalist doctrine, which viewed Turkish minority populations as forcibly Islamicized Bulgarians, practically ended the recognition of Turkish people as a national or ethnic minority and laid the grounds for a politics of assimilation and erasure.

EDUCATION REFORMS AND BULGARIAN HEGEMONY

The changes were most deeply felt in the realm of educational reforms as Bulgarian language and culture were to provide the hegemonic material for socialist integration and mobility. During the early socialist government, Turkish schools had already been subjected to radical changes. The first wave of school reforms in 1951 nationalized and secularized education and vastly expanded the number of Turkish community schools, which had so far been very few and mostly private. By the early 1950s, in addition to hundreds of Turkish primary and secondary schools, the Board of National Education had opened eight Turkish gymnasiums, three specialized secondary schools, and two post-secondary institutes for teachers in regions with concentrated Turkish populations to meet the increased demand for Turkish-speaking teachers. It founded a boarding school for women in Ruse and opened a Department of Turkish Philology at the Sofia University.[62] According to a 1951 party resolution on the "improvement of the work among the Turkish population," the state increased fellowships for Turkish students from working-class and peasant families of "poor and average means" for teachers, doctors, and agricultural specialists, among other vocations. It set up cultural and exchange programs with the Republic of Azerbaijan in the USSR and imported films and books from there. The resolution also called for improved infrastructure and access to health care and physical education, an increase in the number of Turkish people in all political organizations, the translation of political literature into Turkish, an increase and diversification of existing radio programs in Turkish, the opening of art and music collectives, and more.[63]

But the early school reforms were also a measure against the influence of Turkish school teachers and the *hodjas* on the Turkish population, who were seen as the main agents of various strains of Great Turkish nationalism and anti-Bulgarianism, and were generally considered to be agents of anti-communist propaganda. According to the intelligence report from 1947, teachers and *hodjas* held significant political influence on their communities and were some of the most active agitators for organized mass migration among the Turkish people. State documents paint the *hodjas* as ones who cultivated a sense of Turkish identity in young people that was antithetical to communist and socialist politics, and discouraged Turkish youth to join the RMS, the Workers' Youth Organization – those who joined were seen as renouncing their Turkishness, betraying their people, giving up on their "mother country."[64] To interrupt these tendencies, the new government closed the Nüvvab religious school in Shumen, which until the revolution trained *hodjas* and religious leaders, and which the government saw as a hotbed of Turkish nationalism.[65] It also developed a bold plan to restaff the teacher cadres in the schools with communists and to educate a new generation of teachers who would be "included as a productive element in building the People's Republic" and who would transform the Turkish youth "not into enemies and foreigners, but into honest and good citizens."[66] Above all, the report from 1947 argued that the government needed to ensure the equal treatment of the Turkish people and to signal that the future of Bulgarian-born Turkish people is in Bulgaria.[67]

It therefore produced mixed results and ambivalent attitudes toward the new system, fuelling anti-government and anti-communist sentiments. Yet ordinary Turkish people who experienced the changes also spoke of positive effects. According to Ali Eminov's study on education and language among the Turkish population in Bulgaria, "within a few short years there was a drastic increase in the number of Turkish-language schools, students attending school, and teachers staffing them," to reach 150,000 Turkish students in the mid-1950s, up from about 37,000 before 1945.[68] The Turkish language remained the primary language of instruction in the vast majority of primary, secondary, and professional Turkish schools, and Bulgarian language and history constituted only a small fraction of classes in a curriculum centred on Turkish history, literature, and culture.

Eminov reports that during this period Turkish communities enjoyed a thriving local arts and literary scene, which he called a "genuine renaissance of Turkish culture": books of poetry and prose appeared in the Turkish language by local Turkish writers and communist writers from Turkey and the Turkic-speaking people of the USSR, which promoted progressive, revolutionary, and mostly secular content; texts were translated into Turkish from Bulgarian and other languages; regional state theatres and "amateur folk groups at the local level" proliferated.[69] All these activities, Eminov continues, trained a cadre of native Turkish intelligentsia who replaced the traditional religious leaders in Turkish communities and contributed to the emergence of a secular Turkish identity among many Turks, especially among the youth.[70]

This decade of thriving socialist and mostly secular Turkish culture came to an abrupt end in the late 1950s, with the second reform in the minority school system. Until then, many schools had been located beside mosques and shared activities with them, which made the leadership fear that the *hodjas* exerted a "harmful influence" over the students.[71] The resolution from 1958 ordered the separation of primary Turkish schools from the mosques and their relocation to new buildings or to existing Bulgarian schools. Further, inspections conducted in the previous year for the purpose of the resolution had found that children were unwilling to learn Bulgarian and "were not sufficiently educated in patriotic, international, and atheistic spirit."[72] Without knowing Bulgarian, the documents argue, "young people would remain isolated from socialist and progressive Bulgarian culture, and would be more susceptible to ... the influence of bourgeois Turkish nationalism and religious fanaticism."[73] Primary schools were ordered to staff more communist teachers of Turkish descent and to introduce classes in Bulgarian language. The main language of instruction in secondary, post-secondary professional, and higher-education institutions was to change from Turkish to Bulgarian, while Turkish language and literature were to be studied as a separate subject.[74] Autonomous Turkish technical schools and gymnasiums were to be reorganized and merged with the ones for Bulgarian students.[75] Practically speaking, this resulted in a sort of desegregation that consciously eliminated the conditions for the cultural and intellectual autonomy of Turkish communities and established the hegemony of the Bulgarian language and culture.

These policies required drastic changes in the material and cultural lives of ordinary Turkish people and other minorities speaking the Turkish language, which triggered widespread discontent. The anonymous letter from April 1960 with which this chapter opened was written in this context. The two men on the train discussed the difficulties minority students had in keeping up with their Bulgarian schoolmates in the newly merged classes now that all subjects, except of course for the Turkish language, were taught in Bulgarian. Bulgarian children were unjustly advantaged by the fact that they were studying in their own native language while Turkish kids fell behind – and teachers were at a loss trying to navigate the resulting disparities.[76]

At the same time, many Turkish teachers were laid off and replaced by Bulgarians. A letter of appeal from Sami Yusufov Hodzhov, a teacher who worked for a Roma school in Plovdiv, complains that the children of the Roma minority, whose primary language of instruction was Turkish, were also affected.[77] His letter challenged the layoffs as well: instead of remaining there to teach the same material in Bulgarian or being moved to Rüşdiye, the Turkish school in town, Turkish teachers had been laid off and their positions filled by Bulgarian teachers. Hodzhov's father was a member of the Communist Party before the revolution and was sent to a camp as a communist, and his entire family was harassed and beaten by the state militia (*dzhandarmeriiski khaiki*). Since then, he and his "comradess" (*drugarka*) – in fact, his entire family – had been working to put communist ideas into practice. After the revolution, he was active in the movement to form land co-operatives, and as a teacher he educated his Turkish and Roma students in the communist spirit.[78] "I'm asking, comrades, what is democratic here, and what is socialist, and what is communist? Me and my family of five have been left hungry, had my rights taken away."[79] He asked to be placed in the Rüşdiye Turkish school "because most of all, I love the schools and I love the children."[80] The Minority Schools Division of the Ministry of National Education reviewed his appeal and placed him in a Turkish school – not Rüşdiye, but a school in Kuklen, a nearby village.[81]

Many began to see a political logic with nationalist content emerging in the 1958 school reform. They associated it with the assimilationist politics of the pre-revolutionary government, which entertained various expansionist visions and supported right-wing nationalist and fascist forces, and eventually joined the Axis powers in World War II. And indeed, continuities reappeared both in ghostly and direct historical forms.[82] For example, when the "reformists" came to power, members of Rodina, the right-wing nationalist organization operating from 1937 to 1945, attempted to gain rehabilitation for themselves and their organization through their nationalist and assimilationist work among the Pomak populations. Its proponents succeeded in reopening the debate, which led to a revised definition of the organization – from "fascist" to "bourgeois-nationalist" – and managed to rehabilitate some of its members, formerly declared and prosecuted as fascists.[83] In this context, some historians have argued that the socialist regime embraced the nationalist politics of pre-revolutionary Bulgaria and that the Revival Process from the 1970s and '80s should be properly understood in the context of the activity and language of Rodina. But the legacy of Druzhba Rodina continued to generate controversy during the post-Stalinist era as the new leadership refused to entirely lift the ban on the organization. It was in search of a vision of nationalism founded on the socialist principles from the post-Stalinist period – a vision purged of right-wing and bourgeois content, based on a unified socialist peoplehood with its bottom-up history – that the foundations for a politics of assimilation were laid.

These were the subtle political rearticulations of nationalism in the context of post-Stalinist state governance. But to the people, the subtleties of this ideological rewiring made no difference. Osman, one of the passengers described in the anonymous letter, directly characterized this logic as fascist: "It has a fascist character, it's like the discrimination toward the Turkish population before 9 September [the socialist revolution] which was carried out by the fascist governments. To take away the native language of a minority – how do you explain this?"[84] The reform, he continued, was conducted in a non-transparent and non-public manner (*bez glasnost*); it was not based on Marxist principles; it was neither politically sound nor pedagogically appropriate; and finally, it was clearly unconstitutional.[85] He asks,

> Is this how Lenin and Stalin treat the national question? Is it like this in the Soviet Union? After the Great October Socialist Revolution, they created the alphabet of many nationalities who didn't even have an alphabet before. Did the Soviet Union lose from this? Why did everyone fight like one against the enemy in the Great Patriotic War [World War II]? Isn't it because they had equal rights in all spheres of life? And here is what our Dimitrov Constitution states: those who neglect the rights of the national minorities will be punished severely, it says. Doesn't this resolution trample the national rights of the Turkish minority? …
> I had never expected, never even thought, that a solid Marxist party would take such a decision, which calls forth nationalism. And we are talking about proletarian internationalism.[86]

The two passengers also took note of the latest publications on Bulgarian history. These claimed that the "Turks" had committed atrocities during the Ottoman period and during struggles for national liberation, reducing into a sweeping unity the complex class and social strata of Turkish society:

> It's no longer about the Turkish Beys and Sultans. Doesn't this call for hatred toward the Turkish people? Why are the people

> to blame for the deeds of the Turkish Beys – our people have suffered equally from them. This is why the hatred needs to be directed not against the Turkish people but against the Turkish Beys, Paşas, and political administrators [*upravnitsi*] … The Turkish people and the Turkish Beys are now placed under the same umbrella.[87]

The two men continued to discuss the roots of the recent changes, pointing to the fact that there were not enough Turkish people in government to represent ordinary Turkish people's perspectives.[88]

Whether in mediated form or captured directly, the letter contains a sharply worded critique of the state and its efforts to construct a unified ethnic subject, in the process obliterating the analysis of class and social difference within the Turkish minority. By framing Turkish and non-Turkish Muslim minorities as the enemy, these reforms aimed to eliminate their cultural and intellectual autonomy. It was an attack on socialist democracy and pluralism through an erosion of one of socialism's fundamental principles, the right to national self-determination and autonomy, and it resembled the repression and coercive assimilation that many had already experienced in different forms in the two decades prior to the revolution.

ETHNONATIONALIST FOUNDATIONS OF THE POST-STALINIST STATE

In the following two decades, a series of political reforms and events escalated the assimilationist politics of the government, a process that culminated in the 1980s with the Revival Process. While this history has received a great deal of attention from Bulgarian, Balkan, and Turkish historians,[89] it is worth noting here the constitutional reform of 1971. The reform aimed to eliminate contradictions between the first socialist constitution of 1947 and changes in policy that had already taken place in the 1960s. The 1971 constitution expanded the guarantees for social and material equality in the spheres of labour, leisure, and social reproduction (as seen in chapter 2). It also made changes around the relationship between socialist governance and minority identities and languages, which was a reactionary setback from the government of the Otechestven Front. The first socialist constitution upheld the right to national and cultural self-determination and protected minorities; the 1971 document emphasized holistic social and personal development steeped in national and patriotic values.

The "Rights and Duties of the Citizens" section of the 1971 socialist constitution mostly recycled and reshuffled the articles of the old constitution, and it significantly expanded some its original formulations. Like its predecessor, the new constitution guaranteed the equality of all citizens while expanding the categories in the anti-discrimination clause to include nationality, origin, religion, gender, race, education, and social and material status (Article 35). It did not remove the right to freedom of conscience and religion, and added "the right to promote anti-religious propaganda" (Article 53).

Some of the changes were subtle but entailed significant effects. The 1971 reform introduced the term "patriotic" (Article 11) and eliminated the word "minority" (*maltsinstvo*), replacing it with "citizens of non-Bulgarian origin" (*grazhdani ot nebulgarski proizkhod*) (Article 45). Through subtle reformulation, it made significant changes around the contested intersection of education, minority languages, and cultural autonomy. The old constitution guaranteed "national minorities the right to learn *in* their mother [*maichin*] language and to develop their national culture" (Article 79, 1947; emphasis added). By contrast, the new constitution guaranteed "citizens of non-Bulgarian origin" "the right to learn their own language" and it rescinded the right to develop a national culture (Article 45). This was a subtle change that removed constitutional obstacles to establishing the Bulgarian language as the dominant language for Turkish and other minorities, thereby eliminating an important aspect of their administrative and cultural autonomy. As historian Chavdar Marinov puts it, the post-Stalinist constitutional reform "gave a green light to homogenization ... The development of Turkish national culture in Bulgaria practically ended."[90]

The most draconian change in the 1971 constitution, which has not been adequately noted or explored in contemporary scholarship, occurred in the sphere of due process. While guaranteeing the "freedom and inviolability of personhood," the 1971 constitution removed the citizen's right to trial and defence, as well as the guarantee that punishments should be adjudicated only by the courts and be commensurate with the crime – all present in the first socialist constitution from 1947 (compare, for example, Article 82, 1947, with Article 48, 1971). In other words, after 1971 torture, murder, and imprisonment without charge, conviction, or trial became constitutionally available to the state. This constitutional access to violence was used in the brutal repression of organized and everyday resistance to the Revival Process in the 1980s.

5

Violent Revivals

The 1985–89 period, the last years of socialism in Bulgaria, will be remembered above all for the so-called Revival Process and its aftermath. A state-orchestrated campaign that forcefully renamed hundreds of thousands of people of Turkish descent, the Revival Process marks the disastrous culmination of the politics of assimilation pursued by the post-Stalinist government. The renamings caused a profound disruption in people's political, economic, and social lives that left no one unaffected. After years of massive organized resistance, hundreds of thousands of people of Turkish descent fled the country in collective defiance, causing the largest mass migration of any ethnic minority in the country's modern history.

The state "executed" the majority of the renamings in several waves throughout the 1970s and '80s that culminated in 1984–85. Starting in 1959, the government had undertaken small-scale renamings in a rather inconsistent and selective way, targeting separate individuals and families who were part of the military, the party, and the state bureaucracy. By 1965, the state's assimilation efforts took a turn to a systematic campaign targeting entire minority populations, first Pomak and Roma citizens, then citizens of Turkish descent. By 1985, virtually all minorities bearing Turkish and Muslim names were folded into the campaign. This chapter gives an account of the devastating effects of this campaign on people's lives. People experienced broken communities, scrambled webs of kinship, erased histories, fractured individual and collective subjectivities, cultural disorientation, material dispossession, and massive displacement. The chapter also recounts the heroic organized resistance and the everyday forms of defiance people engaged in under conditions of intense surveillance, repression, persecution, and violence.

The ethnic assimilation campaign targeted many aspects of the minorities' lives and collective consciousness, including language, religion, and cultural practice. However, the campaign was obsessively focused on changing the given, middle, and family names of every person – both living and dead. While not historically unique – indeed, the practice built on earlier precedents in the Balkans – the scope of the renaming campaign from the 1970s and '80s in Bulgaria was certainly unprecedented. It was a deliberate attempt at ethnic cleansing, the destruction of social life, and the erasure of historical belonging.

How and why did names become the main vehicle of ethnic assimilation and ethnic cleansing under post-Stalinist socialism? How did names come to stand as the primary signifier of post-Stalinist understandings of ethnic difference? The socialist governments in the Balkans adopted and mastered the practice of renaming as a sort of technology for reshaping or obliterating national and regional identities and their material histories – perfecting what cultural theorist Suzana Milevska has called the "apparatuses of renaming" into a kind "machine of forgetting and forging history."[1] The proper names retained throughout the ages speak to countless layers of turbulent history, contested claims on places and material sites, erased or rewritten historical narratives, redrawn borders and territories, razed, erased, disowned, and exiled populations, and revolutionary beginnings. Underscoring the radically contingent but also powerfully constitutive nature of naming, Milevska discusses the different political uses to which renaming practices were put in the Balkans, from serving projects of assimilation, oppression, and historical erasure, to reproducing patriarchal relations, to embracing the powers of self-naming and self-renaming in emancipatory movements and struggles for self-determination.[2]

Renaming places, towns, and cities, geographic locales, streets and neighborhoods and buildings, is often the first process of political upheaval and revolutionary change or establishing new regimes of power. There is something about both the manifest and unstable nature of proper and "given" names. It opens an ambivalent space in which the tensions between triumphant and subjugated histories, between dominant narratives and what Macarena Gómez-Barris has called "submerged perspectives" are staged.[3] Through the act of naming one is inaugurated into social relations inevitably enmeshed in gender, ethnic, religious, racial, and national differences. Derrida would say that to bear a name is to bear that which always precedes us, to reckon with its historical baggage. Because a name carries meanings that can never be divorced from the historical act of naming, a name is also an inauguration into myriad histories. A name can draw, disrupt, re-enact, or redraw historical trajectories. The power of naming and renaming – including the power of self-renaming – is the power to continue, disrupt, erase, or reclaim parts of these relations and their histories. Sometimes to carry a name is to be locked into an unbearable history that only self-renaming can undo. But it can also be an opportunity to resignify its meanings as they are refracted through personal and collective agency in the present.

The history of the Balkans is replete with name purges and name changes, but as Milevska observes, "name overwriting" is certainly not limited to the region and has a long, ancient history.[4] Scholars in diasporic African, African-American, and Indigenous studies have pointed out the centrality of renaming in the reproduction of slavery and settler colonialism, respectively, underscoring its profoundly disruptive, dehumanizing, and destructive effects on kinship, cultural, historical, linguistic, and communal ties for people of African and Indigenous descent. In his now classic comparative study of societies structured on slave relations, Orlando Patterson highlights the centrality of renaming in unmaking and remaking the subjectivity of the enslaved. Renaming was an important technique that served to violently uproot a newly enslaved person from their prior social environment and reintroduce them into slave society as a marginal or liminal being, a quasi- or non-person. A name, Patterson writes, is a "verbal sign of [one's] whole identity, of their being in the world as a distinct person."[5] Names contain a multiplicity of historical meanings and serve as a kind of compass in a multitude of social hierarchies and registers of belonging and exclusion. Forced name changes were used almost universally as part of the institution and reproduction of slavery, serving as a "symbolic act of stripping a person of his former identity [during which] the slave's former name died with his former self."[6] Changing the person's name was part of a "process of social negation" that Patterson equates to social death, the depersonalization and dehumanization necessary to send the enslaved person into a permanent marginal and liminal existence and to introduce them into the orders of subjection and submission that constitute slave relations.[7]

Renaming was therefore a crucial process in a social reconfiguration that prescribed for the enslaved person a new destiny of social liminality, forced dependence, and exploitation, and in which suffering and death was inconsequential. Slave renamings often involved a ceremony that enacted the material and symbolic severing of social and personal ties bonding the person to their prior social life. It signalled the rejection of the person's former social fabric and ancestral bonds and inaugurated them into a new social order and a new subjectivity. "In a special right of passage," Patterson writes, "the slave was first 'cleansed' of his natal ties, by means of a medicine that denuded him of ancestral protection. Significantly, however, the medicine also eliminated any memory among the master's lineage of the slave's ancestry, so the very act of separation paved the way for the possible assimilation of the slave's descendants."[8] Through renaming, the enslaved person was meant to forget their former attachments and their history and enter a state of abjectness and forced dependence. Without a name they were also stripped of the powers of ancestral history and protection and were "spiritually exposed," lacking the protection of both former and prospective ancestral spirits. Enslaved people were also integrated "into the master's lineage via a naming ceremony" through which they were "forced to deny their natal kin ties and acquired certain fictive kin bonds to the master and their family."[9]

In her famous 1987 essay "Mama's Baby, Papa's Maybe," Hortense Spillers similarly discusses naming and renaming as a technology of conquest, enslavement, and dehumanization in the context of the Atlantic slave trade. Slave traders and slave owners systematically renamed African people sold or captured into slavery, giving them generic names or numbers as part of the process of submission to a new racial order and to shape the subjectivity of the enslaved as an object of ownership and exploitation. Spillers sees it as a deliberate technique aimed at causing social disorganization and a loss of social and historical coordinates. Renaming threw each person's blood and kinship relations into profound crisis and confusion, scrambling orders of consanguinity and the "intricate calculus of descent" and forcing people of African descent into "patterns of dispersal." This was part of the larger process of what Angela Davis has called a "rigidified disorganization" of family life in Black communities under American slavery. It prohibited all forms of social life that would allow Black people to form stable and lasting bonds. In fact, Davis points out, family and kinship relations within the communities of the enslaved were antithetical to the logic of slave property and exchange, and their perpetual disorganization and destruction was one of the direct mechanisms of maintaining the slave ownership system.[10] These historical cases show some of the ways in which forced renamings have played an important role in forced migration, slavery, ethnic cleansing, and the historical erasure of entire populations such as Indigenous Peoples on the American continents.

It is not an accident that names became the central vehicle of the state-driven ethnic assimilation campaign in Bulgaria known as the Revival Process. A renaming mobilized the historical instability of religious, ethnic, national, and cultural differences in the region, of boundaries between collective notions of self and other. In the context of post-Stalinist socialism, the focus on the personal name should also be seen as part of the attempt to shape socialist notions of personhood (*lichnost*). Conceived as a form of personal empowerment and a personalized expression of social integration, socialist personhood became a vehicle of ethnic homogenization and the expropriation of minorities' power to determine their own identity, to speak their own history, and to establish their sense of belonging on a very personal level.

The philosophy of ethnic assimilation from the post-Stalinist period affirmed a concept of ethnicity that is non-determinist and avoids recourse to biological essentialism.[11] This refusal of biological determinism is perhaps the most significant difference from West European colonial, bourgeois-liberal, right-wing, and National Socialist concepts of race and ethnicity. Carrying the awareness that collective subjectivities are always historically contingent and shaped by historical forces, socialist conceptions of ethnic difference retained in their foundation a certain kind of historical-materialist understanding. This is why, as I show in more detail below, the renaming campaign contained a strong performative aspect and took full advantage of the force of iteration in forging a new sense of historical belonging and a new subjectivity. Subjects were to be reconstituted through repeated spoken re-enactments of their names; they were to assume their new subjectivities by passing through daily rituals of utterance. The notion that the human subject is radically malleable, subject to historical making and remaking, defined the social-constructivist and social engineering practices specific to the biopolitical regimes of post-Stalinist socialism, from the post-Stalinist concept of the "holistically developed person" to the intricate population-management systems of the socialist states.

At the same time, the 1970s and '80s abounded in origin-based theories of Bulgarian national identity rooted in blood, kinship, and an ancient past. In this "unique preoccupation with ethnogenesis," Todorova sees a symptom of "nervousness" around the radical instability of collective identities in the region – perhaps the result of a kind of hidden anxiety around the failure to trace a singular "origin," a fear of confronting the historical forces that have made, unmade, and remade these identities.[12]

In the context of the renaming campaigns of the 1970s and '80s in Bulgaria, Neuberger argues that the modern state bureaucracy followed a process of standardizing the nominal system. According to her, before standardization, names were "fluid and there was a considerable gray zone, a prevalent hybridity, until the names were fixed and purged in the twentieth century."[13] But pre-modern nominal systems in the Balkans were far from fluid or arbitrary and followed the most complex and rigorous logic as outward markers of religion, regional origin, occupation, and social status, or of belonging to a *rod* (kinship). "As bearers of historical knowledge," Gruev and Kal'onski argue, "[local nominal systems] unify the past with the present and the future in relationship to both the concrete person and the entire *rod* and even the village. Especially when it comes to kinship [*rodovi*] names [in certain cases turned into signifiers of belonging to a village], passing them to the next generation turns them into bearers of ancestral memory, a custom which is widely developed."[14] They are not just a vehicle of individuation but rather "a signifier of a person's place in a social hierarchy according to their real or symbolic ties" within the larger social habitus – in other words, they have a profound "socializing role."[15]

In addition, as sociologist Cemile Ahmed and historian Antonina Zheliazkova point out, in the Islamic context, renaming severs one's connection to God and "dooms them to eternal suffering – before and after death."[16] The name, Ahmed argues through Bourdieu, is "the last guarantee of the unity of the person" in that it guarantees the coherence and temporal continuity of the self. But for Muslims, she says, a proper name is more than this – by tradition in the region, and often chosen by the mother, it is a mediator between God and the self, and according to local custom, it is given on the third day of birth by an elder after the *aptez* and *namaz* prayers. "It is precisely with this name, whispered in the ear of the child on the third day of their birth, that one appears to Allah, who calls people by their names to judge whether they have lived their lives in sin. Five days before Ramazan Bayram, on *Kadir Gecesi*, God writes down everyone's fate for the following year next to their name."[17]

And further, the name given at birth carries one's personal history as regards their relationship to and practise of faith – that with which one must appear before God at the time of death.[18] And not only that: without the given name, "the soul would not be recognizable to either the Muslim or Christian judge and will be destined to eternal wandering between faiths and spiritual worlds, without finding rest."[19] This is why people experienced renaming as a profound intrusion into their most intimate world and an interruption of the integrity of their spiritual life.

WEBS OF UPRISINGS

In 1964 the state launched its first systematic campaign to rename all Bulgarian-speaking Muslims in the Rhodope Mountains and the Blagoevgrad region further west. In response, the people rose up in fearless defiance, and an open revolt broke out in the village of Ribnovo. After the participants took control of the village, it became a centre of resistance for surrounding settlements, including Avramovo, Buntsevo, Gospodintsi, Kornitsa, and Breznitsa.[20] Caught unprepared, the government backed out, but a few years later, between 1970 and 1974, it launched another carefully planned offensive and renamed by force most Pomaks in the country. Besides Pomaks, the renaming campaigns of the 1960s and '70s also affected Muslims in mixed marriages, Romas with Turkish and Muslim names, and some residents of predominantly Turkish villages in the Eastern and Middle Rhodope Mountains. It is not uncommon for Bulgarians to carry a family or last name with Turkish roots, and some ideologues of the campaign also insisted on changing these names as well.[21]

By 1974, the government had renamed about 220,000 Pomaks and had closed most mosques in their villages. In response, people organized an open and massive resistance movement, which continued for months and was eventually violently and brutally suppressed. During March 1972, miners in Barutin organized an uprising and a blockade of the village that lasted three days; it was eventually quelled with overwhelming military force – resulting in several dead and hundreds of cases of beatings, imprisonment, and torture. As the campaign slowly moved through the small villages nested in the mountains, residents of Yakoruda and Buntsevo, and later of Ribnovo, Ablanitsa, Vulkosel, Kornitsa, Breznitsa, Luzhnitsa, Letnitsa, Lukhovo, and other villages in the Blagoevradski region, rose up in refusal and propelled the dramatic events that are now acknowledged as the prehistory of the Revival Process and the core of the early resistance to it. The aftermath of the so-called Kornishki events, of the winter and spring of 1972–73 – an uprising that turned that village into an autonomous territory of sorts – resulted in dozens of people killed, hundreds wounded, hundreds more beaten, imprisoned, and tortured, and tens of families displaced and exiled to other parts of the country.[22]

The people had no other way forward but to accept their new names and "the Bulgarian-Muslim problem" was considered solved. In light of later developments, scholars and community members read the renaming and assimilation campaigns targeting the Pomaks in the early 1970s as the "general rehearsal" for the renaming of the much larger Turkish population, and indeed, internal discussions at the upper echelons of government suggest that the campaign served as a sort of preparation for the launch of the more massive effort to rename the Turkish people.[23]

Beginning in the 1980s, the state began its offensive against Romas with Turkish and Muslim names, followed by members of mixed marriages who had not been reached during the 1970s. By the end of 1984, the government had moved to deploy a systematic campaign against Bulgarian-born Turks, and soon every town, every neighbourhood, every village in the mountains were folded into this process. By January 1985, between 340,000 and 350,000 Turkish-identifying Bulgarian citizens were renamed – 214,000 in the Kurzhdali region; 41,000 in the Khaskovo region; 22,000 in the Plovdiv region; 5,000 in Pazardzhik; 11,000 in Stara Zagora; 35,000 in the Silistra region; 9,000 in the Burgas region; and 3,000 in the Blagoevgrad region.[24] Documents reveal an organized campaign of daunting proportions mobilizing the state's military and national security apparatuses, bureaucratic and administrative units, the instruments of propaganda, mass media and entertainment, educational institutions, and most political and community organizations. The modern administrative apparatuses of population management, health, education, and social security were the most powerful instruments in the state's ethnic assimilation campaign. Any point of contact with the modern state administration was used to coerce residents into changing their names.

Pensions were withheld unless they were requested under the new names.[25] Passports, identification cards, and personal identification numbers became central vehicles in the name conversions. In the late 1970s, the government introduced a system of personal identification numbers (the EGN) and the new passports issued for every citizen in the 1980s became one of the main vehicles for accounting for and assisting in the renaming of Turkish and Roma citizens.[26] Party administrators and military personnel were at the forefront of the campaign. Leaders of religious organizations and respected members of neighbourhoods and communities were recruited as agents of the campaign. School teachers were under pressure to foment a new national consciousness among minorities in their classrooms. Yaşar Şaban, who worked as a teacher at the time and became involved in parliamentary politics after 1989, recalls that he was instructed to call out the new Bulgarian name of each student at the beginning of class, a call to which everyone was expected to respond.[27] Health-care workers and family doctors, who had more personal contact with minority communities, were called to participate as well: "Because of the nature of their work, they have access to every home, they are in contact with a lot of people."[28] Government authorities also reached out to socially and culturally influential members of the community and asked them to co-operate. These were teachers, artists and intellectuals, spiritual leaders, heads of family and kinship groups, figures of authority and respected members of communities, neighbourhoods, and villages.[29]

Numerous personal accounts continue to emerge from this period, which help us to reconstruct the everyday details of the campaign; indeed, it is through these stories that both the absurdity and the devastating effects of the campaign come to light. To change their Turkish and Muslim names, people had to choose a Bulgarian name phonetically or semantically similar to their own from alphabetized name catalogues kept in various public offices.[30] The names could be processed at multiple locations: at work, at school, at the local precinct, or at office desks often set up at the village square or the local community centre. Some chose Bulgarian (but not Christian) names, while some had their names chosen for them by the administrators processing their documents. Some used the act of renaming as a form of defiance by choosing names with a subversive meaning.

As if these name "restorations" were not a disturbing enough violation of the personal and collective dignity of the people, Bulgarian authorities went even further. Not content with renaming the living, they also targeted the dead. Multiple state registries were changed to give generic, and often identical, Bulgarian names to all deceased people with Turkish and Muslim names found in the state records. In a sequence of ghastly, macabre actions, which according to witnesses were executed mostly by military personnel, even the names on tombstones were etched off and crossed out. People recall that entire Muslim cemeteries were left in ruins, obliterated and razed to the ground.

Ethnophobia and Islamophobia were a major driving force in the design and execution of the ethnic assimilation campaign, and this survey provides just a partial glimpse of its intensity and scope. From the point of view of the ethnonationalists, renaming the dead was a necessary measure, since contemporary Muslim populations of several ethnicities, as if somehow unaware of their own identities, ancestors, and community and family histories, were seen as a product of historical error or injustice. The campaign was also seen as inevitable because of patrilineal naming traditions in the Balkans, which stipulate that middle names, regardless of religion or ethnicity, derive from the father's names. Thus men, often long deceased, acquired their new names through the renaming of their sons and daughters by whom they were survived. Perhaps the erasure of women's historical existence in the patrilineal system of descent spared some mothers and grandmothers who lay buried, resting quietly in the shadows of history.

In line with its doctrine, the party leadership continuously denied any interference with the religious practice of Islam among the Turkish, Pomak, and Roma communities. Yet countless testimonies report that "the reality was different": mosques were closed, praying was prohibited, religious holidays and rituals were banned, every Muslim community was surveilled, *hodjas* and imams were regularly detained, jailed, and persecuted for performing birth, circumcision, and burial services.[31]

In addition to forced renamings and the prohibition of religious practice, the government banned the wearing of traditional clothing and use of the Turkish language in public spaces, public institutions, and at the workplace. In schools, the primary language of instruction had long ago been changed to Bulgarian, but as part of yet another curricular overhaul that aimed to revise the content of primary and secondary school education, the Turkish language was no longer available as a subject.[32] Bulgarian teachers were relocated from other parts of the country to schools in targeted regions, and inspectors were assigned to monitor class content.[33] Yaşar Şaban recalls these disturbing inspections, scheduled during lessons on Bulgarian national history and literature, often with dramatic content depicting Turks as violent, deceptive, and hateful: "These classes were a nightmare. The kids were silent the entire time and I had to go through the class alone, without hurting or provoking them, and show a level of knowledge to the inspectors."[34]

At the same time, the authorities acted swiftly and suppressed all knowledge of these events, or at least contained it to the targeted regions, mostly in the smaller towns and villages in the Rhodope Mountains, as well as northeastern Bulgaria, and away from larger cities and the country's capital. This information blackout was so effective that most Bulgarians living in larger cities and smaller towns who were not in immediate contact with Turkish residents and other Muslim minorities were unaware of the events. But word among those who were targeted travelled fast and when the "Revivalists" (*vuzroditelite*), as people called them, came to their towns and villages, the people had already organized and had been waiting, assembled on the squares in both suspense and defiance.

Demonstrations against the renaming campaign were large, and their size speaks to remarkable levels of organized resistance that prevailed in conditions of intense surveillance, repression, and persecution. The protests continued for months, always in the presence of *militsia* (civil forces), military forces, border patrol, secret services, and a host of party officials and state bureaucrats. Early demonstrations began in the cold December days of 1984 in the Kurdzhaliiski region, in Momchilgrad, Dzhebel, Gruevo, Mlechino, Mogiliane, and Benkovski, and were quickly repressed by an overwhelming military force using live ammunition. The unarmed resistance movement gave its first victims at this time, with dozens wounded and several dead.[35] Among them was the youngest victim of the resistance, the seventeen-month-old Türkan Hasan from the village of Kayaloba, who was killed along with several others in the village of Mogiliane. Her absurd death became a focal point of the movement and its history as monuments and memorial sites in her name were later built throughout the region, from Mogiliane to Edirne. In the Shumenski region of northern Bulgaria, the *Iablanska epopeia*, the blockade mounted by residents of Iablanovo and surrounding villages remains one of the most epic moments in the history of resistance against the Revival Process. People remember the days of the "*Iablanska* Commune" on the village square throughout a cold January marked by extraordinary acts of solidarity, the communal kitchens, and intense sociality and care, and the determination to defend to the death, with all means at their disposal, their "traditions, the memory of their *rod* [kin], and their human dignity."[36]

The wave of unrest from that year was quelled and many organizers were imprisoned, but mobilizations continued in the following years. Many informal organizations emerged, reaching out for international support, and in the meantime many forms of low-grade resistance continued. In 1989, a large wave of demonstrations and uprisings erupted in towns and villages across the country. The so-called May Events of 1989 began when thousands gathered in the town of Dzhebel, in Kurdzhaliiski region, on 19 May. In the following days, peaceful marches and demonstrations were held throughout the country demanding the restoration of people's original names and a lifting of the ban on speaking the Turkish language, as well as the freedom of religion and freedom and amnesty for political prisoners involved in the movements against the Revival Process. On 20 and 21 May long processions formed in the Shumenski region; these soon swelled to the tens of thousands as they passed through various towns and villages, including Pristoe, Kaolinovo, Dulovo, Kliment, Naum, Tukach, Dukhovets, Belentsi, Branichevo, Zagoriche, Silistra, Todor Ikonomovo, Isperikh, Preslav, Novi Pazar, and more. The *militsiia* and military opened fire on several occasions; such was the case in Todor Ikonomovo, where several people were killed and dozens injured. [37]

Demonstrations continued in Razgrad, Tolbukhin, Turgovishte, Isperikh, Benkovski, Kurdzhali, Mlechinsko, Kirkovsko, Momchilgrad, Diakovo, and many other towns and villages across the country.[38] To prevent mobility and public gatherings as well as the spread of information from and into regions with more active mobilizations, the government blocked entire urban areas and installed checkpoints at major roads and intersections. Yet despite the military control of public space and the infrastructure of mobility, large and persistent demonstrations appeared throughout the country, with people travelling from all parts of the country to converge on protest areas. Protests were relentless and defiant, with escalations and clashes with heavily armed militia and the military. The state used tear gas and water canons mixed with sand and gravel, and on multiple occasions rolled out tanks and fired live ammunition.[39] Once again, more people lost their lives and countless were injured, beaten, threatened, and sent to camps, prisons, or psychiatric clinics.[40]

In addition to the protests, the Turkish people engaged in multiple forms of everyday resistance and cultural survival. Speaking and teaching children the Turkish language became a form of defiance and cultural resistance. Wedding and funeral rituals, usually involving celebrations or processions in public spaces, often turned into political rallies and marches. People refused for months to pick up their newly issued passports, their salaries, their pensions, knowing that any contact with the state administration would trigger the name-change process. Some, knowing the authorities would come looking for them, left their homes and hid in the forested mountains for weeks.[41] The workplace became a site of intense collective resistance: workers organized boycotts, wildcat strikes, and sabotaged their workplaces in various ways to stall the production process. They abandoned agricultural fields, refused to harvest the tobacco, abandoned the cattle, and wasted thousands of gallons of milk. Rumen Avramov's study on the political economy of the Revival Process details these actions and shows that the people's efforts to paralyze entire sectors of the economy was one of the most effective forms of political opposition.[42] They set on fire highly flammable sites such as whey storages.[43] In August 1984 and March 1985, deadly explosions occurred in major public and transportation areas throughout the country, killing about ten people and wounding over sixty others.[44]

Many Bulgarians joined the protests and organized solidarity marches and rallies. As news of the events began to spread, solidarity events and informal organizations quickly began to emerge in the larger cities. Some of the most important dissident organizations emerged in opposition to the Revival Process: the Club for the Support of Free Speech and Transformation (*Klub za glasnost i preustroistvo*); the Independent Syndicate Podkrepa (*Nezavisim sindikat Podkrepa*); the Independent Committee for Religious Rights and Freedoms of Conscience (*Nezavisim komitet po religioznite prava i svobodi na suvestta*); the Independent Association for the Defence of Human Rights (*Nezavisimo druzhestvo za zashtita na pravata na choveka*). Many prominent intellectuals and public figures also began public campaigns against the assimilations. However, it would not be accurate to credit the entire dissident movement with the opposition to the Revival Process, which dissidents have often retroactively claimed.

Many of them remained complicit with the campaign or indifferent to the events; some of them embraced nationalist patriotism and joined the revival of Orthodox Christianity; they also welcomed or tolerated the emergence of extreme right-wing and neo-fascist tendencies within their political orbit.

In the summer of 1989, in an act of protest and refusal and an effort to preserve their collective history and dignity, between 310,000 and 340,000 Bulgarian-born Turks left the country en masse for neighbouring Turkey. The party leadership used these developments as an opportunity to purge the country of its largest ethnic and religious minority, orchestrating the biggest population expulsion in the history of the country. The last exodus of such massive proportions had occurred in 1950–51, when over 150,000 Turks and some Pomaks left the country; this was followed by another, smaller wave in the mid-1960s, mostly through family reunification agreements signed between Turkey and Bulgaria. Chapter 4 discussed some of the details of the 1950–51 mass migration, stressing the different political context and the different logics of this earlier exodus. The 1989 expulsions were the subject of detailed record keeping, and internal documents and transcripts of closed meetings, later declassified and published, reveal that the state was actively involved in encouraging, planning, and executing the expatriation of minorities – a "manoeuver," as the process was called by the head of state, that clearly maps onto the logic of ethnic cleansing.[45] They show the ruling party elites planning and strategizing the expulsions in an ethnophobic and Islamophobic language, patronizing and othering ethnic and religious minorities. They also give us an inside look into the laboratory of political power, capturing the process of crafting a public discourse that, steeped in righteous nationalism and patriotism, aims to control the interpretations of events. Indeed, the rhetoric of ethnonationalism enacted its own political imaginary through a skillful reversal of language, which, as Tatiana Vaksberg comments, is impossible to decipher without "a dictionary of antonyms."[46] Names were not "taken away" but "restored"; minorities were not obliterated but "revived" or "reborn"; they called the Turkish people "nationalists" and "chauvinists" to hide their own nationalist agenda. To avoid running afoul of international law, political leaders carefully removed all references to ethnic or religious minorities in official state and public documents. The word "expulsion" (*izselvane*) was replaced with the euphemistic "Great Excursion."[47] Because all citizens now had the freedom to exit and re-enter the country "as they wish," this was not an expulsion, but "free travel," "tourism," an open-ended trip for either temporary or permanent stays.[48]

However, quietly, the government used administrative and bureaucratic means to encourage and propel the exodus, while making the material survival of ethnic and religious minorities impossible and their everyday and cultural lives intolerable. While regulating and enabling the flow of exiles, the state used its bureaucratic-administrative power to add to the suffering, humiliation, and degradation of Turkish families and neighbourhoods preparing to leave. In exchange for an international passport, the state began requiring declarations issued by workplaces and municipalities stating that individuals do not owe anything to the state, their employers, or the municipality. After requesting such declarations or filing an application for a passport, people would find themselves fired from their jobs. Their documents were often stalled, delayed, or revoked, and people waited for hours, even days, on multiple lines, going back and forth between various bureaucracies – the bank, the police precinct, the photo studio, the passport administration, and back.[49]

In addition, in a carefully premeditated manner, the government did everything possible to expropriate all land, property, animals, and income sources from families who ventured to depart.[50] As if the erasure of their belonging, history, and their agency in determining their own identity was not disempowering enough, the authorities made sure to dispossess them materially and send them away to begin their lives in exile empty-handed, materially vulnerable and economically precarious.

The government banned the sale of houses and land to individuals and forced people to sell their property at prices far lower than their value to agrarian industrial collectives (APKs), municipalities, and industrial enterprises. These expropriated estates were to be redistributed to those people (presumably Bulgarians) who would relocate to the abandoned areas.[51] In the meantime, the *militsia* would shut down informal and spontaneous markets where people had started selling their live animals or the meat they had slaughtered.[52] The government placed limits on the amount people could withdraw from their savings, and, while it had to continue paying exiled citizens their pensions, it left them no way to collect their money while abroad.[53] Customs regulations were revised to control and limit the export of cash, luggage, household products, and personal items.[54]

Often having to travel far to get what they needed for their one-way journeys, people formed long lines at stores in order to buy suitcases, travel bags, sleeping bags, tents, clothes, and household items. In predominantly Turkish-populated areas, store managers were ordered to withdraw from their stores commodities that were in short supply – items such as clothes, cotton fabrics, and aged meats and sausages. Instead, managers were urged to emphasize overstock products and to fill their stores with suitcases and travel bags of all kinds.[55] In the meantime, the grey and black markets exploded, a result of the great demand for cars, gold and silver objects, and other items of deficit.

The mass of refugees caused an utter social crisis both in Bulgaria and Turkey, a chaos that reached unfathomable proportions in the summer of 1989. In an attempt to ease the escalating situation, which by this point had gained the attention of international newspapers, Todor Zhivkov delivered his infamous "Unity" speech from 29 May 1989, a public statement broadcast on radio, TV, and printed in major newspapers. The statement denounced the unrest and called for calm. Asking Turkish minorities to remain in the country, he announced that the borders with Turkey were open and everyone who wished to leave was free to do so. The official line put forward in the speech maintained that ethnic Turkish minorities, Bulgarian citizens born and raised for generations on "Bulgarian land," rightfully belonged to the Bulgarian nation and were an indelible "part of the Bulgarian people": "It is particularly important to emphasize that Bulgarian Muslims are our brothers and sisters, an inseparable part of the Bulgarian people, sons and daughters of our dear fatherland – the People's Republic of Bulgaria."[56] Yet at the same time, every citizen had "the right to exit and re-enter the country freely and travel to any part of the world they wish … [and] to use this right as they wish, including permanent departure."[57] The contradictions in Zhivkov's statement expressed the duplicitous attitudes of the regime toward its minorities. It was an effort to quell the protests but propelled the biggest population expulsion in the history of the country.

The government was also struggling to mitigate the economic effects of the exodus. The mass migrations caused profound and large-scale disruptions to Bulgaria's national economy, triggering a crisis in multiple branches of the economy and in the commodity distribution system. For a short period, tens of millions of levs were withdrawn from banks, setting the currency circulation system in crisis. Multiple industries were affected, especially the ones with uninterrupted,

24/7 flows of production. Work stoppages and boycotts in transportation caused nationwide disruptions in public transport. Entire construction brigades abandoned their work sites, halting the construction of major infrastructure projects. Industries involved in the production and use of glass, metal, antibiotics, tiles and ceramics, and fire-resistant material were heavily affected. In Razgrad, 8,700 workers did not show up to work; in Varna, 9,600; in Dulovo, 1,200 workers boycotted a major machine factory and a glass factory. In Lovech, 150 railroad workers left their jobs; 200 left in the sugar industry. Medical personnel and education workers such as doctors, nurses, and teachers opened a void the state scrambled to fill.[58] In the valleys, people working in agriculture abandoned the fields and refused to gather the harvest; in the mountains, those working in animal farming let the animals and the sheep herds walk away – as Evgeniia Ivanova shows, these tactics were used in the Balkans for centuries by the local populations as forms of defiance and resistance to the powers that exploited and oppressed them.[59]

Most severely affected were some branches of agriculture and animal farming such as tobacco, dairy, and poultry, which relied heavily on the labour of the Turkish population. Boycotts and various forms of disobedience at the workplace left animals and crops unattended. As the mass departures happened during prime harvest time, the agricultural sector faced tremendous challenges when it came to bringing in the crops. Party leaders and industry management came up with various disciplinary measures, threatening workers with economic responsibility for the resulting damages and losses of collective property. People were warned that if they boycotted their jobs, their passports would not be issued.[60] While discussing various options, party officials used classic xenophobic and ethnophobic discourse that rendered ethnic and religious minorities inferior, undesirable, and discardable, while showing entitlement to their labour and their social contributions: "We need to tell them, we won't stop you from leaving, but first gather the harvest so that the harvest is inside the storage, and then we'll let you go."[61]

To compensate for the massive labour shortage, the government reached out to retired cadres, especially retired doctors, and invited them to return to work for a generous compensation in addition to their pensions. The Komsomol brigades were employed in affected regions to gather the harvest; army personnel were called to work as drivers of agricultural vehicles; workers in lower administrations such as photographers, bank tellers, cashiers, and passport processing services, were ordered to work on weekends to process documents.[62]

Some people remember with bitterness and disappointment their Bulgarian colleagues, friends, and neighbours standing aside in silence and doing nothing to stop the offensive. Others share emotional stories of solidarity, of Bulgarians joining in their refusal to divide communities along ethnic lines. To many Bulgarians, the campaign was no less confusing and unsettling. In Iablanovo, *kaka* Bonka and *bai* Ionko Taskovi, members of a handful of Bulgarian families in the village, joined in with their *motiki* (mattocks) to defend their neighbours at the blockade. They refused to be spoken for. "The Bulgarian people – this is us, not Todor Zhivkov's people … We've lived here fifty years in peace and quiet as Bulgarians and Turks, and now all of a sudden, 'there are no Turks.' What kind of *divotiia* [lunacy] is this? … I am here with the people I've lived my whole life with. I'm with them in times of fortune and times of hardship."[63]

REVIVING THE LIVING, RESURRECTING THE DEAD

The Revival Process was carried out in the name of unity, social cohesion, and the social, material, and cultural well-being of the national community. But paradoxically – and perhaps predictably – people found themselves torn by discord and antagonism and ravaged by loss, displacement, and abandonment. The campaign left towns and villages heavily depopulated, families separated, neighbourhoods and communities destroyed. It sharply politicized society along ethnic and religious lines, mobilized and intensified collective notions of otherness, antagonized ethnic and religious differences, and polarized the people to an unparalleled degree. Dividing people into "us" and "them," it broke community bonds, severed prior forms of togetherness, destroyed centuries-old cultures of inter-ethnic community life, instilled fear and mistrust among neighbours, wiped out shared religious traditions and rituals, cultures of mutual respect and influence, what some describe as co-adaptive forms of Islam and Orthodox Christianity in the Balkans – regional cultures that had taken centuries to form.

As Ahmed and others report, the renamings introduced into the daily lives of people the nightmare of an unwelcome double social existence: Ahmed shares that to schoolmates and institutions, she was Diliana; in the company of close friends, family, and neighbours, she was Cemile.[64] Stories recount the effects of this abrupt and radical displacement: people found themselves not only without history but without ways of maintaining basic continuity within their own personal lives and everyday existence. They speak of split, fragmented subjectivities descending into a state of disintegration, of selves shattered by a sense of disorientation, interruption, and loss; of scrambled family lineages, relationships, and *rodove* (kinship groups); of the impossibility of narrating their personal lives; of confusion around burying the dead, with people asking themselves and each other, "Are we burying the same person we knew?"

Death, bodies, burials, and graves have a central place in these stories. The question "How do we bury the dead?" would come back with disturbing persistence during these trying times to stand as a poignant reminder of the corporeal materiality of history and to capture the painful effects of the campaign's disruption of historical and cultural orders. The mass departures tore through the large webs of kinship relations. These had already been disrupted multiple times – by government treaties drawing and redrawing nation-state borders after independence, after two Balkan wars and two world wars, and then by the uncompromising Cold War border regime between Bulgaria and Turkey. When families prepared to leave, someone would always stay behind because they couldn't stand the thought of leaving the graves of their ancestors unattended.[65] After the regime changes of 1989, those who chose to retain their Bulgarian names, usually Pomaks, faced multiple conundrums as they navigated their hybrid or ambiguous identities. The fact that they did not belong to established categories had doomed them to an ambivalent existence and marginalization that took various material, cultural, and political forms. In her ethnographic study of Bulgarian-speaking Muslims from the town of Madan, Kristen Ghodsee described how imams would refuse to perform funeral services for the Pomaks because they had non-Muslim names; to ask a priest to perform a funeral service meant that they would be buried as Christians.[66]

Death continues to haunt the history of the Revival Process in another unsettling way because the victims of the campaign have been extremely hard to establish. As scholars and community members continue to grapple with the legacies of these events, the number of dead, imprisoned, beaten and wounded, of exiled, internally displaced, and returnees continues to shift and fluctuate. This was due in large part to the covert nature of the campaign and the cover-ups to which it was subjected, and because a great deal of imprisonments and executions happened without trial. Where bureaucratic records exist, they cannot be trusted because of the state's well-practised instrumental use of statistics. The number of victims has been extremely hard to establish as many died days or months later because of their wounds or due to deadly prison conditions.[67] Death registries and death certificates cannot be trusted, either, as witnesses recount that the reason for death was often inaccurately recorded as "stroke," "heart attack," or "pneumonia."[68] Thus, the death toll, Gruev and Kal'onski reflect, is "diffused" into the "larger surge of violence, in the same way that it is impossible to draw a clear line between "victims and passive observers, collaborators and executioners."[69]

After the fall of the socialist governments in 1989, people's original names were restored and a large number returned from their exile, and some of the returnees were able to reclaim their property.[70] The vast majority of renamed Turkish people restored their maternal names. Many Pomaks and Romas, who have defied fixity throughout history, chose to retain their Bulgarian names. Historically they have maintained a hybrid and flexible subjectivity to navigate the complex, often stigmatizing and ostracizing, social contexts they inhabit and traverse. The number of returnees from abroad are similarly hard to establish – estimates vary, but it is thought that between a third and a half of all refugees returned in the next several years.[71] The gruelling details of the assimilation campaigns came to light in a plethora of voices that helped to reconstruct, through individual and collective stories, historical research, journalistic writings, and oral histories, the profound social cataclysms and the immense toll the Revival Process took on communities, families, and individuals. People describe public humiliation and collective degradation and their testimonies continue to reveal disturbing details of the everyday terror, harassment, repression, and abuse. Rendered alien in their own country, they speak of profound displacement, cultural disorientation, and the disintegration of their personal and collective subjectivity. They share experiences of double or multiple personhood, split realities, separated families and *rodove* (kinship groups), scattered and destroyed communities. They speak of historical and material dispossessions, of taken and abandoned homes, of sold or stolen land and cattle. But they also speak of tremendous strength, endurance, and resilience, of dignity, solidarity, and courage, of political resolve. It took communities a tremendous amount of work to rebuild their homes, reclaim their means of subsistence, and restore the integrity of their families, histories, persons, villages, and neighbourhoods. And the grief of irrecoverable loss, of rupture, and the marks of violence haunt their lives and the places they inhabit into the present.

6

Uncanny Symbioses: Ethnonationalism and the Global Orientations of Bulgarian Socialism

On 17 September 1972, Angela Davis landed at the airport in Sofia to a show of welcome and support. Only a few months prior to her arrival, Bulgarian society had followed the fate of the American political activist with rapt attention: her capture and her prolonged and arduous public trial were covered extensively in the Bulgarian press, and *Narodna mladezh*, a popular socialist youth newspaper, organized a massive letter-writing campaign in support of her liberation. In the following decades, in her political and public work, Davis has never missed an opportunity to make the point that she owes her freedom and her life to the people; indeed, it was only thanks to the relentless mobilizations against her capture and against the political persecutions of Black radicals and communist activists fighting for racial and social justice that she was released from the repressive grind of the justice system and avoided prison and possibly execution by the state. In her autobiography, she wrote that the international campaign in support of her freedom, along with the freedom of all political prisoners in the United States, "had not only exerted serious pressure on the government, it had also stimulated the further growth of the mass movement at home."[1] At the centre of this international movement, she continued, was "the socialist community of nations." "In those countries rallies were attended by more people than I had ever before seen assembled in one place – hundreds of thousands, for example in the GDR, and close to three quarters of a million in Cuba."[2]

During the late 1960s and '70s, Bulgarian society was drawn into a swirl of international events as the socialist public sphere was activated by the global echoes and alignments of struggles for social, economic, and racial justice across borders and continents. These

ДОБРЕ ДОШЛА, АНДЖЕЛА!

«Особено щастлива съм, че мога да посетя родината на Георги Димитров» • Среща на Анджела Дейвис с младата творческа интелигенция

Само няколко месеца ни делят от дните, когато българската младеж целият наш народ заедно с прогресивните хора от петте континента издигаше глас в защита на справедливата кауза на смелата боркиня за свобода и граждански права, младата комунистка Анджела Дейвис „Свобода за Анджела!" — този призив подеха десетки хиляди младежи и девойки от всички краища на България. Мрачните замисли на американската реакция, машинациите на расисткото „правосъдие", решетките на затвора в Сан Рафаел не издържаха пред надигналата се вълна на международната работническа солидарност, пред гневния и справедлив протест на прогресивното човечество. Сега мъжествената и вдъхновена комунистка е на свобода и ние имаме щастието да я приветствуваме със сърдечното българско „Добре дошла" на наша българска земя!

Вчера по покана на Централния комитет на БКП прославената американска боркиня за мир, демокрация и социален прогрес членът на Централния комитет на Американската компартия и лауреат на Димитровска награда Анджела Дейвис пристигна в нашата страна. Заедно с нея са и членовете на ЦК на АКП Кендра Александър и Франклин Александър.

На аерогара София скъпата гостенка бе посрещната от другарите Пеко Таков, кандидат-член на Политбюро на ЦК на БКП и заместник-председател на Държавния съвет Елена Лагадинова, председател на Комитета на българските жени, Иванка Василева секретар на ЦК на ДКМС, Груди Атанасов председател на Националния комитет за защита на мира, ректора на Софийския университет акад. Христо Христов, представители на столичната общественост, много младежи и пионери

„Върховна радост е за нас — изтъкна при пристигането си Анджела Дейвис, — че можахме да дойдем в България в родината на Димитров и страната, която строи социализъм. Ние носим борческите топли привети от Централния комитет на Американската компартия, от всички американски комунисти.

Ние посетихме Съветския съюз, първата социалистическа държава, страната на Ленин, бяхме в Германската демократична република, страната на Маркс и Енгелс, и сме особено щастливи, че сега може да посетим родината на Георги Димитров!"

•

Снощи се състоя сърдечна среща на Анджела Дейвис с представители на младата творческа интелигенция от столицата. На нея присъствуваха председателят на Клуба на младата творческа интелигенция при ЦК на ДКМС Любомир Левчев, първи заместник-председател на Националния съвет на Отечествения фронт, председателката на Комитета на българските жени Елена Лагадинова, секретарят на ЦК на ДКМС инж. Дойчо Динев, млади учени, писатели, артисти, архитекти, художници.

Тук бяха придружаващите Анджела Дейвис Кендра Александър, член на ЦК на Комунистическата партия на САЩ и Франклин Александър, член на Националния съвет на Комунистическата партия на САЩ.

(Продължава на 3-а стр.)

Greetings to the readers of "Narodna mladez"

Peace, Friendship, Solidarity.

Angela Y. Davis

17.9.72

Поздрави на читателите на „Народна младеж". Мир, дружба, солидарност.

Анджела ДЕЙВИС

Figure 6.1 "Welcome, Angela!," *Narodna mladezh*, 18 September 1972. Angela Davis visited Bulgaria in September 1972 after she was acquitted and released from jail. The Bulgarian press covered her trial extensively, and Bulgarian youth organizations and youth journals organized campaigns in support of her freedom.

struggles opened possibilities for the forging of political alternatives across geopolitical and regional confines, to which the socialist countries could make distinct contributions. The Bulgarian press covered the international news in collaboration with reporters from the Soviet Union and other socialist countries strategically located in cities such as New York, London, Havana, and Cairo. In the early 1970s, *Narodna mladezh* followed a dizzying range of political developments around the world, from the war in Vietnam and the anti-war protests in the United States, to teacher strikes in Philadelphia, to Israel's attack on Palestinian refugee camps in Lebanon, to the last throes of Portuguese colonial rule in Mozambique, Guinea-Bissau, and Angola. The newspaper ran regular stories on the economic and social transformation of Chilean society under the short-lived socialist government of Salvador Allende, as well as the right-wing backlash and military coup that took over the state and caused the violence, repression, death, and exile of tens of thousands of people that devastated Chilean society in the following years. Some of these exiled people ended up finding refuge in socialist Bulgaria, mostly in Sofia, forming a small but strong diasporic community that energized the city's radical culture.

In the weeks, months, and years following the assassination of Dr. Martin Luther King Jr. in April 1968, Bulgarian society had become closely acquainted with the social conditions of Black people in the United States, the realities of racism and legal segregation, the history of the civil rights and Black Power movements, the brutality and racism of the police, the structural role of prisons in the perpetuation of class and racial inequality, and more. *Narodna mladezh* began the ongoing column *America: Black and White*, which ran through most of 1972. The column explored the intersections of racism, capitalist exploitation, the criminal justice system and criminalized populations, and the political persecutions of communists and Black radicals. It published coverage of the Attica Prison rebellions in New York State, the war in Vietnam and the anti-war protests, and the persecution of a number of radical political organizers, including Black Panther Party members Bobby Seale, Erica Haggins, and Huey Newton; the Soledad Brothers; the so-called Chicago Seven and Seattle Six, among others.

In this context it was not surprising that, after she was acquitted, Davis visited a number of socialist countries to honour the people who supported her, including the USSR, Czechoslovakia, the People's Republic of Bulgaria, the GDR, Cuba, and Chile. During and after

Figure 6.2 Political cartoon commenting on the arrest of Angela Davis by Ivan Stoichev in the Plovdiv youth newspaper *Komsomolska iskra*, Plovdiv, 11 January 1971.

her trip she shared some of her impressions from these countries, including the housing developments in the Soviet Union, the reconstruction of Tashkent after the April 1966 earthquake that devastated much of the city's built environment, the women's organizations, and "the happy way children live."[3] She told reporters in Moscow that "when we return to the United States, we will speak of the true equality of all peoples in the USSR, the rapid progress of all nations and nationalities living on the territory of [this] country. We will speak about the Soviet people's remarkable accomplishments in the spheres of economy and culture."[4]

Davis spent a total of four days in Bulgaria. She was accompanied by Kendra Alexander, her friend and a veteran of the civil rights movements in the United States who, together with Franklin Alexander (who also accompanied Davis), co-founded and co-chaired the international Free Angela and All Political Prisoners campaign. The guests met with the country's political leadership and with representatives of youth and women's organizations – among them Elena Lagadinova, a high-ranking politician and chair of the Committee of the Bulgarian Women's Movement for many years. Lagadinova's relentless work and organizing throughout the 1970s helped build, along with many others, the extensive infrastructures of care, leisure, and social reproduction that, as discussed in chapter 2, changed the social and material lives of many women and opened the way for the unprecedented reorganization of gender and social relations.

The coverage of the events of September 1972 suggests that Davis and her fellow guests were treated like official visitors: they received the highest honours and their experience was mediated by official programs and their contact with the political elites. It is unclear to what extent they were able to escape the elaborate state rituals and curated encounters with "the people" to experience everyday life on their own. Still, this context presented a stark contrast to the visitors' experiences in their own country, where they were persecuted by the state and vilified by the mainstream press. Audre Lorde, an African-American feminist writer who visited the Soviet Union and Tashkent only a few years later in 1976 as part of the Afro-Asian Writers' Conference sponsored by the Union of Soviet Writers, wrote about the powerful effect this type of unexpected collective welcome had on her.[5] During her short visit, Davis left a lasting impression on the collective experience of an entire generation of young people and was an inspiration for young Bulgarian women in particular, who still remember being captivated by her strength and dignity, her public presence, and her political spirit.

The guests were taken to Varna, a major city on the Black Sea coast, where they visited factories and toured the Black Sea resort of Zlatni Piasatsi. They also visited the town of Septemvri near Plovdiv, where agricultural workers showed them their land co-operatives, their orchards and vineyards. Davis received a painting of women rose gatherers working in the rose valleys, as the socialist state had developed the rose oil industry and exported its products on the international market as part of the symbolic repertoire of Bulgarian nationalism. The party leadership gave her the the International Dimitrov Award, given for contributions in the sphere of political, public, and creative life. Local newspapers found the award particularly relevant because of Dimitrov's own experience and history. The Bulgarian-born communist and Comintern leader was framed together with other communist and anti-fascist activists in the infamous Leipzig trial during the first months of Nazi rule. As for Davis, she took the recognition as an honour and used it as an opportunity to stress the importance of international solidarity among people in struggle. From Dimitrov, she said, we've learned a lot – "not only how to win in court, but like him, we realized that this is not enough ... The only way to win until the end is to unify the progressive forces of our people, and of the entire world."[6] Further, Davis stressed that the elimination of colonialism and racial oppression depended on the full abolition of capitalism and "the building of a socialist culture" and a "socialist way of life." "What we learned," she said, was that "only socialist society will give people the opportunity to enjoy the fruits of their labor, and that building socialism is the only road towards building a new human and a new society."[7]

A number of African and African-American intellectuals shared this idea – that racism and colonialism cannot be uprooted unless capitalism is abolished and that there is a structural juncture between the anti-capitalist and anti-colonial struggles. Indeed, this juncture was rather obvious to many at the time, both in the formerly colonized world and the socialist countries. These bridges became a way of uprooting the colonial legacy in the newly independent countries and served as tools for resisting the various structures that reproduced colonial power. They opened new alliances and tensions and forged transcontinental forms of resistance against capitalist development in the global North and the West, against imperialism, and the reproduction of colonial power in post-colonial contexts. All these were part of the effort to reorder the geographies of power and the circulation of knowledge away from the Euro-American capitalist world.

At the same time, these political landscapes are marked by significant tensions and fractures, leaving a conflicting legacy both in the formerly colonized countries and in the socialist East. This chapter explores the ways in which Bulgarian ethnonationalism from the post-Stalinist period formed a rather disturbing symbiosis with the state's anti-colonial and anti-racist politics as well as its support for various national liberation movements in the global South. Paradoxically, the country's global reorientation and realignment with the formerly colonized nations during the period converged with the politics of repression, erasure, and assimilation vis-à-vis its own minorities. When placed in the context of the global dynamics of the era, the historical experience of Bulgarian socialism during the post-Stalinist period appears as an environment strained by the tensions of these contradictory and discrepant moments.

SOCIALIST AND GLOBAL: COLD WAR FRAMEWORKS AND ALTERNATIVE METHODOLOGIES

The anti-colonial and anti-racist politics adopted by the socialist countries during the 1960s and '70s have usually been examined through research methodologies informed by Cold War political agendas and frameworks, and they are often discounted as state ideology and crude anti-American or anti-Western propaganda. Generations of scholars have seen the relations between the socialist countries and the post-colonial world through this Cold War political framework, emphasizing economic interest and gain, spheres of influence, geopolitical competition, and imperialist expansion. Many of these paradigms have served to render the socialist world, and the Soviet Union in particular, as another form of imperial power that accumulates, although according to a different political logic, economic resources and political influence. Scholars such as Sharad Chari and Katherine Verdery frame both geopolitical formations – the socialist and the capitalist – in terms of imperial powers with expansionist interests, geopolitical competition, tiers, and centre-periphery dynamics, which enfold the formerly colonized world into their spatial orders and colonial logics while fighting for spheres of influence.[8] In their understanding, one formation operates through modes of dispossession specific to contemporary forms of capitalist accumulation and expansion, and the other through the integration and control of what they call "redistributive" or "allocative" power, rather than the accumulation of capital.[9] For them, socialist forms of accumulation and dispossession bear similarities to capitalist forms of dispossession but "in a more radical way, by decisively and rapidly dispossessing the owners of the means of production in favor of the vanguard party and proceeding to develop the productive forces on that basis, allegedly in the public interest."[10] "What, if not accumulation by dispossession," they ask, "were the nationalization and collectivizations the Soviets imposed on their satellites?"[11]

Chari and Verderi therefore see the socialist organization of socio-economic life as part of the expansionist technologies of imperial power with Moscow at the centre. This view is in line with other scholarship that examines the Soviet Union through the framework of imperialism.[12] For these scholars the "post" in the terms "post-socialist" and the "post-colonial" signify the material, social, and political realities that were formed in the wake of crumbling empires – either capitalist-colonial or Soviet-socialist. They are parallel critical projects in rethinking parallel, if different, forms of contemporary imperialism.

But many scholars have already questioned the grounds of these analogies, and in the words of James Mark and Quin Slobodian, they have "often distorted as much as they [have] revealed."[13] A recent body of work in Russian and East European studies positioned at the intersection of socialist and post-colonial studies has returned to these histories to forcefully challenge existing narratives. They have noted that post-colonial and decolonial work has similarly neglected the counter-hegemonic axes of solidarity at the crossroads between the socialist and post-colonial worlds. Focused exclusively on First World–Third World, South–North, and even South–South axes of mobility, they have accepted some of the anti-communist premises of Cold War scholarship on socialism and have left many unexplored questions around the role of the socialist countries in the anti-colonial liberation movements and in forging distinct economic, social, and cultural worlds alternative to global capitalist development and resistant to Western hegemonies. Studying the relations between the Second and Third Worlds from the mid-1950s to the end of the 1980s, this new generation of researchers theorizes the political dynamics between the socialist world and the formerly colonized countries against dominant tropes such as Cold War, First World–Third World, or centre-periphery binaries, opening yet wider horizons for historical revision away from Eurocentric and Western-focused historiographies of the period.

Thus, displacing East–West and South–North axes of analysis, researchers have been recovering alternative routes and locations where decolonial politics with anti-capitalist visions emerged and thrived. Probing into what she calls the blind spots in Black Atlantic and post-colonial studies, Monica Popescu expands on Paul Gilroy's famous study of the transatlantic contours of the African diasporic experience and the way it reshaped concepts and cultures of modernity.[14] "Black solidarities and cultural alliances were not woven only between the African continent, the Americas, and Western Europe," Popescu observes. Instead, she argues for a "more capacious understanding of the black Atlantic during the 1970s and '80s."[15] Her work is part of a growing body of scholarship that traces the lost or forgotten journeys of African, Caribbean, and African-American intellectuals, political and cultural activists, students, and workers to the Soviet Union and other socialist countries in Eastern Europe and elsewhere, restoring the visibility of these marginalized, diasporic cross-continental mobilities and their unanticipated openings and challenges.[16]

Further, David Engerman has argued that relationships between the formerly colonized countries and the socialist world, although deeply entangled in Cold War politics, cannot easily be explained through the main tropes of Cold War political rationality – economic interest and gain, spheres of political and economic influence, imperial expansion, and geopolitical competition.[17] Second and Third World relations were not unidirectional but multifaceted, marked by a "multipolarity" of interactions and dynamics, including Sino-Soviet, pan-African, Sino-African, Afro-Asian relations, and more.[18] Following Engerman and others, Rossen Djagalov and Masha Salazkina trace the lost footprints of the cultural and intellectual convergences between the Soviet Union and the countries of the global South, such as the Tashkent Film Festival and the Afro-Asian Writers' Association.[19] They see these convergences as the sustained zones of encounter in which spaces for reconfiguring global hegemonies of power were opened. For almost two decades, the Tashkent Film Festival, "a confluence of multiple cinematic languages," was a place where African filmmakers could see films and meet fellow filmmakers and intellectuals from other African and global South countries. Together with organizations and venues such as the Afro-Asian Writers' Association and the journal *Lotus*, Tashkent "served as the main forum common to second- and third-world cinemas, providing the latter with a major site for interconnectivity while offering the former its major window on the cinemas of Africa, Asia, and Latin America."[20]

In other words, these venues helped shape a shared discourse about film, literature, and culture from the non-Western world and opened the terrains upon which a Third World literary and visual culture was constructed and a common emancipatory experience emerged.[21] In his work Djagalov makes the compelling argument that these networks not only historically preceded post-colonial thought but enabled it as well – in other words, they formed the material and cultural precondition for the emergence of the post-colonial turn in the 1980s, an important historical contribution disavowed or forgotten in the historiographies and geographies of radical theory pertaining to the global South.

Dominant frameworks have also seen newly independent countries, in Africa in particular, as passive recipients of aid, expertise, education, and various forms of support delivered by the socialist countries in patronizing ways, thereby folding the formerly colonized countries into the developmentalist frameworks of socialist governments. But scholars have challenged these accounts as well and in the process have changed the historical genealogies of dissent in the socialist countries.[22] They show that, on the contrary, students and workers of colour who came to the socialist countries during and after their countries' independence became harbingers of modernity and a door to the world for the socialist youth in the Soviet Union and Eastern Europe.[23] African students in particular taught the socialist youth much about racism, anti-racism, and resistance, generating cultures of nonconformity and inspiring protest and various forms of social discontent during the 1960s and '70s. In other words, these alternative mobilities brought political energy and inspired social radicalism in the socialist East, energizing the socialist youth in unpredictable ways, fuelling social engagement and political activity.[24] These practices were informed by widely popular frameworks of peace, socialist internationalism, and solidarity with and duty to the people in struggle around the world – the international vocabulary of the 1960s and '70s. They imagined a certain kind of globality or internationalism rooted in the people's struggles against racism, colonialism and imperialism, war and militarism, and exploitation and global inequality, and they forged new global alliances, solidarities, and political imaginaries that transcended Cold War and other geopolitical divides.[25] For the socialist youth, these imaginaries shaped a new kind of worldliness that was both alternative and resistant to capitalist and Western hegemonies, what Mark and Slobodian have called a "sense of a world of interconnectedness" in which "one was globally aware and modern."[26]

Many tensions structure and fracture this legacy, leaving an incoherent and contradictory history both in the formerly colonized countries and in the socialist East. For example, scholars have pointed out the unwelcome and counterproductive effects of the socialist countries' involvement in the newly independent post-colonial nations, as well as the race-blind approaches and failures of the socialist governments to challenge racism in their own societies as they opened to the rest of the world.[27] In addition, recent debates have explored some of the tensions present in socialist visions of modernity and their global ambitions and travels. On the one hand, these modernities were organized around distinctly socialist concepts of equality, community, leisure, public access, and social mobility, and woven into the legacies of anti-capitalist, anti-fascist, anti-colonial, and national liberation movements. At the same time, they were committed to social progress, modernization, and industrial and infrastructural development with their own teleologies and universals, often converging with Eurocentric and colonial social and political orders. At times they aligned with Western modernity projects, while at others they departed starkly from them, forging social and material contexts that were discontinuous and incompatible, while simultaneously retaining uneasy and ghastly continuities.[28]

ANTI-COLONIAL NATIONAL LIBERATION AND BULGARIAN ETHNONATIONALISM

The international context of the 1960s and '70s helped to change socialist Bulgaria's orientation in the global sphere. Unlike the Soviet Union or neighbouring Yugoslavia, the People's Republic of Bulgaria was a small socialist country without the political and economic resources that would enable it to exert much influence in the international arena on its own. As the previous chapters have shown, these decades were marked by a strong revival of nationalist politics within the country, which propelled ethnic and religious assimilation campaigns that reached a crescendo in the 1980s. The Revival Process, the series of coercive, state-orchestrated attempts at the ethnic and religious assimilation of Muslim, Turkish, Pomak, and Roma minorities, was developed in the context of a socialist modernization project built on humanist foundations and from within a kind of "progressive" Marxist-humanist socialist discourse.

The ethnic assimilations appear even more uncanny when viewed in the context of the strong anti-colonial and anti-racist rhetoric employed in the socialist public sphere during this time; such a perspective points to inconsistencies that in turn raise several well-founded questions. Paradoxically, Bulgarian socialist politics in support of anti-colonial liberation struggles, the political solidarities and alignments with the formerly colonized countries drawn in the public sphere, became entangled in the ethnonationalist politics of the period and ultimately converged with the assimilation of ethnic and religious minorities within the country.

How do we explain this paradoxical convergence? Many scholars have attributed these contradictions to the discrepancies between "official ideology" and everyday life or the realities of "actually existing socialism," lamenting the hypocrisies of the socialist governments. But these seeming paradoxes were already present in the political discourses employed by these governments and their respective public spheres, especially in their polemical and discursive range. Some of them can be found in the specific political logics of Bulgarian nationalism from the post-Stalinist period.

In previous chapters I have argued that the nationalism of the post-Stalinist period was not the same as the nationalism of the pre-socialist interwar period. Calling itself "socialist patriotism," post-Stalinist nationalism changed the national narrative in order to purge it of its "bourgeois" content and its historical links to the right-wing Bulgarian nationalisms of the pre–World War II era, especially the fascist and irredentist tendencies contained therein. The rise of post-Stalinist nationalism was also embedded in a politics of resistance to both Stalinism and Soviet cultural and political hegemony. In this sense, some aspects of post-Stalinist Bulgarian nationalism contained a subaltern element, which is particularly legible in the work of Liudmila Zhivkova. As previous chapters have shown, Zhivkova's work contains a pronounced universalism and a commitment to national and patriotic ideals that bear an uneasy relationship to the ethnonationalist politics of the period. But her writings also contain a certain kind of awareness of the Bulgarian people as a "minor nation" and a "minor people," and her work in the sphere of culture was crucial to reimagining and reconfiguring the small socialist country in alliance with the countries of the global South, and to exploring links with non-Western cultural histories and traditions, especially from South Asia.

In this already complex discursive formation, Bulgarian national independence from the Ottoman Empire became the framework in which post-Stalinist notions of Bulgarian peoplehood were aligned with the people in struggle against European colonialism and American imperialism. Considering the hegemonic role of the national idea in anti-colonial revolutionary thought, it is not surprising that Lenin's writings on the national question circulated among anti-colonial revolutionaries in Africa and the Caribbean during the 1950s and '60s. Matthieu Renault's work brings out the decolonial and anti-imperialist elements in Lenin's work on national self-determination. Attuned to the different political content and contextual meanings of nationalism, the difference between "oppressor" and "oppressed" nations, Lenin recognized the rebellious, anti-imperialist potentials of national self-determination movements on the periphery of the Russian Empire: to him, they were articulated against the extractivist and exploitative logic of Russian imperialism as well as the ethnic and racial supremacy of Russian imperial nationalism. As Renault has put it, by recognizing and foregrounding these peripheral forces, Lenin "decentered the revolution." In other words, Lenin saw these as heterogeneous revolutionary formations that moved according to their own temporalities and disrupted Eurocentric linearity and stagism.[29]

But although Lenin's "right of nations" principle contained anti-imperialist content, it was a product of a different historical context and was quite inarticulate when it comes to European colonial racism. Therefore anti-colonial intellectuals such as Frantz Fanon, C.L.R. James, and Amilcar Cabral, used Lenin along with their original critiques of racism to articulate the intersections of racism, colonialism, capitalist accumulation, and class power. Similarly, in the context of the socialist 1960s and '70s, the framework of national self-determination and national autonomy did not provide appropriate language against the everyday racisms toward students and workers of colour who came from Africa, Vietnam, and other parts of the global South.

Moreover, post-colonial critics of the nation have spoken out about the pitfalls and paradoxes of national consciousness as it organized the anti-colonial imaginaries during the period of decolonization, of the dead ends and disastrous political consequences of the nation-state both as an anti-colonial vision of political sovereignty and as a political and social organization of post-colonial societies. The work of Partha Chatterjee and Arif Dirlik, among others, reminds us that the national form in the post-colonial contexts, even as it mobilized much of the anti-colonial imaginary, was a European colonial paradigm. This is true both empirically, as it imposed uniform political administrations and homogeneous national cultures, and ideologically, as nations replicated the cultural and political imaginaries of the colonizers, which were utterly unsuited to the social and cultural realities of the former colonies.[30] Post-colonial nations, too, experienced the violence of homogenization and erasure, of ethnic and religious partitioning while constructing their national cultures and histories, all in the name of independence, modernization, social justice, and democracy. As Dirlik observes, "The tragedy of anticolonial revolutionary nationalism has been that it was condemned almost from the beginning to replicate the practices of the colonialists in their very efforts at nation building ... The coloniality of the nation, and the way it was imagined, was already stamped with the legacy of the very colonialism it sought to overthrow."[31]

Chatterjee has cautioned against seeing anti- and post-colonial nationalisms as simple derivatives of European models, since such a move, once again, strips the colonized of political agency and imagination. He reads Indian nationalism as the hegemonic project of the middle classes among the local populations who occupied an ambivalent position – one "of subordination in one relation and ... of dominance in another." "The construction of hegemonic ideologies," Chatterjee continues, "typically involves the cultural efforts of classes placed precisely in such situations."[32] But as Dirlik has also pointed out, the political alternatives to capitalism in the post-colonial worlds, ideas of economic and social justice, democracy, material and social equality, and social mobility for the most part also succumbed to the political form of national self-determination and national sovereignty.[33]

In her vivid narrative of the formation of a Tanzanian national political community in the decades of decolonization, May Joseph remembers that anti-colonial visions of socialist equality and citizenship embraced the multiracial and multi-ethnic populace of the newly formed state, weaving together open visions of Africanness and Tanzanianness through embodied affective bonds among the people across racial and cultural divides. It was a radical experiment in "pulling together" a place, a nation, and a community through socialist belonging that affirmed radical equality, political autonomy and self-governance, and economic self-reliance in alignment with the newly independent countries on the African continent. Julius Nyerere's visions of a future socialist Tanzania rejected belonging based on origin; instead, he imagined a national community that was "against sectarianism, against racialism, and against ethnic separatism."[34] In the early 1970s, Joseph recounts, Tanzanian socialism succumbed to racial, ethnocentric, and origin-based notions of citizenship as the early experiences of anti-colonial becoming embraced socialist ideologies "framed in terms of economic nationalism."[35] Joseph's work inhabits the precarious locations and invisible routes of the regional and cross-oceanic diasporic dispersals of displaced South Asians, Arabs, and Black Africans alienated by or excluded from nationalist notions of Tanzanianness.[36]

These literatures are relevant to the post-Stalinist Bulgarian context. This is not to brush over, in an ahistorical fashion, the specificities of these two historical realities – the socialist and the post-colonial – and their distinct political logics, as Maria Todorova has carefully warned us.[37] But they are important precisely because some part of Bulgarian nationalism from the 1970s incongruously recognized itself in the national independence projects in the post-colonial world. The socialist and nationalist imaginaries, intertwined in their own ways, reverberated across the continents in the socialist and post-colonial worlds. In post-Stalinist Bulgaria, they allowed for the construction of symbolic, political, and historical continuities between nineteenth-century national independence movements in the Balkans and anti-colonial national liberation struggles in Africa and South Asia in the twentieth century. Bulgarian political discourse during the period, anchored in a narrative of centuries-long oppression under Ottoman rule and a history of national liberation struggles from the mid- to late nineteenth century, constructed a shared historical experience with the people of the colonized world, thereby opening possibilities for various forms of political self-identification with the colonized people and their own *natsionalno-osvoboditelni borbi* (national liberation movements). In this context, the political uses of anti-racist and anti-colonial discourses in Bulgaria were recycled within an ethnonationalist framework to form a symbiosis specific to the ethnonationalist narrative of post-Stalinist socialism. Terms such as *robstvo* or *igo* (slavery/yoke) forcefully reappeared in literary, cinematic, and scholarly reconstructions of the Ottoman period during the post-Stalinist years. Those familiar with the historical and cultural reincarnations of nationalist tropes in Bulgaria know that, while part of the lexicon of the 1970s, these terms draw on historical and literary narratives from the eighteenth and nineteenth centuries that played a central role in shaping Bulgarian national consciousness. This language gained new meaning in the 1960s and '70s, as the stories, news, and voices of the anti-colonial liberation struggles echoed in the Bulgarian public sphere.

These symbolic, political, and historical connections were made explicit in a speech by party leader Todor Zhivkov in 1969, when a delegation of Bulgarian politicians visited India to discuss economic and cultural collaboration between the two countries:

> Please allow me to assure you that the Bulgarian people feel the same kind of sympathies and respect for the great multitude of the Indian people. Centuries of struggle against foreign domination developed in our people not only a deep empathy toward the people in struggle for their freedom and independence, but a clearly expressed and genuine solidarity with them. The Bulgarian people followed the oscillations of your struggle. They are familiar with and honour the activists in your national independence movement. This year Bulgaria will celebrate the centennial anniversary of the birth of Mahatma Gandhi, the great leader of India in its struggle against the colonial yoke. Our people remember also the great statesperson and political leader, one of the followers and tireless activists against the colonial system, fighter for national independence and social progress, for peace and solidarity among the peoples – Jawaharlal Nehru ... The emergence of independent India was one of the greatest events in our times ... The once mighty global colonial system is now falling apart. The day is coming when the fires of national liberation struggles will burn the last flags of shameful colonialism. But both we and you and everyone who has waged a costly struggle for their national and social liberation, we know: that in this world we will not get anything for free, that everything has to be fought for and defended.[38]

The visual and monumental arts from the period mobilized these analogies in many ways, one striking example of which is the sculptural composition *Robstvo* (Yoke) from the Bratska Mogila in Plovdiv, depicting the suffering of the Bulgarian people during the Ottoman period. The scene is part of a remarkable architectural ensemble from 1974, a sequence of nineteen monumental sculptural compositions narrating the revolutionary history of the Bulgarian people from the perspective of the 1970s – a nationalist history reimagined and rewritten through the socialist present. Nested in the base of a concrete structure in the shape of a Thracian *mogila*, the sculptures are organized in a circular arrangement and direct an experience that is at once ritual movement, act of commemoration, inauguration into a historical narrative, and orchestrated affective journey. The monument is now abandoned, and although it is currently in the custody of Plovdiv's History Museum, which provides a minimal level of protection and maintenance, much of it was already taken or destroyed years ago. Nowadays few remember that Plovdiv's Bratska Mogila is a temple, a tomb built to harbour the memory of young anti-fascist partisans killed on the battlefields near Plovdiv before and during World War II, a place where their spirits hover and where some of their remains lie in a wall of metal urns in the back of the interior. Yet all the damage, abuse, and neglect that the monument has suffered throughout the years, all the graffiti and litter that have perpetually covered it in the last thirty years, cannot suppress the wondrous otherworldliness of the place and the sacred and spiritual energy it summons. And the spirit of the warriors and their work remains, transcending the nationalist narrative of the 1970s.

Plovdiv's Bratska Mogila is a remarkable material inscription of post-Stalinist visions of socialism, nationhood, and their global entanglements. The symbolic and narrative content of this syncretic structure has arrested the conflicting political logics of the post-Stalinist era and its worldly entanglements in all their monumentality and tension. On the one hand, it contains subaltern and revolutionary elements, which played a crucial role in repositioning socialist Bulgaria in political solidarity with the newly independent nations of the global South and in shaping the socialist people's political identifications with the global South. On the other hand, the faith in development and modernization, the teleologies of revolution and social progress contained in the nationalist and humanist imaginaries of the post-Stalinist era, colluded with universal and West European colonial frameworks. They converged with ethnocentric visions of peoplehood and were open to political uses with ethno-assimilationist agendas. The merger

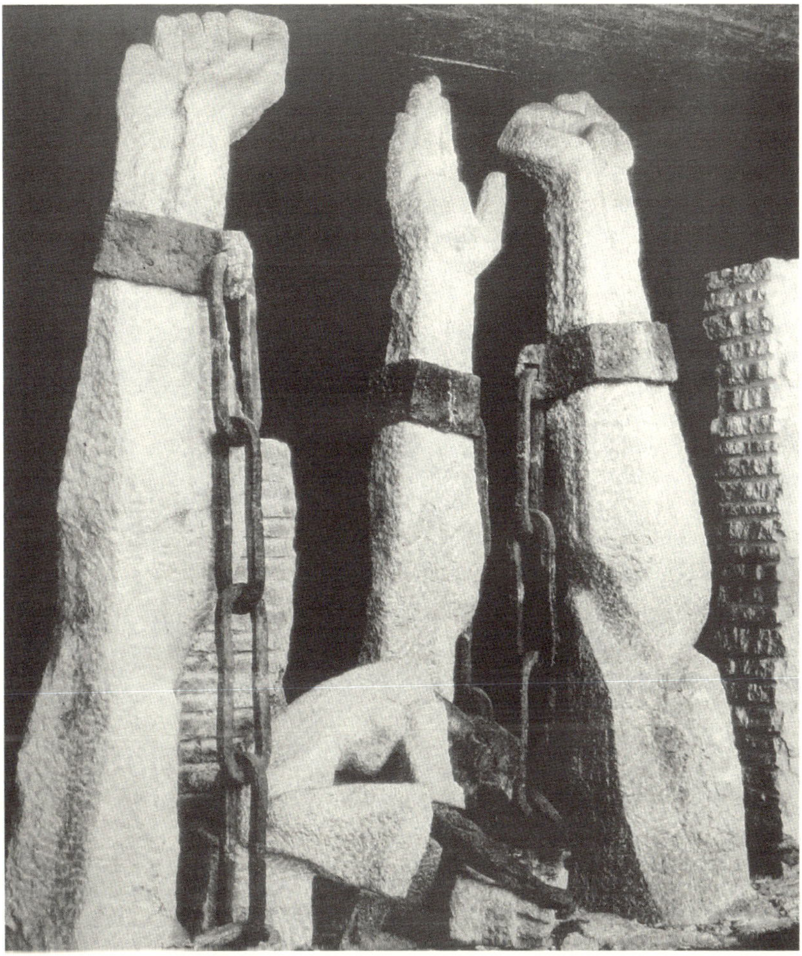

Figure 6.3 *Robstvo* (Yoke) from the Bratska Mogila, Plovdiv (1974), in its original state by sculptors Liubomir Dalchev, Ana Dalcheva, and Petur Atanasov. Currently, most of the metal elements of the composition are missing.

of socialist humanism, socialist modernization, and the national idea propelled ethnic assimilations, mass renamings, departures, and expulsions, and caused the large-scale displacement of ethnic and religious minorities. It led to state-driven erasures of minority histories, lineages, and languages – all in the name of equality, humanism, and social progress. These contradictory moments present a picture unique to the historical context of post-Stalinist socialism, a spectrum of forces that contained and refracted the tensions of the era.

Figure 6.4 The Bratska Mogila in Plovdiv, built in 1974 and designed by a collective of architects, urban planners, engineers, and sculptors under the leadership of architect Liubomir Shinkov and sculptor Liubomir Dalchev. The monument contains the remains of people who died in the anti-fascist struggle near Plovdiv in the 1940s.

CONCLUSION

In the Haunted Landscapes of Post-Socialism

Encounters with swastikas and other fascist symbols are common in the post-socialist city. The anonymous, guerilla-style graffiti covers the walls of subways and pedestrian underpasses, storefront shutters, and boarded-up construction sites and abandoned areas. They target with particular intensity the surfaces of socialist monuments – those abandoned, haunted sites, the public signifiers of the socialist past. In the years after 1989, I have been repeatedly drawn to socialist monuments and their uncanny dwellings, trying to make sense of their ambiguous presence in post-socialist urban life. Many have already been destroyed, relocated, scattered, dismembered, or defaced in ways that may be irreversible. Yet many others quietly persist – some in their full glory, others in the embrace of overgrown wild plants or in the midst of scattered glass and urban trash. As a whole, they have been discarded and neglected as remnants of a useless history. Yet these often dilapidated sites have also become highly politically charged. As such, they remain some of the most active public spaces, offering terrain for grassroots political expression and a convenient place for marginalized subcultures and activities.[1]

"Together against communism," read one piece of anonymous graffiti from 2008 on Plovdiv's Bratska Mogila, flanked by swastikas on each side. The graffiti is no longer there but I have seen different versions of this message in graffiti throughout the years after 1989; in the early years of the so-called *prekhod*, or "transition," especially, it would throw me into confusion. Did "Together against communism" mean to reinforce the analogy between socialism and fascism from a liberal perspective? Or was it giving public expression to a burgeoning reactionary right-wing movement that revived radical neo-fascist, racist, and ethnophobic discourses and sought to castigate the anti-fascist content upon which state socialism was founded? Do the swastikas refer to "communism" or stand for the collective "we" that calls the reader?

Throughout much of the 1990s, political discourse in the public sphere was dominated by the liberal equation of Nazism and communism through the framework of totalitarianism. Dissident liberals, who assumed a central place in political and public life after 1989, introduced one of the most tenacious ideologemes of liberal democracy – the totalitarian state – pitting liberal democracy against fascism, and by analogy, against socialism. The liberal trope of the "totalitarian twins," the evil twins of communism and fascism, gripped the liberal imaginary to condemn the atrocities of the communist regimes.

The 1980s, paradoxically, was a time when revisionist historians of socialism in the West, in an effort to move away from Cold War paradigms, began to question the totalitarian framework and the liberal categories that had informed decades of scholarship on socialism. In their place, they sought to refocus their inquiries on questions of subjectivity, everyday practice, and the multiplicity of social forces "from below" to unsettle earlier conceptions of socialism as a monolithic, static, top-down, and repressive regime.[2] By contrast, East European dissident intellectuals eagerly embraced the totalitarian discourse as their own favourite analytical framework, resisting any approaches that could provide an alternative to the picture of "total ideologization," of top-down, ubiquitous control and repression. After 1989, the totalitarian concept powerfully persisted in post-socialist political life, forming a hegemony of sorts that enabled the unrestrained reign of neo-liberal politics, the massive privatization of communal life, land, public space, infrastructure, and resources, and the widening gap between the poor and the wealthy.

This also meant that during the post-socialist period, "democracy" was imagined via a teleological "transition" toward a capitalist economy, private property, and the free market economy. Boris Buden and Neda Genova have thoroughly critiqued such colonial and developmentalist tropes as "belatedness," "backwardness," and "catching up" with the "developed" countries in the "West," along with the patronizing and infantilizing attitudes toward East European societies. They show that all these were implicated in narratives of "transition" to capitalism and played a central role in the successful and swift channelling of neo-liberal reforms.[3] In addition, dissident discourses from the late 1980s and the early 1990s deployed the language of "normality" to naturalize the regime of private property and the free market and to posit them as the historical norm compared to which the socialist period appears as a failed, deviant, abnormal, and monstrous aberration. Set against the failures of communism, capitalist relations seemed inevitable and "natural," opening the way to aggressive neo-liberal reforms endorsed by right-wing, liberal, neo-liberal, and "socialist" parliamentary parties alike. Self-identified liberals, the vast majority of whom identified as anti-communist, embraced the political rationality of the free market and prioritized the interests of capital to undermine concerns over social and material equality and public access to social services, infrastructure, and resources. Thus anti-communist liberalism positioned itself on the right side of the political spectrum, some parts of which resembled neoliberalism, others libertarianism. What is clear, however, is that a phenomenon with its own logic emerged in the political conditions shaped by the end of socialism.

As various political forces were consolidating around "anti-communism" during the *prekhod* in Bulgaria, Eastern Europe, and the former Soviet Union, post-socialist liberalism became a unique political phenomenon. Sociologists Georgi Medarov and Jana Tsoneva have explored its contradictions and paradoxes in the context of post-socialist Bulgaria, where they argue that "liberalism" was not necessarily antithetical to authoritarianism as long as it opposed "communism."[4]

Anti-communist discourse in the post-socialist context creates jarring contradictions and bewildering political and historical alignments. Tsoneva and I have described it as a kind of "amalgam" that makes possible the seamless convergence of antagonistic historical moments, political ideas, and social phenomena, moulding them into absurd cultural-discursive forms. Tsoneva calls it a kind of "social magic" that causes short circuits between otherwise incompatible political ideas such as liberal democracy and monarchic authoritarianism. In these amalgams, we argue, certain elements of the historical meaning of the past are conveniently and selectively washed out so that even the most anti-liberal and anti-democratic historical moments can be recuperated for the purpose of negating and erasing the socialist past.[5]

But over the last decade, as political links have become more clearly expressed, the amalgams of anti-communism have begun to make a lot more sense. For example, it is hardly a coincidence that the fall of socialism was followed by the revival of self-identified neo-fascist and extreme right-wing nationalist formations. Thirty years after the end of socialism, fascist, xenophobic, and racist graffiti continue to proliferate in subways, streets, and entire neighbourhoods, to signal – this time without any ambiguity as to their political meaning or historical references – that immigrant communities and refugees are unwelcome, that residents of minority ethnic identities and faiths have no place in the lands of their ancestors, and that public spaces are unsafe for gender-queer people and sexual minorities.

Medarov's analysis is important in this respect. It reveals how the "crucial symbiosis" between moderate anti-communist liberals and what are now extreme right-wing nationalist and neo-fascist formations coalesced together around a shared anti-communism. The roots of this convergence take us back to the formation of the peculiar terrains of East European liberal-democratic politics during the early years of post-socialism. In the Bulgarian context, the parties that defined themselves as liberal and were united around Eurocentric, civilizational, and pro-capitalist "transition" narratives also welcomed and tolerated among their ranks elements with nationalist, Islamophobic, and ethnophobic agendas. The latter, ignored and tolerated for much of the 1990s, would later become leaders of what are now extreme right-wing nationalist parties with a majority in parliament in coalition with pro-business and neo-liberal elites.

At the same time, activists and writers continue to point out that the unceasing protests from the 1990s – the years of political and economic turmoil that we can still barely make sense of – were far from simply "anti-communist," but rather revealed a much richer political terrain. They contained a plurality of messages that demanded, along with direct democracy and transparency, more social and material equality for the common people.[6]

As many have already pointed out, in the context of post-socialist East European countries like Poland, Hungary, Ukraine, Romania, and Bulgaria, "Europeanization" has become almost synonymous with "decommunization," a process often ushered through with vaguely worded legislation that criminalizes in absurdly sweeping terms the cultural, material, and symbolic legacies of an entire historical period – that of the "evil" communist regime.[7] Bozhin Traykov shows the role of an imagined "return to Europe," a trope he says was "imported from Central Europe by the Bulgarian liberal elite" to demonize Bulgarian socialism and promote anti-Russian politics while playing into binary oppositions between East and West. The criminalization of communism, he says, is "an attempt to impose a one-sided view on history," a move not far from authoritarianism that aims to suppress the context in which anti-fascist struggles emerged.[8]

In the post-socialist East European context, it is becoming more evident that "Europeanization" has also been forcefully claimed as a right-wing project and has empowered some of the most extreme ethnophobic, Islamophobic, racist, anti-immigrant, and neo-fascist political tendencies in the region. As Martin Marinos has showed, far-right parties such as Bulgaria's Ataka, which entered parliament in 2006, envision a white and Christian European Union while taking advantage of people's "economic discontent" and filling the "vacuum" that has resulted from left-wing parties' capitulation to neo-liberalism and the defeat of social politics in the former socialist countries.[9] Every year from 2003 to 2019, neo-Nazis, neo-fascists, and nationalists congregated in Sofia to commemorate the death of General Khristo Lukov, Bulgaria's war minister from 1935 to 1938 as well as the leader of the Union of Bulgarian National Legions – a fascist, ultranationalist, and pro-Nazi organization active between 1932 and 1944. He was killed by two communist partisans, Violeta Iakova and Ivan Burudzhiev, on 13 February 1943 for his role in a possible plan to send Bulgarian troops to assist the Germans on the Eastern Front. Beginning in 2003, every 13 February for seventeen years, a long and eerie torch-lit march would take to the streets of Sofia as night descended on the city, an event that gained international supporters as fascists and nationalists from Germany and other European countries joined in the name of a "United Europe."[10]

On 18 June 1944, a little over a year after Lukov's assassination, the communist Violeta Iakova, known by the partisan name Ivanka, was captured by the police and tortured to death in the village of Radomir, near the town of Pernik, outside of Sofia. She was only twenty-one years old and did not survive to see the revolution, which came several months later; but as we are told by the hundreds of commemorative sites marking the deaths of young partisans who fought against the pro-fascist regime, "those who die young stay young forever." A modest bust of Iakova carved in granite survives in Radomir to this day; her nose is missing – a result of one of the frequent attacks against the statue – but her head stands firm, her gaze unmoving and strong.

These historical and contemporary alignments show that the rise of the Right in Bulgaria and Eastern Europe goes hand in hand with the demonization of the socialist period and the recuperation of fascism and its legacy from the interwar period. Many of us have called attention to the alarming tendency in the post-socialist years to restore and even fetishize the material culture of the interwar period, a lot of it carrying monarchic, military-authoritarian, nationalist, and outright fascist content.[11] Moderate liberals have advocated for these kinds of restorations by romanticizing bourgeois values from the pre-socialist period without much consciousness of the layered historical meanings inscribed in this material culture; indeed, many have disavowed the local histories of fascism and dismissed or minimized Bulgaria's alliance with the Nazis during World War II. Neo-fascists and national patriots consciously push for the historical recuperation and restoration of historical figures and material cultures from the period while fully aware of their antisemitic, Islamophobic, nationalist, ethnophobic, or expansionist content. As a result of this fusion of anti-communist liberalism, neo-liberal capitalism, fascist nationalism, and various kinds of right-wing nationalisms, pronounced fascists and Nazi supporters are now rehabilitated as victims of communist repression. Right-wing nationalist organizations from the 1940s, banned by the socialist government for their assimilationist work among minorities and for their pro-fascist leanings (such as Druzhba Rodina, discussed in chapter 4) have now reestablished their public presence and activity. Outright fascist figures are now memorialized in commemorative monuments as "victims of communism."[12]

Such is the case with the military memorial from 1934 in the centre of Sofia, which was restored in the place where 1,300 Years Bulgaria had stood. In the summer of 2017, the Municipality of Sofia moved to demolish 1,300 Years Bulgaria – the landmark work of socialist modernism from 1981 created in the humanist tradition (discussed in chapter 3). With a jarring collision of political meanings reflected in its visual content, the monument has had an active presence in public space during the post-socialist years.[13] This socialist creature, protruding from the ground in strange angular shapes in the city's most central location, survived for years despite the city's deliberate neglect. During this time it became one of the most politically charged and contested sites in the city. Intense and divisive discussions would chronically flare up around it, often ending in a cacophony of rants and rumbles. Some insisted that it should be demolished because it was a visible symbol of the communist regime, and that it was never liked by the people even then. Many found it "ugly," even illegible, as it was easily among the wildest statements made in the socialist-modernist tradition of monumental public sculpture. Others argued that it should be restored to its original state, while some wanted it preserved in its current condition, arguing that even as it was, stripped to its bare structure, the monument had a remarkable effect and was even "better than before." Yet others, mainly collectives of young architects and urbanists, developed and presented various imaginative projects to transform it in ways that preserve its diverse everyday uses.

This time around, we had little hope that what remained of the monument would survive the latest round of pressure from above. Allied with extreme nationalist elements in parliament, the political forces in power worked hard to clear the way for corporate development and business interests, dismounting public services and erasing all remaining traces, material and symbolic, of the "evil communist regime." In addition, Bulgaria was to host its first presidency of the Council of the European Union at the nearby National Palace of Culture, and the city was determined to dismember the modernist giant in a rush to tidy the surrounding area. Undeterred by protests against the demolition, the municipal government responded with workers on cranes, bulldozers, trucks, and demolition machines and destroyed the socialist structure over several days.

In the meantime, various anti-communist liberal, patriotic, and nationalist groups used the opportunity to put pressure on the city government to replace 1,300 Years Bulgaria with a restored version of the memorial from 1934, a monument to the fallen soldiers of the Balkan Wars and World War I. And yet, as Tsoneva and I have shown, the memorial is not just an innocent commemoration of these fallen soldiers. Originally installed soon after the military coup of 19 May 1934, which took power from the monarch and abolished parliament, it marks a turn toward military authoritarianism in Bulgarian history. It is a public declaration of the expansionist ambitions of an emergent state regime with a pro-fascist orientation and an open platform of nationalist supremacy.

The Lion, as the monument has come to be known, refers to the titular figure in the centre of the composition. It is holding a map, an interwar revisionist projection of "Greater Bulgaria," which includes parts of present-day North Macedonia, Serbia, Greece, Turkey, and Romania.[14] Designed as part of a complex of military barracks, it

Figure 7.1 A human chain surrounding the 1,300 Years Bulgaria monument in the centre of Sofia to protect it from demolition, July 2017. After 1989, Sofia's residents initiated multiple actions to protest the government's neglect of the monument and pleaded with it to save, transform, or restore it. And yet, despite these initiatives, the municipal government demolished it in the summer of 2017.

was severely damaged by aerial bombardment during World War II. The wartime ruins remained in place, boarded off, until 1980, when socialist city planners began a major overhaul of the area to build the National Palace of Culture and the recreational zone around it. At that time the surviving parts of the monument were moved to the Museum of Military History in Sofia.

Those of us who were alarmed by the possibility that parts of this monument might be restored could hardly foresee how quickly this would become a reality. But a few months later, in November 2017, the Lion landed triumphantly in the newly cleared site. I saw the Lion for the first time the following June, a few months after it was installed. It was a disorientating experience, similar to the ways I have felt at other post-socialist spaces haunted by these abrupt reinscriptions. I felt dizzy from the weird twists and warps of meanings, my body detached as if flying two feet above the ground. Before arriving, I had

Figure 7.2 The central figure of the Memorial to the First Sofia Division of the Bulgarian Army from 1934 (the Lion). Formerly in the Museum of Military History in Sofia, the monument was installed in place of 1,300 Years Bulgaria in November 2017. The Lion, a symbol of the Bulgarian people, holds a map of "Greater Bulgaria," a vision of the nationalist and expansionist ambitions of the interwar governments.

imagined a stern and empty space, but the Lion was standing in the embrace of a neatly manicured rose garden, and people seemed to have effortlessly integrated the monument into their daily lives. There was no trace of the socialist giant, and yet its presence and its dramatic transformations were etched into my memory as if still present at the site. Even in its most derelict state, stripped to its "bones," its dense concrete and metal armature exposed, it had retained some kind of dignity and grandeur. I had also been seeing pictures of the memorial from 1934 circulating on social media – in its original design, the Lion marked the centre of an austere monumental and symmetrical neoclassical composition, reminiscent of some European fascist architecture from the 1930s. In the current version, the Lion standing in the middle of a rose garden, some flashy corporate event happening around it – it all felt like a collage of paper cut-outs, these historical collisions and recurrences causing discords that my senses couldn't immediately process. But life seemed to continue unbothered on this lively pedestrian area as young people had enveloped it in joyful play and socializing.

Like the 1,300 Years Bulgaria monument, the public infrastructures of social reproduction and care that feminists fought to build in the 1970s are being slowly dismembered. The architects of these textbook neo-liberal reforms have successfully mobilized nationalist, xenophobic, and racist anti-Roma arguments and popular sentiments to achieve their goals.[15] These changes have affected the elderly and lower-income populations, as well as ethnic, racial, and religious minorities and immigrant communities the most. They also have had larger social effects leading to the loss of women's autonomy and the re-entrenchment of patriarchal relations and values in the mainstreams of Bulgarian and East European society. Waged on the terrain of social reproduction, this kind of neo-liberal assault has intensified class inequalities and subjugation, deepening women's dependence on men and further marginalizing women, migrants, and ethnic and cultural minorities, rendering entire regions abject and thereby exploitable.[16]

Maria Dinkova, the feminist theorist and fierce organizer who was at the forefront of the "women's revolution" of the 1960s and '70s, has spoken of the relentless determination of her contemporaries' work. They were driven not only by the sense that their accomplishments would have tangible material and social effects on collective life in the present and into the near future. What gave them "confidence" was, strikingly, a sense that they "worked for eternity."[17] It is difficult to read Dinkova's reflections today, at a time when these women's work and struggle over decades is disappearing bit by bit. Was their consciousness of "eternity" rooted in some kind of evolutionary historical understanding or a lack of historical foresight – a sense that the "social progress" they accomplish would remain in history in irreversible ways?

It seems that their sense of eternity did not come from some belief in the historical progress, but rather from the hope that their work would leave some historical trace, that it would conjure a reality that, even as it is now pushed into the corners of history, would be carried into the present through collective memory or collective material and social practice, through struggle, and that it would speak to us through its promises, even through its radical inversions. As Dinkova writes,

> In effect, the product of our efforts lasted for thirty years. When I think about it, I can say that even this should not be

> underestimated ... These thirty years had spanned the lives of at least three generations of women. The social politics toward women, which were designed and realized from the beginning of the 1970s, are part of the history of Bulgaria and the beginning of a tradition that at this moment is being destroyed, but it would hardly be fully crossed out if women manage to stand up for their own interests.[18]

The political and economic developments that have shaped Eastern Europe in the three decades since 1989 – the rapid privatization of public infrastructure and property; the enclosure of land, public space, and resources through countless mechanisms of dispossession; the introduction of debt; the rise or escalation of neo-fascism, nationalism, and ethnophobia; and the re-entrenchment of patriarchal relations – all these should be seen not as continuities with the imperial or totalitarian tendencies within the socialist projects, but, on the contrary, as a result of the decline of their political values. Each of these are due to the decline of the anti-capitalist, anti-colonial, feminist, and anti-racist politics that the socialist countries forged in their own societies and in the global sphere during the twentieth century.

At the same time, it is important to stay attentive to the uneven legacies of the twentieth-century socialist projects, both in their radical political promises and the disturbing political directions that they took. They also abounded in discourses of development, modernization, and social progress, which, as I have shown throughout this book, folded their own minorities into frameworks of backwardness and otherness that propelled ethnic assimilation, expulsion, and ethnic and national homogenization projects with devastating effects for hundreds of thousands of people. While undoing deep historical structures of patriarchy, they also naturalized women's reproductive activities, heterosexuality, and binary gender orders. Sometimes they converged with Western modernity projects and their colonial and expansionist imaginaries, while at others they departed starkly from them, leaving an ambivalent history.

The tension between rupture and continuity with these uneven histories continues to shape the contemporary political terrain in Eastern Europe, forming an open and contested relationship to the socialist past. The present-day Bulgarian Socialist Party, successor to the Bulgarian Communist Party, has inherited without much critique the frameworks of national patriotism that led to the ethno-assimilationist politics of the 1970s and '80s. When it comes to pushing through homophobic legislation in parliament, upholding patriarchal cultures, and fuelling the scare of "gender ideology," the Socialist Party is eager to align with the far-right nationalist parties in parliament. Forged across divides between "Right" and "Left," these nationalist alignments see women's economic and cultural autonomy, queer sexualities, and gender-nonconforming people and practices as a threat to the Bulgarian nation in the same way that they see migrants and refugees as a threat to national integrity and the "survival" of the nation, and they regularly encourage racist and ethnophobic sentiments in the public sphere toward the country's ethnic, racial, and religious minorities.[19]

These tendencies are also an important reminder that the political movements working to challenge neo-liberal capitalism, Eurocentrism, and the escalation of nationalism, xenophobia, racism, and anti-immigrant politics in the Balkans and Eastern Europe ought to be forged across ethnic, racial, cultural, linguistic, religious, and national lines and be rooted in the rich multi-ethnic, multicultural, multiracial, cross-border, and diasporic history of the region, the rebel struggles and cultural practices that have made it an unruly and impermeable place, ungovernable zone, a space of insubordination and defiance throughout history.

The massive turn to neo-liberal and right-wing politics in the post-socialist countries, a direct effect of the demise and devaluation of the socialist worlds of the twentieth century, also sheds light on the global resurgence of right-wing governments and grassroots forces today as the global effect of post-socialism. As neo-liberal and right-wing agendas are emboldened from the "top down" and the "bottom up," strikingly reverberating across continents, how we read and mobilize the history of twentieth-century socialisms in Eastern Europe and the rest of the world becomes a crucial question.

Calling attention to the erasure of the socialist countries in a range of critical knowledge formations, Nikolay Karkov and I have proposed alternative ways of thinking about the geo-political and historical legacy of twentieth-century East European socialism. The state-socialist projects, with all their limitations, ought to be acknowledged as a front of resistance to capitalism and as one of the forces of disobedience and insubordination vis-à-vis Western colonial projects. They were defiant mammoths that formed open, messy, and intractable environments, discontinuous histories, and resistant geographies that disrupted global capitalist and colonial projects, their teleological narratives, and their totalizing geographic and temporal orders. They interrupted, if only partially, the flows of global capital as well as the continuity of West European colonial orders of governance. Stationed at their ends, the socialist worlds formed a kind of abject or surplus geography and history, a remainder unsubsumed by the totalizing ambitions and reach of capitalist and Western hegemonies. Even as they have now been left behind as the old utopias of "past futures" (in the words of David Scott) driven into dead ends by the tragic unfolding of their limits, of their nationalist and revolutionary teleologies, their ruptural and transformative energies continue to hold the possibility of "reanimat[ing] this present and even engender[ing] in it new and unexpected horizons."[20]

By reopening the post-Stalinist period in Bulgaria and Eastern Europe, this book has sought not to overdetermine the meaning of this history but to pry open its contradictions, tensions, and ambivalent moments. It offers the socialist past as a sort of unfinished history in its unsettling multiplicity, a history that cannot be put to rest with ease.

Notes

INTRODUCTION

1 Castro, "'The Universal Conscience' Speech to the Cultural Congress of Havana," 186–206.
2 Malcolm X, "I Don't Mean Bananas," 218.
3 On the history of Western Marxist and socialist humanism, see Kevin Anderson, "Sources of Marxist Humanism: Fanon, Kosík and Dunayevskaya"; "Introduction," in *The Dunayevskaya-Marcuse-Fromm Correspondence*; "Fromm, Marx, and Humanism." See also Epstein, "On the Disappearance of Socialist Humanism"; Alderson and Spencer, eds, *For Humanism*.
4 Most scholarship on East European humanism is from the 1970s and early 1980s. For more recent work, see Mervart, "Czechoslovak Humanist Marxism and the Revolution"; Robertson, "On Czech Marxism: An Interview with Ivan Landa and Jan Mervart." Earlier histories of Polish, Hungarian, Czechoslovakian, and Yugoslavian Marxism include Satterwhite, *Varieties of Marxist Humanism*; Sher, *Praxis: Marxist Criticism and Dissent in Socialist Yugoslavia*; Sher, ed., *Marxist Humanism and Praxis*; Marković and Cohen, eds, *Yugoslavia: The Rise and Fall of Socialist Humanism*; Crocker, *Praxis and Democratic Socialism*.
5 The English-language *Praxis International* (1981–91), founded by Richard Bernstein and Seyla Benhabib, continued these exchanges.
6 Marković, "Humanism and Dialectic," 90.
7 Thompson, "Socialist Humanism," 108.
8 Ibid., 132.
9 Ibid., 109.

10 Ibid., 125.
11 Mitev, "Problemi na aktivnata zhiznena pozitsiia na mladata lichnost," 135. Unless otherwise noted, all translations from the Bulgarian, Russian, and Serbo-Croatian are mine.
12 Thompson, "Socialist Humanism," 122.
13 Althusser, *For Marx*, 224–36.
14 For a more extended discussion of hegemonic humanism in Western thought as well as Althusser's critique, see Valiavicharska, "Herbert Marcuse, the Liberation of 'Man,' and Hegemonic Humanism."
15 Gordon, *Fanon and the Crisis of European Man*, 5–14, 86–103; Maldonado-Torres, *Against War*, 93–121; Maldonado-Torres, "Lewis Gordon: Philosopher of the Human"; Henry, "Lewis Gordon, Africana Phenomenology and the Crisis of European Man."
16 For a relevant discussion of Wynter's critical project, see Weheliye, *Habeas Viscus*, 17–32; McKittrick, ed., *Sylvia Wynter: On Being Human as Praxis*, and in particular, the conversation between Wynter and McKittrick, "Unparalleled Catastrophe for Our Species?"; Ferreira da Silva, "Before Man: Sylvia Wynter's Rewriting of the Modern Episteme"; Mignolo, "Sylvia Wynter: What Does it Mean to Be Human?"; Scott, "The Re-Enchantment of Humanism."
17 Joseph, *Sea Log: Indian Ocean to New York*.
18 For an extended discussion, Valiavicharska, "Social Reproduction in the Making."
19 Among them, Battacharya, ed., *Social Reproduction Theory*; the special issue on social reproduction in *Viewpoint* 5 (2015), in particular Katsarova, "Repression and Resistance on the Terrain of Social Reproduction"; Giardini and Simone, "Reproduction as Paradigm"; Barbagallo, "Leaving Home"; Nadasen, "Domestic Worker's Rights"; Cramer, "Race, Class, and Social Reproduction in the Urban Present"; Farris, "Social Reproduction, Surplus Populations and the Role of Migrant Women"; Serra, "Reproducing the Struggle." See also Arruzza, Bhattacharya, and Fraser, *Feminism for the 99%*. Taha and Salem, "Social Reproduction and Empire in an Egyptian Century"; Federici, "Social Reproduction Theory"; Mezzandri, "On the Value of Social Reproduction"; Vora, "After the Housewife."
20 Weeks, *The Problem with Work*, 101, 85.
21 See Ghodsee, *Second World, Second Sex*; "Pressuring the Politburo"; "Rethinking State Socialist Mass Women's Organizations"; "Feminism-by-Design."
22 Karkov and Valiavicharska, "Rethinking East-European Socialism."

23 Karkov, "Decolonizing Praxis in Eastern Europe," 191.
24 Karkov and Valiavicharska, "Rethinking East-European Socialism."
25 Karkov, "Decolonizing Praxis in Eastern Europe," 192.
26 Ibid., 193.
27 Historians Maria Todorova and Mary Neuburger have both explored these elements in different ways. See Todorova, "The Ottoman Legacy in the Balkans," 70, and *Imagining the Balkans*; Neuburger, *The Orient Within*.
28 Neuburger, *The Orient Within*; Büchsenschütz, *Minderheiten Politik in Bulgarien*. I reference here the Bulgarian translation, Biuksenshiuts, *Maltsinstvenata politika v Bulgariia*, 31–3.
29 For Balkan federalist visions within the communist movements of the late nineteenth and early twentieth centuries, see Robertson, "Imagining the Balkans as a Space of Revolution"; Lalkov, *Ot nadezhda kum razocharovanie*; Marinov, "Ot 'internatsionalisum' kum natsionalizum – chast 1." I offer further discussion of this topic in chapter 4.
30 See, among others, Popescu, *South African Literature Beyond the Cold War*; "Lewis Nkosi in Warsaw; "On the Margins of the Black Atlantic." See also Engerman, "The Second World's Third World"; Djagalov, *From Internationalism to Postcolonialism*; Djagalov and Salazkina, "Tashkent '68"; Kret, "'We Unite with Knowledge'"; Ghodsee, "Historiographical Challenges of Exploring Second World–Third World Alliances"; Katsakioris, "The Patrice Lumumba University in Moscow."
31 Engerman, "The Second World's Third World," 197; Djagalov and Salazkina, "Tashkent '68," 281–2.
32 For an informative discussion of the debates on modernity in the field of Soviet and socialist history, see David-Fox, *Modernity, Ideology, and Culture in Russia and the Soviet Union*, 1–73; "Modernost' v Rossii i SSSR."

CHAPTER ONE

1 Marks and Engel's, *Iz rannikh proizvedenii*.
2 *Literaturnoe nasledstvo*, 143–4.
3 Ibid., 145.
4 Ibid., 153.
5 Marks, "Podgotvitel'nye raboty dlia 'Sviatogo semeistva.'"
6 Morozova, "Sochineniia K. Marska i F. Engel'sa"; Stepanova, "O sobiranii i nauchnoi publikatsii v SSSR." Fragments of the *1844 Manuscripts* also appeared in the collected volume *Marks i Engel's ob iskusstve* (edited by Mikhail Lifshits and Frants Shiller), first published in 1933 and subsequently expanded and republished multiple times.

7 *History of the Communist Party (Short Course)*. The chapter "Dialectical Materialism and Historical Materialism" is attributed to Stalin.
8 Ibid., 110.
9 Ibid., 111.
10 Lefebvre, *Dialectical Materialism*, 1.
11 Ibid., 2.
12 Ibid., 7.
13 For more on the discursive formation and the history of the doctrine, see Valiavicharska, "The Production of 'Leninism' and its Political Journeys."
14 Marković, "Humanism and Dialectic," 90.
15 Ibid., 91.
16 *Literaturnoe nasledstvo*, 320
17 "Predislovie ko vtoromu izdaniiu," v–ix; Morozova, "Sochineniia K. Marska i F. Engel'sa."
18 *Literaturnoe nasledstvo*, 354–62.
19 Morozova, "Sochineniia K. Marska i F. Engel'sa"; *Literaturnoe nasledstvo*, 319.
20 "Predislovie ko vtoromu izdaniiu," v–vi.
21 *Literaturnoe nasledstvo*, 321.
22 "Predislovie ko vtoromu izdaniiu," vi; "Predislovie k pervomu tomu," in Marks and Engel's, *Sochineniia*, vol. 1: xv–xvi.
23 For example, *Iz rannikh proizvedenii* became very influential in Bulgaria. It was used and referenced in Bulgaria until the *1844 Manuscripts*' first translation from Russian appeared twenty-five years later, 1981, in an anthology of texts on the young Hegelians and the young Marx. Some excerpts from the *1844 Manuscripts*, however, appeared in Bulgarian in 1951 with the translation of the volume *Marks i Engel's ob iskusstve*. See Mitev and Mineva, eds, *Antologiia po istoriia na marksistkata filosofiia*. In Bulgaria, another important collection was the anthology on "new Soviet Marxism," translated and published in the 1970s. See Mitev and Raichev, eds, *Izsledvaniia vurkhu istoriiata na marksistkata filosofiia*.
24 Lapin, "O genezise marksizma kak tsel'nogo ucheniia"; Oizerman, *Formirovanie filosofii marksizma*; Rozental, ed., *Istoriia marksistkoi dialektiki*; Mitev, "Formiraneto, razvitieto i razprostranenieto na filosofskite vuzgledi na Marks i Engels."
25 Lapin, *Molodoi Marks*.
26 Althusser and Balibar, *Reading Capital*.
27 Keshelava, *Mif o dvukh Marksakh*.
28 Lapin, *Mladiiat Marks*, 469. For an analogous critique in Bulgaria, see Mitev, "Filosofski predshestvenik na marksizma."

29 Rozental', *Dialektika Kapitala Karla Marksa* (first published in 1955 as *Voprosy dialektiki v Kapitale K. Marksa*); Bagaturiia and Vygodskii, *Ekonomicheskoe nasledie Karla Marksa* (here used in Bulgarian translation: Bagaturiia i Vigodski, *Ikonomicheskoto nasledstvo na Karl Marks*); Vygodskii, *K istorii sozdaniia "Kapitala"*; Vaziulin, *Logika "Kapitala" K. Marksa*; Il'enkov, *Dialektika abstraktnogo i konkretnogo v "Kapitale" Marksa*; Tipukhin, *Metod voskhozhdeniia ot abstraktnogo k konkretnomy v "Kaptale" K. Marksa*; Iovchuk, ed., *"Kapital" Marksa, filosofiia i sovremennost'*.

30 See the discussion by Bagaturiia and Vygodskii, *Ikonomicheskoto nasledstvo na Karl Marks*, 3–7. *Theories of Surplus Value* was first published in German in 1910 by Karl Kautsky with significant changes and omissions. This edition circulated until the 1960s in various translations.

31 On Soviet and socialist interpretations of the *1844 Manuscripts*, see Pazhitnov, *U istokov revoliutsionnogo perevorota v filosofii*; Bagaturiia and Vigodski, "Nachalo na izgrazhdaneto na dialektiko-materialisticheskata metodologiia." On alienation, see Narskii, "Ob istoriko-filosofskom razvitii poniatiia 'otchuzhdenie'"; Sitnikov, *Problema "otchuzhdeniia" v burzhoaznoi filosofii*; Smolentsev, "Problema cheloveka v tvorchestve K. Marksa"; Zhelubovskaia, ed., *Marks – istorik*.

32 Georgii Badaturiia, "Ekonomichesko-filosofskiie rukopisi," 791–2. See also Georgii Bagaturiia and Vitalii Vygodskii, *Economicheskoe nasledie Karla Marksa*, esp. ch. 14 (here used in Bulgarian translation).

33 Mitev, "Formiraneto, razvitieto i razprostranenieto," 58.

34 Ibid.

35 Petur-Emil Mitev, *Ot sotsialniia problem kum svetogledni otkritiia*, 172.

36 Anderson and Rockwell, eds, *The Dunayevskaya-Marcuse-Fromm Correspondence*, 125.

37 Ibid., 12, 29.

38 Dunayevskaya, "Marx's Humanism Today," 81n10.

39 *Economic and Philosophic Manuscripts of 1844*, translated by Martin Milligan. This translation also appeared almost unchanged in *Marx-Engels Collected Works*, vol. 3, the full body of work in English that Moscow began producing with International Publishers. For a brief and excellent history of Progress Publishers with a focus on its role in the non-Western world, see Djagalov, "Progress Publishers: A Short History."

40 Dunayevskaya, "Marx's Humanism Today," 81n10.

41 Ibid.

42 Erich Fromm, ed., *Socialist Humanism*; Oglesby, ed., *The New Left Reader*. See also Raya Dunayevskaya's formulation of these links in her *Philosophy and Revolution*.

43 Lefebvre, *Dialectical Materialism*, 5.
44 Thompson, "Socialist Humanism," 143.
45 C.L.R. James, *State Capitalism and World Revolution*; Dunayevskaya, *Marxism and Freedom*, 215–57.
46 As in Dunayevskaya, *Philosophy and Revolution*, 247–66.
47 Narskii, "Za istoriko-filosofksoto razvitie na poniatieto 'otchuzhdenie,'" 119.
48 Lapin, *Mladiiat Marks*, 474–5.
49 Ibid., 297. Lapin's analysis bears similarities to the one Lukács developed in 1924, but the latter wasn't available to Soviet Marxists at the time of Lapin's publication.
50 Oizerman, *Problema otchuzhdeniia i burzhoaznaia legenda o marksizme*, 5–6.
51 Ibid., 14.
52 Ibid., 37.
53 Karkov, "Decolonizing Praxis in Eastern Europe," 190. See also Karkov and Valiavicharska, "Rethinking East-European Socialism."
54 Pešić-Golubović, *Problemi savremene teorije ličnosti*; Golubović, *Staljinizam i socijalizam.*
55 Stoianov, *Suchineniia v dva toma*, vol. 2: 69.
56 Ibid., 98.
57 Ibid., 143.
58 Ibid., 178–9.
59 Ibid., 70–4.
60 Ibid., 73–4.
61 Ibid., 73.
62 Ibid., 80.
63 Ibid., 82.
64 Ibid., 75.
65 Ibid., 83.
66 Ibid., 182
67 Ibid., 183.
68 Ibid., 179.
69 Ibid., 76–7.
70 Ibid., 181.
71 Ibid., 178.
72 Ibid., 184.
73 Ibid., 187.
74 Ibid., 197.
75 Marković, "Humanism and Dialectic," 96.

76 Mitev, "Formiraneto, razvitieto i razprostranenieto," 75.

77 Gajo Petrović, "Man and Freedom," 273–5.

78 For more on Yugoslavian members of the Praxis School, see Karkov, "Decolonizing Praxis in Eastern Europe"; Karkov and Valiavicharska, "Rethinking East-European Socialism."

79 Lapin, *Mladiiat Marks*, 430.

80 Ibid.

81 Mitev, "Sotsialnoto tvorchestvo na mladezhta," 6.

82 Ibid., 6–7.

83 Lapin, *Mladiiat Marks*, 429.

84 Puteva, "Mladata zhena – trud, bit, otdikh" (1985), 171.

85 Marcuse, *One Dimensional Man*, 3.

86 See Kathi Weeks, who uses the work of Moishe Postone and Italian autonomists to critique what she calls the "productivist work ethic" in 1970s Marxist feminism. Weeks, *The Problem with Work*.

87 Ibid., 97.

88 Puteva, "Svobodnoto vreme i kharmonichnoto razvitie na mladata lichnost."

89 Mitev, "Problemi na aktivnata zhiznena pozitsiia na mladata lichnost," 136.

90 "Marks i mladezhta: Diskusiia," 33.

91 Gospodinov, "Realizatsiia i sotsializatsiia na mladezhta," 36–47.

92 For an extended critique, see Valiavicharska, "Herbert Marcuse, the Liberation of 'Man,' and Hegemonic Humanism."

CHAPTER TWO

1 For a history of the concept and a survey of the literature, see Valiavicharska, "Social Reproduction in the Making."

2 See, among others, Spade, *Normal Life*.

3 Some classical contributions from the 1970s to the 1990s include Davis, "The Approaching Obsolescence of Housework" and "Reflections on the Black Woman's Role in the Community of Slaves"; Spillers, "Mama's Baby, Papa's Maybe"; Jones, *The Labor of Love, the Labor of Sorrow*; and Roberts's now classic *Killing the Black Body*.

4 As in the work of Wacquant, *Punishing the Poor*, and Gilmore, *Golden Gulag*. For further discussion and references, see Whitener, "Detroit's Water Wars."

5 Ghodsee, "Pressuring the Politburo"; "Feminism-by-Design"; "Historiographical Challenges of Exploring Second World–Third World

Alliances"; "Rethinking State Socialist Mass Women's Organizations"; *Second World, Second Sex.*

6 Ghodsee, *Second World, Second Sex*, 11–13.

7 Mohanty, "Under Western Eyes." For a more elaborate analysis, see Valiavicharska, "Social Reproduction in the Making."

8 Some of the early interventions include Edholm, Harris, and Young, "Conceptualizing Women"; Rosaldo: "The Use and Abuse of Anthropology"; Parmar and Amos, "Challenging Imperial Feminism"; Bhavnani and Coulson, "Transforming Socialist Feminism." See also interventions in the two special issues of *Feminist Review*, "Many Voices, One Chant: Black Feminist Perspectives," no. 17 (Autumn 1984), and "Socialist Feminism: Out of the Blue," no. 23 (Summer 1986). For discussion on the history of these debates, as well as some further interventions, see Mirza, "Introduction: Mapping a Genealogy of Black British Feminism," in *Black British Feminism*, 1–28; Mohanty, Russo, and Torres, eds, *Third World Women and the Politics of Feminism*; Alexander and Mohanty, "Introduction," in *Feminist Genealogies, Colonial Legacies, Democratic Futures*; Mohanty, "'Under Western Eyes' Revisited"; Jayawardena, ed., *The White Woman's Other Burden*; Burton, *Burdens of History*.

9 Carby, "White Woman Listen!"

10 Puteva, "Razvitieto na devoikata i mladata zhena v sotsialisticheskoto obshtestvo," 34.

11 "Ravenstvo, razvitie, mir," 15. On Elena Lagadinova's life, see Ghodsee, *The Left Side of History*, 101–25.

12 Dinkova, "Strasti po velikata zhenska revoliutsiia," 43.

13 Dinkova, "Strasti po velikata zhenska revoliutsiia (produlzhenie ot br. 5)," 31.

14 Ibid.

15 For a classic critique, see hooks, "Black Women: Shaping Feminist Theory"; *Feminist Theory: From Margin to Center.*

16 Mohanty, "Cartographies of Struggle." See also, among others, Sinha, "Historically Speaking: Gender and Citizenship in Colonial India"; Shenabuddin, "Gender and the Figure of the 'Moderate Muslim.'"

17 Mohanty, "Cartographies of Struggle."

18 Puteva, "Razvitieto na devoikata i mladata zhena," 34.

19 For a more detailed history of the document, see Sharkova, "Sotsialisticheskata zhena mezhdu publichnoto i chastnoto (1967–73)."

20 *Za izdigane roliata na zhenata v izgrazhdaneto na razvito sotsialistichesko obshtestvo*, 5.

21 Ibid., 6–7.

22 Dinkova, *Sotsialen portret na bulgarskata zhena*, 21.
23 An excellent take on warrior-women mobilized in the military during the Great Patriotic War in Stalinist Soviet Union, see Krylova, *Women in Combat: A History of Violence on the Eastern Front*. On gender and labour under Stalinism, see Goldman, *Women at the Gates: Gender and Industry in Stalin's Russia*.
24 Ghodsee, "Historiographical Challenges" and *Second World, Second Sex*.
25 Dukhteva, "Panorama na zhenskiia trud," 3.
26 Ibid.
27 *Za izdigane roliata na zhenata v izgrazhdaneto na razvito sotsialistichesko obshtestvo*, 7–8.
28 Ibid., 15.
29 Dinkova, "Strasti po velikata zhenska revoliutsiia (produlzhenie ot br. 5)," 32.
30 Dinkova, "Strasti po velikata zhenska revoliutsiia," 35.
31 Dinkova, "Strasti po velikata zhenska revoliutsiia (produlzhenie ot br. 5)," 24–5.
32 Ibid.
33 Ibid.
34 Dinkova, "Strasti po velikata zhenska revoliutsiia," 35.
35 Dinkova, "Strasti po velikata zhenska revoliutsiia (produlzhenie ot br. 5)," 23–5.
36 Ibid.
37 Dukhteva and Dinkova, "Zhenata v stroitelstvoto [Part 1]," 4–5; "Zhenata v stroitelstvoto [Part 2]," 6–7.
38 Dukhteva and Dinkova, "Zhenata v stroitelstvoto [Part 1]"; "Zhenata v stroitelstvoto [Part 2]."
39 "Da otmenim 'vtorata smiana'!"; Ignatova, "Na vtorata smiana – ne!"
40 "Da otmenim 'vtorata smiana'!," 1.
41 Dinkova, "Strasti po velikata zhenska revoliutsiia," 43.
42 Ibid.
43 Ibid.
44 Puteva, "Spored vutreshnite potrebnosti i interesi," 70.
45 Ibid., 71.
46 Ibid., 71–2.
47 Ibid., 72.
48 Ibid.
49 Velev, "Interesi i deinosti v sferata na svobodnoto vreme"; Puteva, "Mladata zhena – trud, bit, otdikh."
50 Puteva, "Mladata zhena i neinoto svobodno vreme," 40.

51 Puteva, "Svobodnoto vreme na mladata zhena."

52 Puteva, "Mladata zhena – trud, bit, otdikh," 28; "Mladata zhena i neinoto svobodno vreme," 40–7.

53 Puteva, "Mladata zhena – trud, bit, otdikh."

54 Dinkova, "Strasti po velikata zhenska revoliutsiia," 28. See also Ghodsee's discussion of the survey, in which she quotes 16,060 responses. Ghodsee, "Pressuring the Politburo," 548.

55 Dinkova, "Strasti po velikata zhenska revoliutsiia," 28.

56 Ibid., 28.

57 Ibid., 44.

58 Dinkova, *Sotsialen portret na bulgarskata zhena*, 110.

59 Dinkova, "Strasti po velikata zhenska revoliutsiia," 41–2.

60 Dinkova, *Sotsialen portret na bulgarskata zhena*, 21.

61 Topolova, "Promeniashtata se rolia na pola i sotsialnata politika na NR Bulgariia," 114.

62 Haraway, *Simians, Cyborgs, and Women.*

63 Dinkova, "Strasti po velikata zhenska revoliutsiia," 44.

64 *Za izdigane roliata na zhenata v izgrazhdaneto na razvito sotsialistichesko obshtestvo*, 10.

65 Dinkova, "Strasti po velikata zhenska revoliutsiia," 45. See also Ghodsee's discussion of child-care benefits in "Pressuring the Politburo."

66 Dinkova, "Tendentsii i problemi vuv formiraneto, funktsioniraneto i razvitieto na mladoto semeistvo," 11–21.

67 Ibid., 12.

68 Some formulations here, especially on kinship and parenthood, first appeared in Schultes, "Under Assault."

69 Ghodsee, "Pressuring the Politburo," 549–53; Sharkova, "Sotsialisticheskata zhena," 74.

70 Dinkova, "Tendentsii i problemi vuv formiraneto, funktsioniraneto i razvitieto na mladoto semeistvo," 12.

71 Totev, "Za broia na detsata v semeistvoto," 42.

72 Ibid.

73 "Ukaz za nasurchavane na razhdaemostta," *Durzhaven vestnik: ofitsialen organ na narodnoto subranie* (23 February 1968): 1–2; ibid. (15 March 1968): 1; ibid. (10 August 1973): 1; ibid. (1 March 1974): 1; ibid. (10 January 1975): 1. See also Totev, "Za broia na detsata v semeistvoto," 39–42.

74 See, for example, Dinkova, "Labirinti na lekomislieto i bezotgovornostta"; Moneva, "Abortut po zhelanie."

75 Ghodsee, "Pressuring the Politburo," 553.

76 Sharkova, "Sotsialisticheskata zhena mezhdu publichnoto i chastnoto," 75.

77 *Za izdigane roliata na zhenata v izgrazhdaneto na razvito sotsialistichesko obshtestvo*, 6.

78 Ibid., 24.

79 Dinkova, "Pogled vurkhu istoriiata na bulgarskoto semeistvo," 29.

80 Puteva, "Mladiiat chovek – liubov, brak, semeistvo."

81 Dinkova, "Pogled vurkhu istoriiata na bulgarskoto semeistvo."

82 Dinkova, "Suvremenna zhena? Da! A Suvremenen muzh?," 4.

83 Ibid.

84 Ivanova, *Otkhvurlenite "priobshteni," ili protsesut, narechen "vuzroditelen,"* 155–6.

CHAPTER THREE

1 For a more elaborate political analysis of the monument, see Valiavicharska, "History's Restless Ruins."

2 Neuburger, *The Orient Within*, 57.

3 See Avramov's otherwise impressively researched study of the political economy of the Revival Process, *Ikonomikata na "Vuzroditelniia protses."* See also Ivanova, *Otkhvurlenite "priobshteni," ili protsesut narechen "vuzroditelen"*; Kalinova and Baeva, "'Vuzroditelniiat protses' – vurkhut na aisberga."

4 On Soviet minority politics during the Stalinist period, see Martin, *Affirmative Action Empire*; Slezkine, *Arctic Mirrors*. For studies that register policy changes toward minorities from Stalinism to post-Stalinism, see Eminov, "The Turks of Bulgaria: 1945–1983"; Marinov, "Ot 'internatsionalisum' kum natsionalizum – chast 1"; "Ot 'internatsionalisum' kum natsionalizum – chast 2." For an extensive study of the early socialist period, see Gruev, *Mezhdu petoluchkata i polumesetsa*.

5 Zhivkov, *Bulgaria: Ancient and Socialist*; Zhivkova, "Trinadeset veka bulgarska durzhava."

6 Neuburger, *The Orient Within*, 55–68; Todorova, "The Ottoman Legacy in the Balkans," 70.

7 For an extensive empirical study of the state's cultural policies during the Zhivkova era, see Elenkov, *Kulturniiat front*.

8 For more on Zhivkova's eclectic philosophical and spiritual interests, see Atanasova, "Lyudmila Zhivkova and the Paradox of Ideology and Identity in Communist Bulgaria."

9 Zhivkova, "Opoznavaneto na zakonite na krasotata i kharmonichnoto razvitie na choveshkiia individ," 169.

10 Ibid.
11 Ibid., 176.
12 Ibid., 167.
13 Zhivkova, "Bulgariia i kulturata," 542–3.
14 Zhivkova, "Opoznavaneto na zakonite na krasotata i kharmonichnoto razvitie na choveshkiia individ," 174.
15 Ibid.
16 Zhivkova, "Igrazhdaneto na kulturata na razvitoto sotsialistichesko obshtestvo," 648.
17 Elenkov, *Kulturniiat front*, 413–73.
18 Ibid., 456–7.
19 See also Neuburger's discussion of the idea of "blood-based sameness" in *The Orient Within*, 68–84.
20 Iankov, "Formiraneto i razvitieto na bulgarskata natsiia i Vuzroditelniiat protses," 28.
21 Ibid.
22 Ibid.
23 Transcript of Atanasov's words, *Istinata za "Vuzroditelniia protses,"* 11.
24 Ibid., 7.
25 Zhivkov, "Edinstvoto na bulgarskiia narod e grizha i sudba na vseki grazhdanin na nasheto milo otechestvo."
26 Zagorov, "Istorichesko suznanie i vuzroditelen protses," 183.
27 Zagorov's clearest theoretical elaboration of the principles behind the Revival Process as part of the "consolidation of the socialist nation" are developed in his book *Bulgarsko sotsialistichesko suznanie.*
28 Zagorov, "Istorichesko suznanie i vuzroditelen protses," 184.
29 Ibid., 185.
30 Zhivkova, "Bulgariia i kulturata," 539.
31 Ibid., 549.
32 Zhivkova, "Dostoini za doverieto na svoia narod," 743.
33 Transcript of Todor Zhivkov's statement, *Istinata za "Vuzroditelniia protses,"* 121.
34 Zhivkova, "Da bude Bulgariia!," 519.
35 Zhivkova, "Znamenatelen iubilei," 508.
36 Ibid.
37 Todorova, "Identity Transformation among Bulgarian Muslims"; "The Ottoman Legacy in the Balkans."
38 See Todorova on the work of historians Iliia Todorov, Strashimir Dimitrov, Evgeni Radushev, and others in "Conversion to Islam as a Trope in Bulgarian Historiography, Fiction, and Film." For an important earlier

intervention, see Zheliazkova, "The Problem of the Authenticity of Some Domestic Sources on the Islamization of the Rhodopes."

39 A tremendous amount of research on the shared Bulgarian roots of the Muslim and Orthodox Christian populations was published during the period in journals such as *Nov Zhivot*, *Nova Svetlina*, and *Rodopi* (see for example the work of Ekaterina Venedikova). Also important are the volumes *Iz minaloto na bulgarite-mokhamedani v Rodopite* and *Izvori i izsledvaniia za bulgarskiia kharakter na naselenieto ot iztochnite Rodopi.* See Zagorov, "Istorichesko suznanie i vuzroditelen protses," 188–93, for an overview of the literature.

40 For an excellent history of the formation of this narrative, see Eminov, *Turkish and Other Muslim Minorities in Bulgaria* and "Social Construction of Identities: Pomaks in Bulgaria."

41 Transcript of Atanasov's statement, *Istinata za "Vuzroditelniia protses,"* 8.

42 Zagorov, *Edinenieto*; *Obshtuvane i dukhovno nasledstvo*; "Istorichesko suznanie i vuzroditelen protses"; Petrov and Miusliumov, eds, *Druzhni i edinni prez vekovete*; Iankov, *Niakoi osobenosti na razvitieto na bulgarskata natsiia*; Iankov, ed., *Stranitsi ot bulgarskata istoriia*; Petrov, *Po sledite na nasilieto* and "Iziava na bulgarska prinadlezhnost."

43 Mizov, "Etnoreligiozni aspekti na vuzroditelniia protses," 166.

44 Ibid.

45 Transcript of Atanasov's statement, *Istinata za "Vuzroditelniia protses,"* 9.

46 Ibid.

47 For an earlier critical analysis of official state discourse, see the work of Cemile Ahmed, which I discuss in chapter 6, in Dzhemile Akhmed, "Ime, preimenuvane i dvoinstvena identichnost," 169. See also Neuburger, *The Orient Within*, 76–84.

48 Zhivkova, "Bulgariia i kulturata," 540–1.

49 Ibid.

50 Zhivkova, "Izgrazhdaneto na kulturata," 684.

51 Zhivkova, "Opoznavaneto na zakonite na krasotata," 170.

52 Zhivkova, "Da bude Bulgariia!," 519.

53 Zhivkova, "Bulgaria i kulturata," 539.

54 Neuburger, *The Orient Within*, 55–68.

55 Iankov, "Formiraneto i razvitieto na bulgarskata natsiia," 31.

56 Todorova, "The Ottoman Legacy in the Balkans," 70.

57 Ibid., 70–2. For more detailed analysis, see Todorova's *Imagining the Balkans.*

58 Iankov, "Formiraneto i razvitieto na bulgarskata natsiia," 30.

59 Ibid.

60 Zhivkov, "Edinstvoto na bulgarskiia narod."
61 Ibid., 39.
62 Ibid., 39–40. Numbers are from the 2001 census.
63 Dureva, "Boiana, ulitsa Sekvoia."
64 Transcript of Atanasov's statement, *Istinata za "Vuzroditelniia protses,"* 12.
65 *Istinata za "Vuzroditelniia protses,"* 90.
66 Transcript of Atanasov's statement, *Istinata za "Vuzroditelniia protses,"* 13.
67 Ibid., 34.
68 Iankov, ed., *Stranitsi ot bulgarskata istoriia*, 80.
69 Ibid.
70 Ibid.
71 Zagorov, "Istorichesko suznanie i vuzroditelen protses," 189–90.
72 Ibid., 189.
73 Transcript of Zhivkov's statement, *Istinata za "Vuzroditelniia protses,"* 34.
74 *Istinata za "Vuzroditelniia protses,"* 25.
75 See Todorova on how the meanings of "Turkish" and "Muslim" became compounded in nationalist discourse, a form of reductionism that Pomak and other ambivalently positioned identities consistently challenged: Todorova, "Identity (Trans)Formation among Bulgarian Muslims."
76 Transcript of Zhivkov's statements, *Istinata za "Vuzroditelniia protses,"* 31.
77 Todorova, "Identity (Trans)Formation among Bulgarian Muslims," 474.
78 Todorova develops this point with respect to the Pomak minority, who could never adapt to fixed identity modalities. They "retained fluid consciousness" and maintained the more cosmopolitan and inclusive character of the millet identity from the Ottoman period. "Identity (Trans) Formation among Bulgarian Muslims."
79 On the ambitious scope of the campaign, see Elenkov, *Kulturniiat front*, 357–412.

CHAPTER FOUR

1 TsDA f. 1, op. 28, arkh. ed. 16, 1–2. On the multiple forms and expressions of discontent during the post-Stalinist period in the Soviet Union, see Kozlov, Fitzpatrick, and Mironenko, eds, *Sedition: Everyday Resistance in the Soviet Union under Khrushchev and Brezhnev.*
2 TsDA f. 1, op. 28, arkh. ed. 16, 1 (front).
3 TsDA f. 1, op. 28, arkh. ed. 16, 1 (front and back).
4 See, for example, Gruev and Kal'onski, *Vuzroditelniiat protses*; Gruev, *Mezhdu petoluchkata i polumesetsa*; Ivanova, *Otkhvurlenite "priobshteni"*; Avramov, *Ikonomikata na "Vuzroditelniia protses."*
5 Mary Neuburger, *The Orient Within*, 60.

6 Ibid., 57. For example, Neuburger writes that "By the 1960s and 1970s, the Bulgarian Communist Party had fully embraced and even surpassed the methods and formulations of pre-Communist Bulgarian nationalists in its approach to the Muslim minority question" (75–6). At times, Neuburger acknowledges that the first years of socialist government saw radical changes in the government's approach to minorities. For example, it revoked the fascist "Law on Names" and guaranteed minorities protection from further assaults on their names or identities. Yet because the post-1956 shift remains unexamined, Neuburger attributes the 1958–60 clothing reforms and the subsequent name changes among the Pomaks and Romas to the party's "consolidation of power." See Neuburger, *The Orient Within*, 154 and throughout.

7 Avramov, *Ikonomikata na "Vuzroditelniia protses"*; Gruev and Kal'onski, *Vuzroditelniiat protses.*

8 Eminov, "The Turks of Bulgaria"; Marinov, "Ot 'internatsionalizum' kum natsionalizum – chast 1" and "Ot 'internatsionalizum' kum natsionalizum – chast 2"; Ivanova, *Otkhvurlenite "priobshteni"*; see also Gruev's later work, "Ideologicheskiiat zavoi kum natsionalizum."

9 Martin, *Affirmative Action Empire*."

10 Ibid., 9–27.

11 Slezkine, "The USSR as a Communal Apartment."

12 Brubaker, *Nationalism Reframed*, 23–54.

13 As in the work Hirsch, *Empire of Nations*; Slezkine, *Arctic Mirrors*; Stronsky, *Tashkent: Forging a Soviet City.*

14 Iğmen, *Speaking Soviet with an Accent*, 37.

15 Smith, "The Battle for Language: Opposition to Khrushchev's Education Reform."

16 Gruev and Kal'onski, *Vuzroditelniiat protses*, 21, 118; Gruev, *Mezhdu petoluchkata i polumesetsa*, 107–16; Avramov, *Ikonomikata na "Vuzroditelniia" protses.*

17 Kalinova and Baeva, *"Vuzroditelniiat protses": Bulgarskata durzhava i bulgarskite turtsi.*

18 See Avramov, *Ikonomikata na "Vuzroditelniia protses,"* 35–51.

19 On the history and prehistory of Rodina, see Ivanova, *Otkhvurlenite "priobshteni,"* 24–58; Gruev and Kal'onski, *Vuzroditelniiat protses*, 13–20; Neuburger, *The Orient Within*, 153–4; Todorova, "Conversion to Islam."

20 Gruev and Kal'onski, *Vuzroditelniiat protses*, 18; Ivanova, *Otkhvurlenite "priobshteni,"* 29–58.

21 For more on the history of Macedonian national identity and territorial autonomy as viewed through the political relationship between socialist

Bulgaria and Yugoslavia, see Marinov, "Ot 'internatsionalizum' kum natsionalizum – chast 1"; Lalkov, *Ot nadezhda kum razocharovanie*; Minchev, *Makedonskiiat vupros i bulgaro-iugoslavskite otnosheniia*.

22 For discussion, see Eminov, "The Turks of Bulgaria"; Republika Bulgariia, Natsionalen suvet po etnicheski i demografski vuprosi, "Natsionalen doklad suglasno chl. 25, al. 1 ot Ramkovata konventsiia za zashtita na natsionalnite maltsinstva."

23 Kazasov, *Konstitutsiiata na narodnata republika Bulgariia*, 15.

24 TsDA, f. 214b, op. 1, arch. ed. 716, 10.

25 Ibid., 12.

26 Ibid., 19–20.

27 Ibid., 20.

28 Ibid., 55, 58.

29 Ibid., 57.

30 Gruev and Kal'onski, *Vuzroditelniiat protses*, 20–1; Republika Bulgariia, "Natsionalen doklad," 10; Marinov, "Ot 'internatsionalisum' kum natsionalizum – chast 2."

31 TsDA, f. 214b, op. 1, arch. ed. 716, 22.

32 Ibid., 13.

33 Ibid., 8.

34 Ibid., 50. Eventually Turkey's Ministry Council moved to give political asylum to Bulgarian-born Turkish people and help them relocate, but such a resolution, the report continues, could not be accomplished and would remain only on paper.

35 TsDA, f. 214b, op. 1, arch. ed. 716, 7–9.

36 Ibid., 49–50.

37 Ibid., 9.

38 Ibid., 13–15.

39 Ibid., 21.

40 Ibid., 15–21.

41 Ibid., 34–5.

42 Ibid., 36. Recorded statement by Mekhmed Muradov Merdvinov from Sukhindol.

43 TsDA, f. 1, op. 27, arkh. ed. 19, 6–7.

44 Dimitrova, "Nazum Khikmet v Bulgariia," 41–125.

45 Dimitrova, "Belezhki, poiasneniia," 299–303.

46 Ibid., 299.

47 Dimitrova, "Nazum Khikmet v Bulgariia," 54.

48 TsDA, f. 1, op. 27, arkh. ed. 19, 5–6.

49 Dimitrova, "Nazum Khikmet v Bulgariia," 108.

50 TsDA, f. 1, op. 27, arkh. ed. 19, 4–14.
51 Ibid., 9.
52 Ibid., 11.
53 Ibid., 10–11.
54 Ibid., 7–9.
55 Zhivkov, *Memoari*, 444.
56 Ibid.
57 TsDA, f. 1b, op. 5, arch. ed. 353, 350–470. The protocol contains minutes from the party's Central Committee meeting and discussion outlining the content of the document and a final version of the "Theses."
58 TsDA, f. 1b, op. 6, arkh. ed. 3645, 50–7, 58–64.
59 Ibid., 51.
60 TsDA, f. 1b, op. 5, arkh. ed. 353, 368.
61 Ibid., 374–5.
62 TsDA f. 1b, op. 6, arkh. ed. 3645, 60–1; Eminov, "The Turks of Bulgaria," 589; Marinov, "Ot 'internatsionalizum' kum natsionalizum – chast 2." See also the resolution from 1951, "Za podobriavane rabotata na Partiiata sred turskoto naselenie," 26 April 1951. TsDA, 1b, op. 6, 1298, 37–43.
63 TsDA, 1b, op. 6, 1298, 37–43.
64 TsDA f. 214b, op. 1, arch. ed. 716, 38–45.
65 Ibid., 37–47.
66 Ibid., 47.
67 Ibid., 54.
68 Eminov, "The Turks of Bulgaria," 589.
69 Ibid.
70 Ibid.
71 TsDA f. 1b, op. 6, arkh. ed. 3645, 59–60.
72 Ibid., 52.
73 Ibid.
74 Ibid., 61.
75 Ibid., 55; Marinov, "Ot 'internatsionalizum' kum natsionalizum – chast 2."
76 TsDA, f. 1., op. 28, arkh. ed. 16, 1 (back).
77 TsDA, f. 1., op. 28, arkh. ed. 10, 6 (front).
78 Ibid., 6–7.
79 Ibid., 6 (front).
80 Ibid., 7 (front).
81 Ibid., 5 (front).
82 Todorova, "Conversion to Islam."
83 Gruev and Kal'onski, *Vuzroditelniiat protses*, 47–50; Ivanova, *Otkhvurlenite "priobshteni,"* 70–3.

84 TsDA, f. 1, op. 28, arkh. ed. 16, 2 (front).
85 Ibid.
86 Ibid.
87 Ibid., 2–3.
88 Ibid., 3.
89 Gruev and Kal'onski, *Vuzroditelniiat protses*; Avramov, *Ikonomikata na "Vuzroditelniia protses"*; Ialumov, *Istoriia na turskata obshtnost v Bulgariia*; Ivanova, *Otkhvurlenite priobshteni*; collections of primary documents in Angelov, *Goliamata ekskurziia*, vols 1 and 2; *Protestnite aktsii na turtsite v Bulgariia*; Baeva and Kalinova, eds, *"Vuzroditelniiat protses": Bulgarskata durzhava i bulgarskite turtsi*; *"Vuzroditelniiat protses": Mezhdunarodni izmereniia.*
90 Marinov, "Ot 'internatsionalizum' kum natsionalizum – chast 2."

CHAPTER FIVE

1 Milevska, "In the Wake of Renaming," 9–10; "The Renaming Machine in the Balkans," 11.
2 Milevska, "In the Wake of Renaming," 9–10.
3 Gómez-Barris, *The Extractive Zone.*
4 Milevska, "In the Wake of Renaming," 78–92.
5 Patterson, *Slavery and Social Death*, 55.
6 Ibid.
7 Ibid., 38–46.
8 Ibid., 53.
9 Ibid., 53–4.
10 Spillers, "Mama's Baby, Papa's Maybe," 72–3; Wolfe, "Settler Colonialism and the Elimination of the Native"; Davis, "Reflections on the Black Woman's Role in the Community of Slaves."
11 I thank Jana Tsoneva for giving me a lead on this particular formulation (informal discussion, New York, 2016).
12 Todorova, "The Ottoman Legacy in the Balkans," 71.
13 Neuburger, *The Orient Within*, 148.
14 Gruev and Kal'onski, *Vuzroditelniiat protses*, 65.
15 Ibid.
16 Akhmed, "Ime, prezime, i dvoistvena lichnost," 177; Zheliazkova, "Sotsialna i kulturna adaptatsiia na bulgarskite izselnitsi v Turtsiia," 20.
17 Akhmed, "Ime, prezime, i dvoistvena lichnost," 177. See also Gruev and Kal'onski, *Vuzroditelniiat protses*, 65n144.
18 Gruev and Kal'onski, *Vuzroditelniiat protses*, 65.

19 Ibid.
20 For more details, see Ivanova, *Otkhvurlenite "priobshteni,"* 72–85; Marinov, "Ot 'internatsionalizum' kum natsionalizum – chast 2"; Trifonov, "Miusiulmanite v politikata na bulgarskata durzhava (1944–89)," 217–19; Gruev and Kal'onski, *Vuzroditelniiat protses*, 49–56.
21 Gruev and Kal'onski, *Vuzroditelniiat protses*, 70–1.
22 For a carefully researched and written account of the 1970–74 events, see Ivanova, *Otkhvurlenite "priobshteni,"* 104–20; Gruev and Kal'onski, *Vuzroditelniiat protses*, 64–87.
23 For further details, see Gruev and Kal'onski, *Vuzroditelniiat protses*, 64–105; Akhmed [Ahmed], "Ime, preimenuvane i dvoistvena identichnost," 168.
24 Different sources vary on these numbers, but they range from 310,000 to 350,000 and above. The numbers here follow Ivanova, *Otkhvurlenite "priobshteni,"* 175; see also *Istinata za "Vuzroditelniia protses,"* 8; Zagorov, *Vuzroditelniiat protses*, 29. A most useful discussion can be found in Veselin Angelov's introduction to the collection of primary sources on the "Great Excursion," in which Angelov also acknowledges the difficulty of establishing accurate numbers: see "Goliamata ekskurziia: Prinuditelnoto izselvane na bulgarskite turtsi."
25 "Nasilieto ne se zabravia lesno."
26 Gruev and Kal'onski, *Vuzroditelniiat protses*, 129.
27 Mutafchieva, "Iashar Shaban," 751.
28 Transcript of Atanasov's statement, *Istinata za "Vuzroditelniia protses,"* 15.
29 Ibid., 18.
30 "They gave people a name book with lists of names they could choose from, close to the Turkish one in structure, phonetically, and in pronunciation (Cemile-Diliana, Yumer-Iulian, Ali-Aleko, and so on). It was required that the name is Bulgarian, and not Western, Russian, and so on. After the name was chosen, a new temporary permit was issued with the new name. The permit served as a temporary ID. You could go to the police station to get your new ID issued. You were required to carry it everywhere, and the lack of an ID was interpreted as a form of resistance." See Akhmed, "Ime, preimenuvane, i dvoistvena identichnost," 167–8.
31 Ibid., 169.
32 *Istinata za "Vuzroditelniia protses,"* 71.
33 Ibid., 70–1.
34 Mutafchieva, "Iashar Shaban," 751.
35 Vaksberg, "Tekhnologiia na zloto (3)," 12.

36 Khalif and Tsankova, "Apokrifnata Iablanska epopeia: Chast 1"; "Apokrifnata Iablanska epopeia: Chast 2."
37 Angelov, "Maiskite protesti na turtsite v Bulgariia."
38 Gorcheva and Skochev, "Az ne sum chuzhdenets, az sum tvoi sin."
39 *Istinata za "Vuzroditelniia protses,"* 94.
40 Akhmed, "Ime, prezime, i dvoistvena identichnost," 167.
41 Ivanova gives an account of the various forms of everyday resistance among the Pomak and Turkish populations. See *Otkhvurlenite "priobshteni."*
42 Avramov, *Ikonomikata na "Vuzroditelniia protses."*
43 As in Shivachevo, Sliven region. See *Istinata za "Vuzroditelniia protses,"* 112.
44 For a narrative of the events, see Marinov, "Ot 'internatsionalizum' kum natsionalizum – chast 2."
45 *Istinata za "Vuzroditelniia protses,"* 60.
46 Vaksberg, "Tekhnologiia na zloto (3)," 12.
47 *Istinata za "Vuzroditelniia protses,"* 99.
48 Ibid., 72–3.
49 Ibid., 98.
50 Avramov has reconstructed this process in great detail in his *Ikonomikata na "Vuzroditelniia protses."*
51 *Istinata za "Vuzroditelniia protses,"* 67–8. See also Avramov, *Ikonomikata na "Vuzroditelniia protses,"* 470–570.
52 "Monday and Tuesday [people] started selling their animals in some places. A sheep together with a lamb would sell for 10–15 levs; in some places they would slaughter the cows and sell the beef for 1 lev per kilogram. We need to mobilize the municipalities so that meat could not be sold without the permission of the agrarian co-operatives and the veterinarians." Statement by Nikolai Zhishev, *Istinata za "Vuzroditelniia protses,"* 109.
53 Ibid., 72.
54 "They start dragging everything they can get a hold of – washing machines, TVs, refrigerators ... We need to strengthen the customs in these regions with additional labour for the summer season." Statement by Todor Zhivkov, *Istinata za "Vuzroditelniia protses,"* 109. For discussion and more details, see Avramov, *Ikonomikata na "Vuzroditelniia protses,"* 425–45.
55 *Istinata za "Vuzroditelniia protses,"* 106.
56 Todor Zhivkov, "Edinstvoto na bulgarskiia narod," 47.
57 Transcript of Todor Zhivkov's statement, *Istinata za "Vuzroditelniia protses,"* 84.

58 Ibid., 85–127. For a detailed reconstruction of the effects on industry, see Avramov, *Ikonomikata na "Vuzroditelniia protses,"* 445–54.

59 Ivanova, *Otkhvurlenite "priobshteni,"* 138.

60 "The most important thing is to convince them to come back to work. If they do not come back to work, we have to take alternative measures. We'll tell them that they would be interned to a different part of the country and their houses expropriated and given to others who would replace them on the job." Statement by Zhivkov, *Istinata za "Vuzroditelniia protses,"* 65. See also the following statement by Zhivkov: "If they don't work, they won't receive passports" – *Istinata za "Vuzroditelniia protses,"* 66.

61 Statement by Pencho Kubadinski, *Istinata za "Vuzroditelniia protses,"* 66.

62 Ibid., 65–8.

63 Khalif and Tsankova, "Apokrifnata Iablanska epopeia (Chast 2)," 16.

64 Akhmed, "Ime, prezime, i dvoistvena lichnost," 166–7.

65 "Nasilieto ne se zabravia lesno," 6.

66 Ghodsee, *Muslim Lives in Eastern Europe*, 34–7.

67 Gruev and Kal'onski, *Vuzroditelniiat protses*, 84.

68 Ibid.

69 Ibid.

70 On the events of the post-1989 period, see Kalinova, "Remembering the 'Revival Process' in Post-1989 Bulgaria," 567–93. On the experiences of Bulgarian-Turkish refugees in Turkey, see Zheliazkova, ed., *Mezhdu adaptatsiiata i nostalgiiata*; Maeva, *Bulgarskite turtsi-preselnitsi v Republika Turtsiia;* Parla, *Precarious Hope*.

71 Some of the most reliable information about the returnees can be found in the collection of primary documents edited and with an introduction by Veselin Angelov, which, however, provides numbers only up until January 1990 (about 56,000 people). See Angelov, ed., *Obratnata vulna*.

CHAPTER SIX

1 Davis, *An Autobiography*, 398.

2 Ibid., 398–9.

3 "Shte razkazvam za suvetskite khora."

4 Ibid.

5 Lorde, "Trip to Russia," 22.

6 "Dobre Doshla, Andzhela!" See also "Vulnuvashti sreshti s Andzhela Deivis."

7 "Dobre Doshla, Andzhela!"

8 Chari and Verdery, "Thinking between the Posts."

9 Ibid., 15.

10 Ibid., 16.

11 Ibid., 14.

12 Slezkine, *Arctic Mirrors*; Martin, *The Affirmative Action Empire*; Francine, *Empire of Nations*.

13 Mark and Slobodian, "Eastern Europe," 3.

14 Popescu, "On the Margins of the Black Atlantic."

15 Ibid., 92–3.

16 Matusevich, "Journeys of Hope"; "Black in the U.S.S.R"; "Probing the Limits of Internationalism"; Quist-Adade, "From Paternalism to Ethnocentrism"; Popescu, *South African Literatures Beyond the Cold War*; Engerman, "The Second World's Third World"; Djagalov, *From Internationalism to Postcolonialism*; Djagalov and Salazkina, "Tashkent '68"; Baldwin, *Beyond the Color Line and the Iron Curtain.*

17 Engerman, "The Second World's Third World," 183–211.

18 Ibid., 197.

19 Djagalov, *From Internationalism to Postcolonialism*; "Premature Postcolonialists"; Djagalov and Salazkina, "Ţashkent '68."

20 Djagalov and Salazkina, "Tashkent '68," 280; Halim, "Afro-Asian Third-Worldism into Global South."

21 Ibid., 281–2.

22 Matusevich, "Journeys of Hope"; "Black in the USSR"; Popescu, *South African Literature Beyond the Cold War*; Mark and Slobodian, "Eastern Europe."

23 Matusevich, "Journeys of Hope."

24 Mark and Slobodian, "Eastern Europe."

25 On concepts of international debt, duty, and solidarity in the political economies of the socialist world, see Apostolova, "Duty and Debt under the Ethos of Internationalism."

26 Mark and Slobodian, "Eastern Europe," 7–8.

27 Mark and Slobodian, "Eastern Europe"; Law, *Red Racisms*; Matusevich, "Journeys of Hope"; "Probing the Limits of Internationalism"; Quist-Adade, "Paternalism to Ethnocentrism"; Baldwin, *Beyond the Color Line and the Iron Curtain.*

28 Karkov and Valiavicharska, "Rethinking East-European Socialism."

29 Renault, "The Idea of Muslim National Communism"; "The Revolution Decentered"; Reno, "Detsentrirana revoliutsiia."

30 Dirlik, "Rethinking Colonialism"; Chatterjee, *Nationalist Thought and the Colonial World.*

31 Dirlik, "Rethinking Colonialism," 437.

32 Chatterjee, *The Nation and Its Fragments*, 36.
33 Dirlik, "Rethinking Colonialism," 438.
34 Joseph, "Indian Ocean Ontology," 53.
35 Ibid., 54. See also Joseph, *Sea Log*, 84–98.
36 Joseph, *Sea Log*, 84–98.
37 Todorova, "Balkanism and Postcolonialism"; Johnson, "To the Center via the Periphery: Interview with Maria Todorova."
38 "Poseshtenieto na dr. Todor Zhivkov v India."

CONCLUSION

1 Valiavicharska, "History's Restless Ruins."
2 See, among others, Fitzpatrick, "Revisionism in Soviet History" and "Revisionism in Retrospect"; David-Fox, Holquist, and Poe, eds, *The Resistance Debate in Russian and Soviet History*. For further discussion, see Valiavicharska, "How the Concept of Totalitarianism Appeared in Late Socialist Bulgaria."
3 Genova, "Material-Semiotic Transformations of the Berlin Wall"; "Za dvete litsa na komunizma dnes: Interview with Boris Buden"; Buden, "Kogato svobodata imashe nuzhda ot detsa."
4 For a discussion of the contradictions in the "liberal vs. authoritarian" opposition in post-socialist Bulgaria, see Medarov, "Mezhdu (anti)avtoritarizma i demokratsiiata." For a critique of post-communist liberalism, see Medarov, "Komunizmut e zlo"; Tsoneva, "Komunizmut e greshka."
5 Tsoneva and Valiavicharska, "Obshtinata planira da vurne pametnika na Purva sofiiska diviziia ot 1934 g."
6 Apostolova et al., *Vremeto e nashe?*; Medarov, "Zagubeni v protivorechiiata na prekhoda."
7 Stanoeva, "Vizualna lustratsiia ili krai na debatite za minaloto?"; Tsoneva, "Of the Past Let Us Make a Crime"; Tsoneva and Valiavicharska, "Obshtinata planira da vurne pametnika na Purva sofiiska diviziia ot 1934 g."
8 Traykov, "From Anti-Communism to Fascism."
9 Marinos, "Anti-Neoliberal Neoliberalism."
10 This trend was interrupted in 2020 thanks to a broad coalition of antifascist activists, who pressured the city to cancel the event.
11 Traykov, "From Anti-Communism to Fascism"; Tsoneva and Valiavicharska, "Obshtinata planira da vurne pametnika na Purva sofiiska diviziia ot 1934 g."; Ghodsee, *The Left Side of History*, 187–200; Medarov, "Zagubeni v protivorechiiata na prekhoda."

12 Traykov, "From Anti-Communism to Fascism."
13 Valiavicharska, "History's Restless Ruins"; "Smutnite ruini na istoriiata."
14 The map was initially misidentified as the map of the territories of Bulgaria as established by the San Stefano Treaty of 1878. But it is unclear if the map has an actual historical referent or represents an imaginary projection of Greater Bulgaria. For a discussion of the different interpretations of the map and its possible representations, see Stefan Dechev, "Pretoplenata mandzha 'San Stefanska Bulgariia.'"
15 On the links between the dismantling of public services and anti-Roma discourses in mainstream media and parliamentary politics, see Kratunkova, "Bulgaria (Not) Only for Bulgarians."
16 For further analysis, see Schultes, "Under Assault: Class and Gender in Bulgaria and Europe Today" (interview with LevFem Collective)."
17 Dinkova, "Strasti po velikata zhenska revoliutsiia," 45
18 Ibid., 46.
19 For further elaboration, see Schultes, "Under Assault: Class and Gender in Bulgaria and Europe Today."
20 Scott, *Conscripts of Modernity*, 1.

Bibliography

GENERAL

Akhmed, Dzhemile. "Ime, preimenuvane i dvoinstvena identichnost (Bulgarskite turtsi po vreme na 'Vuzroditelniia protses')." *Sotsiologicheski problemi* 1–2 (2003): 166–78.

Alderson, David, and Robert Spencer, eds. *For Humanism: Explorations in Theory and Culture*. London: Pluto Press, 2017.

Alexander, M. Jacqui, and Chandra Talpade Mohanty, eds. *Feminist Genealogies, Colonial Legacies, Democratic Futures*. New York: Routledge, 1997.

– "Introduction." In *Feminist Genealogies, Colonial Legacies, Democratic Futures*, edited by M. Jacqui Alexander and Chandra Talpade Mohanty, xiii–xvii. New York: Routledge, 1997.

Allen, Amy. *The End of Progress: Decolonizing the Normative Foundations of Critical Theory*. New York: Columbia University Press, 2016.

Althusser, Louis. *The Humanist Controversy and Other Writings*. Edited by Francois Matheron. London: Verso, 2006.

– *For Marx*. London: Verso, 1999.

– *Philosophy of the Encounter: Later Writings, 1978–1987*. New York: Verso, 2006.

Althusser, Louis, and Etienne Balibar. *Reading Capital*. London: Verso, 1997.

Amos, Valerie, and Pratibha Parmar. "Challenging Imperial Feminism." *Feminist Review* 17 (Autumn 1984): 3–19.

Amrita Basu, ed. *The Challenge of Local Feminisms: Women's Movements in Global Perspective*. Boulder, CO: Westview Press, 1995.

Anderson, Benedict. *Imagined Communities*. London: Verso, 1991.
– *The Spectre of Comparisons: Nationalism, Southeast Asia and the World*. London: Verso, 1998.
Anderson, Bridget. *Doing the Dirty Work? The Global Politics of Domestic Labor*. London: Zed Books, 2000.
Anderson, Kevin. "Fromm, Marx, and Humanism." In *Towards a Human Science: The Relevance of Erich Fromm for Today*, edited by Rainer Funk and Neil McLaughlin, 209–19. Giessen, DE: Psychosozial-Verlag, 2015.
– *Lenin, Hegel, and Western Marxism: A Critical Study*. Urbana: University of Illinois Press, 1995.
– "Lenin's Encounter with Hegel Eighty Years Later: A Critical Assessment." *Science and Society* 59, no. 3 (1995): 298–319.
– *Marx at the Margins: On Nationalism, Ethnicity, and Non-Western Societies*. Chicago: University of Chicago Press, 2010.
– "Sources of Marxist Humanism: Fanon, Kosík and Dunayevskaya." *Quarterly Journal of Ideology* 10, no. 4 (1986): 15–29.
Anderson, Kevin, and Russell Rockwell, eds. *The Dunayevskaya-Marcuse-Fromm Correspondence (1954–1978): Dialogues on Hegel, Marx, and Critical Theory*. Lanham, MD: Lexington Books, 2012.
Anderson, Perry. *Considerations on Western Marxism*. London: Verso, 1976.
– *In the Tracks of Historical Materialism*. London: Verso, 1983.
Anderson, Perry, and Patrick Camiller. *Mapping the West European Left*. New York: Verso, 1994.
Angelov, Veselin. "Goliamata ekskurziia: Prinuditelnoto izselvane na bulgarskite turtsi, nespoluchliviiat opit za etnichesko prochistvane i nai-goliamoto v Evropa preselenie na choveshki masi ot edna v druga durzhava sled Vtorata svetovna voina (iuni–avgust 1989 g.)." In *Goliamata ekskurziia: Prinuditelnoto izselvane na etnicheski turtsi ot Bulgariia, iuni–avgust 1989 g*, vol. 1, edited by Veselin Angelov, 7–36. Sofia: n.p., 2011.
– ed. *Goliamata ekskurziia: Prinuditelnoto izselvane na etnicheski turtsi ot Bulgariia*. 2 vols. Sofia: n.p., 2011.
– "Maiskite protesti na turtsite v Bulgariia prez 1989g." *Vreme za istoriia*, 27 May 2009. http://angelovveselin.blogspot.com/2009/05/1989_27.html.
– ed. *Obratnata vulna: Vrushtane na grazhdanskite prava na bulgarskite turtsi (septemvri 1989–ianuari 1990)*. Sofia: n.p., 2012.
– *Protestnite aktsii na turtsite v Bulgariia, ianuari–mai 1989 g: Dokumenti*. Sofia: n.p., 2010.

Anzaldúa, Gloria. *Borderlands/La Frontera: The New Mestiza*. San Francisco: Aunt Lute Books, 1987.
– *The Gloria Anzaldúa Reader*. Edited by AnaLouise Keating. Durham, NC: Duke University Press, 2009.
– *Light in the Dark: Rewriting Identity, Spirituality, Reality*. Edited by AnaLouise Keiting. Durham, NC: Duke University Press, 2015.
Anzaldúa, Gloria, and Cherríe Moraga. *This Bridge Called My Back: Writings by Radical Women of Color*. Albany: SUNY Press, 2015.
Apostolova, Raia. "Duty and Debt under the Ethos of Internationalism: The Case of the Vietnamese Workers in Bulgaria." *Journal of Vietnamese Studies* 12, no. 1 (2017): 101–25.
– "Moving Labor Power and Historical Forms of Migration: The Internationalist Socialist Worker, the Social Benefit Tourist and the Economic Migrant." PhD diss., Central European University, 2017.
Apostolova, Raia, Stanislav Dodov, Kalina Drenska, and Konstantin Mravov, eds. *Vremeto e nashe?* Sofia: DVersia, 2019.
Appadurai, Arjun. *Modernity at Large: Cultural Dimensions of Globalization*. Minneapolis: University of Minnesota Press, 1996.
Arendt, Hannah. *Between Past and Future: Eight Exercises in Political Thought*. New York: Penguin, 1993.
– *The Origins of Totalitarianism*. New York: Harcourt Brace and Co., 1973.
Arkhiv K. Marksa i F. Engel'sa. Vol. 3. Moscow and Leningrad: Gosudarstvennoe izdatel'stvo, 1927.
Arruzza, Cinzia, Tithi Bhattacharya, and Nancy Fraser. *Feminism for the 99%*. New York: Verso, 2019.
Asad, Talal, ed. *Anthropology and the Colonial Encounter*. New York: Humanity Books, 1973.
– *Formations of the Secular: Christianity, Islam, Modernity*. Stanford, CA: Stanford University Press, 2003.
Atanasov, Georgi. *Istinata za "Vuzroditelniia protses": Dokumenti ot arkhiva na Politbiuro i TsK na BKP*. Sofia: Institut za izsledvane na integratsiiata, 2003.
Atanasova, Ivanka Nedeva. "Lyudmila Zhivkova and the Paradox of Ideology and Identity in Communist Bulgaria." *East European Politics and Societies* 18, no. 2 (2004): 278–315.
Avramov, Rumen. *Ikonomikata na "Vuzroditelniia protses."* Sofia: Center for Advanced Study, 2016.
Baeva, Iskra, and Evgeniia Kalinova, eds. *Vuzroditelniiat protses. Bulgarskata durzhava i bulgarskite turtsi (sredata na 30-te–nachaloto*

na 90-te godini na XX vek). Vol. 1. From the series *Akhivite govoriat*, vol. 55. Sofia: Durzhavna Agentsiia "Arkhivi," 2009.

– eds. *"Vuzroditelniiat protses." Mezhdunarodni izmereniia (1984–1989)*. Vol. 2. From the series *Akhivite govoriat*, vol. 61. Sofia: Durzhavna Agentsiia "Arkhivi," 2009.

Baeva, Iskra. "Choveshkite izmereniia na 'vuzroditelniia protses.'" In *Novi izvori za "vuzroditelniia protses,"* 83–94. Sofia: Paradigma, 2011.

– *Iztochna Evropa sled Stalin, 1953–56*. Sofia: Universitetsko izdatelstvo "Sv. Kliment Ohridski," 1995.

– "Sotsialnoikonomicheski predpostavki za i posleditsi ot 'vuzroditelniia protses,'" In *Evraziiski khorizonti: Minalo i nastoiashte. Sbornik v chest na prof. d.i.n. Valeri Stoianov*, 154–70. Sofia: III-BAN, 2011.

– "'Vuzroditelniiat protses' kato mezhdunaroden problem. Bulgarskata durzhava i 'vuzroditelniiat protses' na mezhdunarodnata arena." In *"Vuzroditelniiat protses." Mezhdunarodni izmereniia (1984–1989)*. From the series *Arkhivite govoriat*, vol. 61, edited by Iskra Baeva and Evgeniia Kalinova, 5–13. Sofia: Durzhavna Agentsiia "Arkhivi," 2009.

– "'Vuzroditelniiat protses' v Bulgariia kato natsionalen i regionalen konflikt (Prichini za vuznikvane i nachini za preodoliavane)." In *Granichni i etnonatsionalni konflikti v Sredna i Iugoiztochna Evropa*, 99–121. Sofia: BAN, Institut po balkanistika, 2008.

Bagaturiia, Georgii. "Ekonomichesko-filosofskiie rukopisi." In *Filosofskii entsiklopedicheskii slovar*, 791–2. Moscow: Sovetskaia entsiklopediia, 1983.

Bagaturiia, G.A., and V.S. Vigodskii. *Ekonomicheskoe nasledie Karla Marksa: Istoriia, soderzhnie, metodologiia*. Moscow: Mysl', 1976.

– *Ikonomicheskoto nasledstvo na Karl Marks: Istoriia, sudurzhanie, metodologiia*. Sofia: Nauka i izkustvo, 1983.

Baker, Catherine. "Postcoloniality without Race? Racial Exceptionalism and Southeast European Cultural Studies." *Interventions: International Journal of Postcolonial Studies* 20, no. 6 (2018): 759–84.

Bakić-Hayden, Milica. "Nesting Orientalisms: The Case of Former Yugoslavia." *Slavic Review* 54, no. 4 (1995): 917–31.

Baldwin, Kate. *Beyond the Color Line and the Iron Curtain: Reading Encounters between Black and Red, 1922–1963*. Durham, NC: Duke University Press, 2002.

Balibar, Etienne, and Immanuel Wallerstein. *Race, Nation, Class: Ambiguous Identities*. London: Verso, 1988.

Barbagallo, Camille. "Leaving Home: Slavery and the Politics of Reproduction." *Viewpoint Magazine*, 31 October 2015. https://www.

viewpointmag.com/2015/10/31/leaving-home-slavery-and-the-politics-of-reproduction.

Battacharya, Tithi, ed. *Social Reproduction Theory: Remapping Class, Recentering Oppression*. London: Pluto Press, 2017.

Bhabha, Homi. *The Location of Culture*. London: Routledge, 1994.

Bhavnani, Kum-Kum, and Margaret Coulson. "Transforming Socialist Feminism: The Challenge of Racism." *Feminist Review* 23 (1986): 81–92.

Biuksenshiuts, Ulrihk. *Maltsinstvenata politika v Bulgariia: Politikata na BKP kum evrei, romi, pomatsi i turtsi, 1944–1989*. Sofia: Mezhdunaroden tsentur po problemite na maltsinstvata i kulturnite vzaimodeistviia, 2000.

Bjelić, Dušan. "Toward a Genealogy of the Balkan Discourses on Race." *Interventions: International Journal of Postcolonial Studies* 20, no. 6 (2018): 906–29.

Boseva, Rositsa, and Varvara Kirilova. "Drugite maiki na nashite detsa." *Zhenata dnes* 11 (1968): 12–13.

Bridgewater, Pamela. *Breeding a Nation: Reproductive Slavery, the Thirteenth Amendment and the Pursuit of Freedom*. Brooklyn, NY: South End Press, 2014.

Bringa, Tone. *Being Muslim the Bosnian Way: Identity and Community in a Central Bosnian Village*. Princeton, NJ: Princeton University Press, 1995.

Brown, Wendy. *Edgework: Critical Essays on Knowledge and Politics*. Princeton, NJ: Princeton University Press, 2005.

– *Politics Out of History*. Princeton, NJ: Princeton University Press, 2001.

– *Regulating Aversion: Tolerance in the Age of Identity and Empire*. Princeton, NJ: Princeton University Press, 2006.

– *States of Injury: Power and Freedom in Late Modernity*. Princeton, NJ: Princeton University Press, 1995.

Brubaker, Rogers. *Nationalism Reframed: Nationhood and the National Question in the New Europe*. Cambridge: Cambridge University Press, 1996.

Büchsenschütz, Ulrich. *Minderheiten Politik in Bulgarien: Die Politik der Bulgaristischen Partei gegenüber den Juden, Roma, Romaken, and Türken 1944 bis 1989*. Berlin: Freien Universitat, 1997.

Buck-Morss, Susan. *Dreamworld and Catastrophe: The Passing of Mass Utopia East and West*. Cambridge, MA: MIT Press, 2000.

Buden, Boris. "Kogato svobodata imashe nuzhda ot detsa." In *Vremeto e nashe?*, edited by Raia Apostolova, Stanislav Dodov, Kalina Drenska, and Konstantin Mravov, 119–41. Sofia: DVersia, 2019.

Burton, Antoinette. *Burdens of History: British Feminists, Indian Women, and Imperial Culture, 1865–1915*. Chapel Hill: University of North Carolina Press, 1994.

Butler, Judith. *Excitable Speech: A Politics of the Performative*. New York: Routledge, 1997.

– *Gender Trouble*. New York: Routledge, 1990.

– *The Psychic Life of Power: Theories in Subjection*. Stanford, CA: Stanford University Press, 1997.

Cabral, Amilcar. *Return to the Source: Selected Speeches of Amilcar Cabral*. New York: Monthly Review Press with Africa Information Service, 1973.

Carby, Hazel. "White Woman Listen!" In *Black British Feminism*, edited by Heidi Safia Mirza, 45–53. London: Routledge, 1997.

Carew, Joy Gleason. *Blacks, Reds, and Russians: Sojourners in Search of the Soviet Promise*. New Brunswick, NJ: Rutgers University Press, 2008.

Castro, Fidel. "'The Universal Conscience' Speech to the Cultural Congress of Havana." In *The New Left Reader*, edited by Carl Oglesby, 186–206. New York: Grove Press, 1969.

Césaire, Aimé. *Discourse on Colonialism*. New York: Monthly Review Press, 1972.

Chakrabarty, Dipesh. *Provincializing Europe: Postcolonial Thought and Historical Difference*. Princeton, NJ: Princeton University Press, 2000.

Chang, Grace. *Disposable Domestics: Immigrant Women Workers in the Global Economy*. Brooklyn, NY: South End Press, 2000.

Chari, Sharad, and Katherine Verdery. "Thinking between the Posts: Postcolonialism, Postsocialism, and Ethnography after the Cold War." *Comparative Studies in Society and History* 51, no. 1 (2009): 6–34.

Chatterjee, Partha. *The Nation and Its Fragments: Colonial and Postcolonial Histories*. Princeton, NJ: Princeton University Press, 1993.

– *Nationalist Thought and the Colonial World: A Derivative Discourse*. Minneapolis: University of Minnesota Press, 1986.

Cheah, Pheng. *Spectral Nationality: Passages of Freedom from Kant to Postcolonial Literatures of Liberation*. New York: Columbia University Press, 2003.

"Chovekut i sotsializmut." *Zhenata dnes* 8 (1974): 16–17.

Chukhrov, Keti, Aleksei Penzin, and Valeri Podoroga. "Marx against Marxism, Marxism against Marx." *Stasis* 5, no. 2 (2017): 266–88.

Clark, Katerina. *The Soviet Novel: History as Ritual*. Chicago: University of Chicago Press, 1981.

Cramer, Jon. "Race, Class, and Social Reproduction in the Urban Present: The Case of the Detroit Water and Sewage System." *Viewpoint Magazine*, 31 October 2015. https://www.viewpointmag.com/2015/10/31/race-class-and-social-reproduction-in-the-urban-present-the-case-of-the-detroit-water-and-sewage-system/.

Crocker, David. *Praxis and Democratic Socialism: The Critical Theory of Markovic and Stojanovic*. Atlantic Highlands, NJ: Humanities Press; Brighton, UK: Harvester Press, 1983.

"Da otmenim 'vtorata smiana'!" *Zhenata dnes* 6 (1967): 1.

Dalla Costa, Mariarosa. *Family, Welfare, and the State: Between Progressivism and the New Deal*. Brooklyn, NY: Common Notions, 2015.

David-Fox, Michael. *Crossing Borders: Modernity, Ideology, and Culture in Russia and the Soviet Union*. Pittsburgh: University of Pittsburgh Press, 2015.

– "'Modernost' v Rossii i SSSR: Otsustvuiushtaia, obshtaia, al'ternativnaia ili perepletennaia?" *NLO* 140 (2016): 19–46.

David-Fox, Michael, Peter Holquist, and Marshall Poe, eds. *The Resistance Debate in Russian and Soviet History*. Bloomington: Indiana University Press, 2003.

Davis, Angela. "The Approaching Obsolescence of Housework: A Working-Class Perspective." In *Women, Race, and Class*, 222–44. New York: Vintage Books, 1983.

– *An Autobiorgraphy*. New York: International Publishers, 1974.

– "Racism, Birth Control, and Reproductive Rights. In *Women, Race, and Class*, 2020–21. New York: Vintage Books, 1983.

– "Reflections on the Black Woman's Role in the Community of Slaves." In *The Angela Y. Davis Reader*, edited by Joy James, 111–28. Malden, MA: Blackwell, 1998.

– *Women, Culture, Politics*. New York: Vintage Books, 1990.

– *Women, Race, and Class*. New York: Vintage Books, 1983.

Dechev, Stefan. "Pretoplenata mandzha 'San Stefanska Bulgariia.'" *Marginalia*, 3 February 2018. www.marginalia.bg/aktsent/pretoplenata-mandzha-sanstefanska-balgariya.

Deivis, Andzhela. "Solidarnost." *Komsomolska iskra* (Plovdiv), 1 February 1971, 4.

Delphy, Christine. *Close to Home: A Materialist Analysis of Women's Oppression*. Amherst: University of Massachusetts Press, 1984.

Delphy, Cristine, and Diana Leonard. *Familiar Exploitation: A New Analysis of Marriage in Contemporary Western Societies*. Oxford: Polity Press, 1992.

Derrida, Jacques. *Limited Inc.* Evanston, IL: Northwestern University Press, 1988.

– *Margins of Philosophy.* Chicago: University of Chicago Press, 1982.

– *Specters of Marx: The State of the Debt, the Work of Mourning, and the New International.* New York: Routledge, 1994.

Dimitrova, Blaga. "Belezhki, poiasneniia." In *Subrani tvorbi* vol. 4, 297–323. Sofia: Tikh-Ivel, 2004.

– "Nazum Hikmet v Bulgariia: Putepis." In *Subrani tvorbi* vol. 4, 41–125. Sofia: Tikh-Ivel, 2004.

Dinkova, Maria. "Labirinti na lekomislieto i bezotgovornostta." *Zhenata dnes* 4 (1972): 12–13.

– "Pogled vurkhu istoriiata na bulgarskoto semeistvo." In *Moeto budeshto semeistvo*, edited by Pavlina Popova, 11–36. Sofia: Narodna mladezh, 1984.

– "Semeistvoto i sotsialnata realizatsiia na mladiia chovek." In *Mladezhta – Probelmi i izsledvaniia*, edited by Petur-Emil Mitev, 57–73. Sofia: Narodna mladezh, 1985.

– *Sotsialen portret na bulgarskata zhena.* Sofia: Profizdat, 1980.

– "Strasti po velikata zhenska revoliutsiia." *Vezni* 5 (2003): 23–37.

– "Strasti po velikata zhenska revoliutsiia (produlzhenie ot br. 5)." *Vezni* 6–7 (2003): 23–46.

– "Strasti po velikata zhenska revoliutsiia. Chast vtora: speechwriter." *Vezni* 6 (2008): 31–62.

– "Suvremenna zhena? Da! A Suvremenen muzh?" *Zhenata dnes* 9 (1966): 4–5.

– "Tendentsii i problemi vuv formiraneto na mladoto semeistvo." In *Mladoto semeistvo*, edited by Maria Dinkova, 96–163. Sofia: Narodna mladezh, 1985.

– "Tendentsii i problemi vuv formiraneto, funktsioniraneto i razvitieto na mladoto semeistvo." In *mladoto semeistvo*, edited by Maria Dinkova, 9–42. Sofia: Narodna mladezh, 1985.

Dirlik, Arif. "Rethinking Colonialism: Globalization, Postcolonialism, and the Nation." *Interventions: International Journal of Postcolonial Studies* 4, no. 3 (2002): 428–48.

"Diskusiia: Mladezhta v perspektivata na 80te godini. Problemi i tendentsii." In *Mladezhta – problemi i izsledvaniia*, edited by Petur-Emil Mitev, 203–28. Sofia: Narodna mladezh, 1985.

Djagalov, Rossen. *From Internationalism to Postcolonialism: Between the Second and the Third Worlds.* Montreal: McGill-Queen's University Press, 2020.

– "Premature Postcolonialists: The Afro-Asian Writers Association and Soviet Engagement with Africa." *LeftEast*, 3 November 2017. https://www.criticatac.ro/lefteast/premature-postcolonialists-the-afro-asian-writers-association-and-soviet-engagement-with-africa.

– "Progress Publishers: A Short History." In *The East Was Read: Socialist Culture in the Third World*, edited by Vijay Prashad, 78–86. New Delhi: LeftWord Books, 2019.

Djagalov, Rossen, and Masha Salazkina. "Tashkent '68: A Cinematic Contact Zone." *Slavic Review* 75, no. 2 (2016): 279–98.

"Dobre doshla, Andzhela!" *Narodna mladezh*, 17 September 1972, 1, 3.

Dosev, P. *Teoriia otrazheniia: Ocherki po teorii poznaniia dialekticheskogo materializma.* Moscow: Gosudarstvenoe sots.-ekon. izdatel'stvo, 1936.

Du Bois, W.E.B. *The Souls of Black Folk*. Boston: Bedford Books, 1997.

Dukhteva, Penka. "Panorama na zhenskiia trud." *Zhenata dnes* 4 (1971): 3–4, 19.

Dukhteva, Penka, and Maria Dinkova. "Zhenata v stroitelstvoto: problemi i perspektivi [Part 1]." *Zhenata dnes* 7 (1967): 4–5.

– "Zhenata v stroitelstvoto: problem i perspektivi [Part 2]." *Zhenata dnes* 8 (1967): 6–7.

Dunayevskaya, Raya. *Marxism and Freedom: From 1776 to Today.* New York: Humanities Books, 2000 [1958].

– "Marx's Humanism Today." In *Socialist Humanism: An International Symposium*, edited by Erich Fromm, 68–83. New York: Anchor Books, 1966.

– *Philosophy and Revolution: From Hegel to Sartre, and from Marx to Mao*. New York: Delacorte, 1973.

Dureva, Velislava. "Boiana, ulitsa Sekvoia." Interview with Todor Zhivkov. *Duma* 56, 25 February 1991.

Dussel, Enrique. *Twenty Theses on Politics*. Durham, NC: Duke University Press, 2008.

Edholm, Felicity, Olivia Harris, and Kate Young. "Conceptualizing Women." *Critique of Anthropology* 3 (1978): 101–30.

Ehrenreich, Barbara. *Nickel and Dimed: On (Not) Getting by in America*. New York: Henry Holt, 2001.

Ehrenreich, Barbara, and Arlie Hochschild, eds. *Global Woman: Nannies, Maids, and Sex Workers in the New Economy.* New York: Henry Holt, 2002.

Elenkov, Ivan. *Kulturniiat front: Bulgarskata kultura prez epokhata na komunizma – politichesko upravlenie, ideologicheski osnovaniia, institutsionalni rezhimi*. Sofia: Ciela/Institut za izsledvane na blizkoto minalo, 2008.

Eminov, Ali. "Education in the Mother Tongue: Turkish in Bulgaria." In *Beyond the Borders*, edited by Lora Tasheva, 118–32. Sofia: Izdatelska Kushta Marin Drinov, 2019.

– "Social Construction of Identities: Pomaks in Bulgaria," *JEMIE* 2 (2007). www.ecmi.de/publications/detail/issue-22007-59.

– *Turkish and Other Muslim Minorities in Bulgaria*. New York: Routledge, 1997.

– "Turks and Tatars in Bulgaria and the Balkans." *Nationalities Papers* 28, no. 1 (2000): 129–64.

– "The Turks of Bulgaria: 1945–1983." In *The Turkish* World, vol. 6, edited by Celal Güzel, C. Cem Oğuz, and Osman Karatay, 584–91. Ankara: Yeni Türkiye, 2002.

Engerman, David. "The Second World's Third World." *Kritika: Explorations in Russian and Eurasian History* 12, no. 1 (2011): 183–211.

Epstein, Barbara. "On the Disappearance of Socialist Humanism." *Brumaria* 22 (2010): 51–70.

Esmeir, Samera. *Juridical Humanity: A Colonial History*. Stanford, CA: Stanford University Press, 2012.

Fanon, Frantz. *Alienation and Freedom*. Edited by Jean Khalfa and Robert J.C. Young. London: Bloomsbury Academic, 2018.

– *Black Skin, White Masks*. New York: Grove Press, 1967.

– *A Dying Colonialism*. New York: Grove Press, 1965.

– *The Wretched of the Earth*. Translated by Richard Philcox. New York: Grove Press, 2004.

Farris, Sara. "Social Reproduction, Surplus Populations and the Role of Migrant Women." *Viewpoint Magazine*, 31 October 2015. https://www.viewpointmag.com/2015/11/01/social-reproduction-and-surplus-populations.

Federici, Silvia. *Caliban and the Witch: Women, the Body, and Primitive Accumulation*. Brooklyn, NY: Autonomedia, 2004.

– *Revolution at Point Zero: Housework, Reproduction, and Feminist Struggle*. Oakland, CA: PM Press, 2012.

– "Social Reproduction Theory: History, Issues and Present Challenges." *Radical Philosophy* 2, no. 4 (2019): 55–7.

Feher, Ferenc, and Agnes Heller. *Eastern Left, Western Left: Totalitarianism, Freedom, and Democracy*. Atlantic Highlands, NJ: Humanities Press International, 1987.

Ferreira da Silva, Denise. "Before Man: Sylvia Wynter's Rewriting of the Modern Episteme." In *Sylvia Wynter: On Being Human As Praxis*, edited by Katherine McKittrick, 90–105. Durham, NC: Duke University Press, 2015, 90-105.

Firestone, Shulamith. *The Dialectic of Sex: The Case for Feminist Revolution*. New York: Farrar, Straus and Giroux, 2003.

Fitzpatrick, Sheila. "Afterword: Revisionism Revisited." *Russian Review* 45, no. 4 (1986): 409–13.

– *The Cultural Front: Power and Culture in Revlutionary Russia*. Ithaca, NY: Cornell University Press, 1992.

– *Everyday Stalinism: Ordinary Life in Extraordinary Times*. New York: Oxford University Press, 1999.

– "New Perspectives on Stalinism." *Russian Review* 45, no. 4 (1986): 357–73.

– "Revisionism in Retrospect: A Personal View." *Slavic Review* 67, no. 8 (2007): 682–704.

– "Revisionism in Soviet History." *History and Theory* 46, no. 4 (2007): 77–91.

– *Stalin's Peasants: Resistance and Survival in the Russian Village after Collectivization*. New York: Oxford University Press, 1994.

Foner, Philip S., ed. *The Black Panthers Speak*. Chicago: Haymarket Books, 2014.

Fortunati, Leopoldina. *The Arcane of Reproduction: Housework, Prostitution, Labor, and Capital*. Brooklyn, NY: Autonomedia, 1995.

Foucault, Michel. *The Birth of Biopolitics: Lectures at the College de France, 1978–1979*. New York: Palgrave Macmillan, 2008.

– *The History of Sexuality: An Introduction*. Vol. 1. New York: Vintage Books, 1990.

– *Security, Territory, Population: Lectures at the College de France, 1977–1978*. New York: Palgrave Macmillan, 2007.

– *Society Must Be Defended: Lectures at the College de France, 1975–1976*. New York: Picador, 2003.

Fox, Cybelle. *Three Worlds of Relief: Race, Immigration, and the American Welfare State from the Progressive Era to the New Deal*. Princeton, NJ: Princeton University Press, 2012.

Fromm, Erich. *Marx's Concept of Man*. London: Continuum, 2003.

– ed. *Socialist Humanism: An International Symposium*. New York: Anchor Books, 1966.

Funk, Nanette, and Magda Mueller, eds. *Gender Politics and Post-Communism: Reflections from Eastern Europe and the Former Soviet Union*. New York: Routledge, 1993.

Funk, Rainer, and Neil McLaughlin, eds. *Towards a Human Science: The Relevance of Erich Fromm for Today*. Giessen, DE: Psychosozial-Verlag, 2015.

Gal, Susan, and Gail Kligman. *The Politics of Gender after Socialism: A Comparative Historical Essay.* Princeton, NJ: Princeton University Press, 2000.

Genova, Neda. "Material-Semiotic Transformations of the Berlin Wall in Post-Communist Bulgaria." *Identities: Journal for Politics, Gender, and Culture* 16, nos 1–2 (Summer–Winter 2019): 78–90.

– "Za dvete litsa na komunizma dnes." Interview with Boris Buden. In *Borbi bez vreme*, 47–62. Sofia: DVersia, 2018.

Geyer, Michael, and Sheila Fitzpatrick. *Beyond Totalitarianism: Stalinism and Nazism Compared.* Cambridge: Cambridge University Press, 2009.

Ghamari-Tabrizi, Behrooz. *Foucault in Iran: Islamic Revolution after the Enlightenment.* Minneapolis: University of Minnesota Press, 2016.

Ghodsee, Kristen. "Feminism-by-Design: Emerging Capitalisms, Cultural Feminism, and Women's Nongovernmental Organizations in Postsocialist Eastern Europe." *Signs: Journal of Women in Culture and Society* 29, no. 3 (Spring 2004): 727–53.

– "Historiographical Challenges of Exploring Second World–Third World Alliances in the International Women's Movement." *Global Social Policy* 14, no. 2 (2014): 244–64.

– *The Left Side of History: World War II and the Unfulfilled Promise of Communism in Eastern Europe.* Durham, NC: Duke University Press, 2015.

– *Muslim Lives in Eastern Europe: Gender, Ethnicity, and the Transformation of Islam in Postsocialist Bulgaria.* Princeton, NJ: Princeton University Press, 2010.

– "Pressuring the Politburo: The Committee of the Bulgarian Women's movement and State Socialist Feminism." *Slavic Review* 73, no. 3 (Fall 2014): 538–61.

– "Rethinking State Socialist Mass Women's Organizations: The Committee of the Bulgarian Women's Movement and the United Nations' Decade of Women, 1975–84." *Journal of Women's History* 24, no. 4 (2012): 49–73.

– *Second World, Second Sex: Socialist Women's Activism and Global Solidarity during the Cold War.* Durham, NC: Duke University Press, 2019.

Giardini, Federica, and Anna Simone. "Reproduction as Paradigm: Elements for a Feminist Political Economy." *Viewpoint Magazine*,

31 October 2015. https://www.viewpointmag.com/2015/10/31/reproduction-as-paradigm-elements-for-a-feminist-political-economy.
Gilmore, Ruth. *Golden Gulag: Prisons, Surplus, Crisis, and Opposition in Globalizing California*. Berkeley: University of California Press, 2007.
Gilroy, Paul. *The Black Atlantic: Modernity and Double Consciousness*. Cambridge, MA: Harvard University Press, 1993.
Goldman, Wendy. *Women at the Gates: Gender and Industry in Stalin's Russia*. Cambridge: Cambridge University Press, 2002.
– *Women, the State, and Revolution: Soviet Family Policy and Social Life, 1917–1936*. Cambridge: Cambridge University Press, 1993.
Golubović, Zagorka. *Staljinizam i socijalizam: nastanak staljinizma u ideologiji i praksi sovjetskog društva*. Belgrade: Filozofsko društvo Srbije, 1982.
Gómez-Barris, Macarena. *The Extractive Zone: Social Ecologies and Decolonial Perspectives*. Durham, NC: Duke University Press, 2017.
Gorcheva, Daniela, and Borislav Skochev. "Az ne sum chuzhdenets, az sum tvoi sin." *Mediapool*, 8 June 2016. http://www.mediapool.bg/az-ne-sam-chuzhdenets-az-sam-tvoi-sin-news149481.html.
Gordon, Lewis. *Bad Faith and Antiblack Racism*. New York: Humanity Books, 1999.
– *Fanon and the Crisis of European Man: An Essay on Philosophy and the Human Sciences*. New York: Routledge, 1995.
– "Shifting the Geography of Reason in an Age of Disciplinary Decadence." *Transmodernity: Journal of Peripheral Cultural Production of the Luso-Hispanic World* 1, no. 2 (2011): 95–102.
Gospodinov, Konstantin. "Realizatsiia i sotsializatsiia na mladezhta: Filosofsko-sotsiologicheski uvod." *Problemi na mladezhta* 4 (1983): 36–47.
Greenhalgh, Susan. *Just One Child: Science and Policy in Deng's China*. Berkeley: University of California Press, 2008.
Greenhalgh, Susan, and Edwin A. Winkler. *Governing China's Population: From Leninist to Neoliberal Politics*. Stanford: Stanford University Press, 2005.
Gruev, Mikhail. "Ideologicheskiiat zavoi kum natsionalizum i politikata na BKP kum miusiulmanskoto naselenie v stranata v kraia na 50-te godini i prez 60-te godini na 20 vek." *Liberalen pregled*, 7 April 2014. http://www.librev.com/index.php/2013-03-30-08-56-39/prospects/science/2351-50-60-20.
– *Mezhdu petoluchkata i polumesetsa: Buglarite miusiulmani i politicheskiiat rezhim (1944–1959)*. Sofia: IK Kota, 2003.

– *Preorani slogove: Kolektivizatsiia i sotsialna promiana v bulgarskiia severozapad 40-te i 50-te godini na XX vek*. Sofia: Ciela/Institut za izsledvane na blizkoto minalo, 2009.

Gruev, Mikhail, and Aleksei Kal'onski. *Vuzroditelniiat protses: Miusiulmanskite obshtnosti i komunisticheskiia rezhim*. Sofia: Ciela/ Institut za izsledvane na blizkoto minalo, 2008.

Guha, Ranajit. *Elementary Aspects of Peasant Insurgency in Colonial India*. Durham, NC: Duke University Press, 1999.

Guha, Ranajit, and Gayatri Chakravorty Spivak, eds. *Selected Subaltern Studies*. New York and Oxford: Oxford University Press, 1988.

Halberstam, Jack. *In a Queer Time and Place: Transgender Bodies, Subcultural Lives*. New York: New York University Press, 2005.

Halberstam, Judith. *Female Masculinity*. Durham, NC: Duke University Press, 1998.

Halfin, Igal, and Jochen Hellbeck. "Rethinking the Stalinist Subject: Stephen Kotkin's *Magnetic Mountain* and the State of Soviet Historical Studies." *Jahrbücher für Geschichte Osteuropas* 3, no. 44 (1996): 456–63.

Halim, Hala. "Afro-Asian Third-Worldism into Global South: The Case of *Lotus* Journal." *Global South Studies: A Collective Publication with The Global South*, 22 November 2017. https://globalsouthstudies.as.virginia.edu/key-moments/afro-asian-third-worldism-global-south-case-lotus-journal.

Haraway, Donna. *Simians, Cyborgs, and Women: The Reinvention of Nature*. London: Free Association Books, 1991.

Hellbeck, Jochen. *Revolution on My Mind: Writing a Diary under Stalin*. Cambridge, MA: Harvard University Press, 2006.

Hellbeck, Jochen. "Speaking Out: Languages of Affirmation and Dissent in Stalinist Russia." In *The Resistance Debate in Russian and Soviet History*, edited by Michael David-Fox, Peter Holquist, and Marshall Poe, 102–37. Bloomington: Indiana University Press, 2003.

Hendessi, Mandana. "Fourteen Thousand Women Meet: Report from Nairobi, July 1985." *Feminist Review* 17 (Autumn 1984): 147–56.

Henry, Paget. "Lewis Gordon, Africana Phenomenology and the Crisis of European Man." *C.L.R. James Journal* 14, no. 1 (Spring 2008): 71–101.

Hirsch, Francine. *Empire of Nations: Ethnographic Knowledge and the Making of the Soviet Union*. Ithaca, NY: Cornell University Press, 2005.

History of the Communist Party of the Soviet Union (Bolsheviks): Short Course. New York: International Publishers, 1939.

Hoffmann, David L., and Annette F. Timm. "Urban Biopolitics: Reproductive Policies, Gender Roles, and Sexuality in Nazi Germany and the Soviet Union." In *Beyond Totalitarianism: Stalinism and Nazism Compared*, edited by Michael Geyer and Sheila Fitzpatrick, 87–132. Cambridge: Cambridge University Press, 2009.

Hoffmann, David L. and Yanni Kostonis, eds. *Russian Modernity: Politics, Knowledge, Practices*. New York: Palgrave Macmillan, 2000.

hooks, bell. "Black Women: Shaping Feminist Theory." In *The Black Feminist Reader*, edited by Joy James and T. Denean Sharpley-Whiting, 131–45. Malden, MA: Blackwell, 2000.

– *Feminist Theory: From Margin to Center*. 2nd ed. Cambridge, MA: South End Press, 2000.

– "Sisterhood: Political Solidarity between Women." *Feminist Review* 23 (Summer 1986): 125–38.

Horvat, Srećko, and Igor Štiks, eds. *Welcome to the Desert of Post-Socialism: Radical Politics after Yugoslavia*. London: Verso, 2015.

Humphrey, Caroline. *The Unmaking of Soviet Life: Everyday Economies after Socialism*. Ithaca, NY: Cornell University Press, 2002.

Hutchful, Eboe. "Eastern Europe: Consequences for Africa." *Review of African Political Economy* 50, no. 18 (1991): 51–9.

Ialumov, Ibrakhim. *Istoriia na turskata obshtnost v Bulgariia*. Sofia: IK Ilinda-Evtimov, 2002.

Iankov, Georgi. "Formiraneto i razvitieto na bulgarskata natsiia i Vuzroditelniiat protses." In *Problemi na razvitieto na bulgarskata narodnost i natsiia*, edited by Georgi Iankov, Strashimir Dimitrov, and Orlin Zagorov, 7–32. Sofia: Bulgarska Akademiia na Naukite, 1988.

– *Niakoi osobenosti na razvitieto na bulgarskata natsiia*. Sofia: BAN, 1988.

– *Stranitsi ot bulgarskata istoriia: Ocherk za isliamiziranite bulgari i natsionalnovuzroditelniia* protses. Sofia: Nauka i izkustvo, 1989.

Iankov, Georgi, Strashimir Dimitrov, and Orlin Zagorov, eds. *Problemi na razvitieto na bulgarskata narodnost i natsiia*. Sofia: Bulgarska Akademiia na Naukite, 1988.

Iğmen, Ali. *Speaking Soviet with an Accent: Culture and Power in Kyrgyzstan*. Pittsburgh: University of Pittsburgh Press, 2012.

Ignatova, Liuba. "Na vtorata smiana – ne!" *Zhenata dnes* 5 (1968): 10.

Il'enkov, E.V. *Dialektika abstraktnogo i konkretnogo v "Kapitale" Marksa*. Moscow: Nauka, 1960.

Ilyenkov, Evald. *Leninist Dialectics and the Metaphysics of Positivism*. London: New Park, 1982.

Iovchuk, M.T., ed. *"Kapital" Marksa, filosofiia i sovremennost'*. Moscow: Nauk, 1968.

Ivanova, Evgeniia. *Otkhvurlenite "priobshteni," ili protsesa, narechen "vuzroditelen" (1912–1989)*. Sofia: Institut za iztochnoevropeiska khumanitaristika, 2002.

Ivanova, Veneta. *Bulgarska monumentalna skulptura: razvitie i problemi*. Sofia: Bulgarski khudozhnik, 1978.

Izvori i izsledvaniia za bulgarskiia kharakter na naselenieto ot iztochnite Rodopi. Khaskovo: Okruzhen Istoricheski Muzei, 1985.

James, C.L.R. *The Black Jacobins: Toussaint L'Ouverture and the San Domingo Revolution*. New York: Vintage Books, 1989.

– *Marxism for Our Times*. Jackson: University Press of Mississippi, 1999.

– *Notes on Dialectics: Hegel, Marx, Lenin*. London: Allison and Busby, 1980.

– *On the "Negro Question."* Jackson: University Press of Mississippi, 1996.

– *State Capitalism and World Revolution*. Chicago: Charles Kerr, 1986.

James, Joy, and T. Denean Sharpley-Whiting, eds. *The Black Feminist Reader*. Malden, MA: Blackwell, 2000.

James, Selma. *Sex, Race, and Class: The Perspective of Winning. A Selection of Writings, 1952–2011*. Oakland, CA: PM Press, 2012.

Jay, Martin. *Marxism and Totality*. Berkeley: University of California Press, 1984.

Jayawardena, Kumari. *Feminism and Nationalism in the Third World*. London and New York: Verso, 2016.

– ed. *The White Woman's Other Burden: Western Women and South Asia during British Rule*. New York: Routledge, 1995.

Johnson, Dana. "To the Center via the Periphery: Interview with Maria Todorova." *Europe Now Journal*, 5 June 2018. https://www.europenowjournal.org/2018/06/24/to-the-center-via-the-periphery-an-interview-with-maria-todorova/.

Johnson, Walter. *River of Dark Dreams: Slavery and Empire in the Cotton Kingdom*. Cambridge, MA: Harvard University Press, 2013.

Jones, Jacqueline. *The Labor of Love, the Labor of Sorrow: Black Women, Work, and the Family from Slavery to the Present*. New York: Basic Books, 2010 [1985].

Joseph, May. "Indian Ocean Ontology." In *Reimagining Indian Ocean Worlds*, edited by Smriti Srinivas, Bettina Ng'weno, and Neelima Jeychandran, 42–57. London: Routledge, 2020.

– *Sea Log: Indian Ocean to New York*. New York: Routledge, 2019.

Kaganovsky, Lilya. *How the Soviet Man Was Unmade: Cultural Fantasy and Male Subjectivity under Stalin*. Pittsburgh: University of Pittsburgh Press, 2008.

Kalinova, Evgenia. "Remembering the 'Revival Process' in Post-1989 Bulgaria." In *Remembering Communism: Private and Public Recollection of Lived Experience in Southeast Europe*, edited by Maria Todorova, Augusta Dimou, and Stefan Troebst, 567–93. Budapest and New York: Central European University Press, 2014.

Kalinova, Evgeniia. "Bulgaro-Iugoslavskite otnosheniia 1953–63 – mezhdu ideologiiata i pragmatizma." In *Problemut Iztok-Zapad. Bulgariia i Balkanite: Statii, dokumentalni materiali i diskusiia*, edited by Tamara Stoilova, 224–51. Sofia: Asotsiatsiia Klio-96, 2006.

– "Moskva, 'vuzroditelniiat protses' i bulgaro-turskite vzaimootnosheniia, 1985–89." In *Georgi Markov: Istorikut-izsledovatel i populiarizator. Sbornik v chest na 70-godishninata na akad. Georgi Markov*, 338–425. Sofia: Zakharii Stoianov, 2017.

– "Nasilvstvenata smiana na imenata na bulgarskite turtsi i otrazhenieto i vurkhu bulgaro-turskite otnosheniia (dekemvri 1984 g.–mart 1985 g.)." In *Bulgariia i Balkanite v sferata na evropeiskite vliianiia prez XIX–XXI vek*, 316–26. Veliko Turnovo: Ivis, 2020.

– "Nauchni podkhodi v izsledvaniiata za politikata kum turskoto naselenie v Bulgariia v perioda 1944–89." In *Predizvikatelstva na promianata*, edited by Iskra Baeva and Plamen Mitev, 302–7. Sofia: Universitetsko izdatelstvo Sv. Kliment Okhridski, 2006.

Kalinova, Evgeniia, and Iskra Baeva. "'Vuzroditelniiat protses' – vurkhut na aisberga. Bulgarskata durzhava i turskata etnicheska obshtnost v stranata (sredata na 30-te godini – nachaloto na 90 te godini na 20-ti vek." In *"Vuzroditelniiat protses": Bulgarskata durzhava i bulgarskite turtsi (sredata na 30-te godini – nachaloto na 90-te godini na XX vek)*. Vol. 1. From the series *Arkhivite govoriat*, vol. 55, edited by Iskra Baeva and Evgeniia Kalinova, 5–40. Sofia: Durzhavna Agentsiia "Arkhivi," 2009.

Kaneff, Deema. *Who Owns the Past? The Politics of Time in a "Model" Bulgarian Village*. New York: Bergahn Books, 2004.

Karkov, Nikolay. "Decolonizing Praxis in Eastern Europe: Toward a South-to-South Dialogue." *Comparative and Continental Philosophy* 7, no. 2 (November 2015): 180–200.

Karkov, Nikolay, and Zhivka Valiavicharska. "Rethinking East-European Socialism: Notes Toward a Decolonial Anti-Capitalist Methodology." *Interventions: International Journal of Postcolonial Studies* 20, no. 8 (2018): 785–813.

Karpushin, B.A. "Razrabotka K. Marksom materialisticheskoi dialektiki v 'Ekonomichesko-filosofskikh rukopisakh 1844 goda.'" *Voprosy Filosofii* 3 (1955): 102–14.

Katsakioris, Constantin. "The Patrice Lumumba University in Moscow." Lecture at the NYU Jordan Center for Russian Studies, 20 April 2017. Available at https://www.youtube.com/watch?v=62xyYdpfcFM.

Katsarova, Rada. "Repression and Resistance on the Terrain of Social Reproduction." *Viewpoint Magazine*, 31 October 2015. https://www.viewpointmag.com/2015/11/02/issue-5-social-reproduction/.

Kazasov, Dimo. *Konstitutsiiata na narodnata republika Bulgariia garantira pravata i svobodite na bulg. grazhdani*. Sofia: Izdatelstvo na natsionalniia suvet na Otechestveniia front, 1949.

Keshelava, Varlam. *Mif o dvukh Marksakh*. Moscow: Izdatel'stvo politicheskoi literatury, 1963.

Khakov, Dzhengiz. "Bulgaro-turskite otnosheniia i turskoto naselenie v Bulgariia." In *Izsledvaniia v chest na chl. kor. Strashimir Dimitrov*, vol. 2, 691–3. Sofia: BAN, 2001.

Khalif, Omar, and Diana Tsankova. "Apokrifnata Iablanska epopeia: Apogeiat na suprotivata sreshtu 'Vuzroditelniia' protses. Chast 1." *Sedem* 11, 23–9 March 2005, 16.

– "Apokrifnata Iablanska epopeia. Bulgari i turtsi zaedno se vuzpravikha sreshtu diktaturata na Todor Zhivkov. Chast 2." *Sedem* 12, 30 March–5 April 2005, 16.

Kharkhordin, Oleg. *The Collective and the Individual in Russia: A Study of Practices*. Berkeley: University of California Press, 1999.

Khikmet, Nazum. *Izbrani stikhotvoreniia*. Sofia: Bulgarski pisatel, 1952.

Khristov, Khristo, ed. *Stranitsi ot bulgarskata istoriia: Ocherk za isliamiziranite bulgari i natsionalnovuzstanovitelniia protses*. Sofia: Nauka i izkustvo, 1989.

Khristov, Khristo, and Veselin Khadzhinikolov. *Iz minaloto na bulgarite-mokhamedani v Rodopite*. Sofia: Bulgarska Akademiia na Naukite, 1985.

Kirov, Maksimilian. "Zlatka Dubova." *Zhenata dnes* 5 (1972): 10.

Koleva, Svetla. *Sotsiologiiata kato proekt: Nauchna identichnost i sotsialni izpitaniia v Bulgariia, 1945–1989 godina*. Sofia and Moscow: Pensoft, 2005.

Koliovski, Petur. "'Prestuplenieto' na Andzhela. Oshte edin opit za razprava i terror." *Komsomolska iskra* (Plovdiv), 11 January 1971, 4–5.

Kollontai, Axelandra. *Selected Writings*. New York: W.W. Norton and Co., 1977.

"Komsomoltsite ot Plovdivskata okruzhna organizatsiia v zashtita na mladata amerikanska komunistka." *Komsomolska iskra* (Plovdiv), 1 February 1971, 4.

Kotkin, Stephen. *Magnetic Mountain: Stalinism As Civilization*. Berkeley: University of California Press, 1995.

– "Modern Times: The Soviet Union and the Interwar Conjuncture." *Kritika* 2, no. 1 (2001): 111–64.

– "1991 and the Russian Revolution: Sources, Conceptual Categories, Analytical Frameworks." *Journal of Modern History* 72, no. 2 (1998): 384–425.

Kozlov, Vladimir A., Sheila Fitzpatrick, and Sergei V. Mironenko, eds. *Sedition: Everyday Resistance in the Soviet Union under Khrushchev and Brezhnev*. New Haven, CT: Yale University Press, 2011.

Kratunkova, Rositsa. "Bulgaria (Not) Only For Bulgarians." *LeftEast*, 2 March 2018. http://www.criticatac.ro/lefteast/bulgaria-not-only-for-bulgarians.

Kret, Abigail Judge. "'We Unite with Knowledge': The Peoples' Friendship University and Soviet Education for the Third World." *Comparative Studies of South Asia, Africa, and the Middle East* 33, no. 2 (2013): 239–56.

Krylova, Anna. *Women in Combat: A History of Violence on the Eastern Front*. Cambridge: Cambridge University Press, 2010.

Laclau, Ernesto. *Emancipations*. London: Verso, 1996.

Laclau, Ernesto, and Chantal Mouffe. *Hegemony and Socialist Strategy: Towards a Radical Democratic Politics*. London: Verso, 1985.

Lahusen, Thomas, and Evgeny Dobrenko, eds. *Socialist Realism without Shores*. Durham, NC: Duke University Press, 1997.

Lalkov, Milcho. *Ot nadezhda kum razocharovanie: Ideiata za federatsiia v balkanskiia Iugoiztok (1944–1948)*. Sofia: Vek 22, 1994.

Lapin, Nikolai. *Bor'ba vokrug ideinogo naslediia molodogo Marksa*. Moscow: Gosudarstvennoe izdatel'stvo "Vysshaia shkola," 1962.

– *Mladiiat Marks*. Sofia: Izdatelstvo na Bulgarskata Komunisticheska Partiia, 1969.

– *Molodoi Marks*. Moscow: Politizdat, 1968.

– "Nachalo marksizma." *Voprosy filosofii* 1 (1983): 27–48.

– "O genezise marksizma kak tsel'nogo ucheniia." In *Istoriia obshtestvennoi mysli: Sovremennye Problemy*, edited by Vasilii Oreshkin, 50–77. Moscow: Nauka, 1972.

Law, Ian. *Red Racisms: Racism in Communist and Post-Communist Contexts*. New York: Palgrave Macmillan, 2012.

Lazarus, Neil. "Spectres Haunting: Postcommunism and Postcolonialism." *Journal of Postcolonial Writing* 48, no. 2 (2012): 117–29.

Lefebvre, Henri. *Dialectical Materialism.* Minneapolis: University of Minnesota Press, 2009.

– *The Production of Space.* Malden, MA: Blackwell, 1991.

Lewis, Reina, and Sara Mills. *Feminist Postcolonial Theory: A Reader.* New York: Routledge, 2003.

Lifshits, Mikhail, and Frants Shiller, eds. *Marks i Engel's ob iskusstve.* Moscow: Sovetskaia literatura, 1933.

Literaturnoe nasledstvo K. Marksa i F. Engel'sa: Istoriia publikatsii i izucheniia v SSSR. Moscow: Izdatel'stvo politicheskoi literatury, 1969.

Lobkowicz, Nicholas, ed. *Marx and the Western World.* Notre Dame, IN: University of Notre Dame Press, 1967.

Lorde, Audre. "The Master's Tools Will Never Dismantle the Master's House." In *This Bridge Called My Back*, edited by Cherríe Moraga and Gloria Anzaldúa, 94–7. Albany: SUNY Press, 2015.

– *Sister Outsider.* Berkeley, CA: Crossing Press, 1984.

Lukács, Georg. *History and Class Consciousness: Studies in Marxist Dialectics.* Cambridge, MA: MIT Press, 1972.

– *Marxism and Human Liberation.* Edited with an introduction by E. San Juan Jr. New York: Delta Books, 1973.

Luxemburg, Rosa. *Rosa Luxemburg Speaks.* Edited with an introduction by Mary-Alice Waters. New York: Pathfinder Press, 1970.

– *Selected Political Writings.* New York: Monthly Review Press, 1971.

Maese-Cohen, Marcekke. "Introduction: Toward Plenary Decolonial Feminisms." *Qui Parle* 18, no. 2 (2010): 3–27.

Maeva, Mila. *Bulgarskite turtsi-preselnitsi v Republika Turtsiia.* Sofia: Mezhdunaroden tsentur po problemite na maltsinstvata i kulturnite vzaimodeistviia, 2006.

Mahmood, Saba. *Politics of Piety: The Islamic Revival and the Feminsit Subject.* Princeton, NJ: Princeton University Press, 2005.

Maldonado-Torres, Nelson. *Against War: Views from the Underside of Modernity.* Durham, NC: Duke University Press, 2008.

– "Lewis Gordon: Philosopher of the Human." *C.L.R. James Journal* 14, no. 1 (Spring 2008): 103–37.

– "On the Coloniality of Being: Contributions to the Development of a Concept." *Cultural Studies* 21, nos 2–3 (2007): 240–70.

– "Thinking through the Decolonial Turn: Post-Continental Interventions in Theory, Philosophy, and Critique – An Introduction." *Transmodernity: Journal of Peripheral Cultural Production of the Luso-Hispanic World* 1, no. 2 (2011): 1–15.

Mamardashvili, Merab. *Izbrano: Klasicheska i neklasicheska ratsionalnost*. Vol. 1. Edited by Deian Deianov and Liliana Deianova. Sofia: Iztok-Zapad, 2004.

– *Soznanie i tsivilizatsiia*. Moscow: Logos, 2004.

Marcuse, Herbert. *One Dimensional Man*. Boston: Beacon Press, 1991 [1964].

Marinos, Martin. "Anti-Neoliberal Neoliberalism: Post-Socialism and Bulgaria's 'Ataka' Party." *TripleC: Communications, Capitalism, and Critique* 13, no. 1 (2015): 274–97.

Marinov, Chavdar. "Ot 'internatsionalisum' kum natsionalizum – chast 1." *Liberalen pregled*, 23 July 2013. http://www.librev.com/index.php/2013-03-30-08-56-39/discussion/bulgaria/2127-from-internationalism-to-nationalism-1.

– "Ot 'internatsionalizum' kum natsionalizum – chast 2." *Liberalen pregled*, 5 August 1013. http://www.librev.com/index.php/discussion-bulgaria-publisher/2133-int-nat-2.

Mark, James, and Quinn Slobodian. "Eastern Europe in the Global History of Decolonization." In *The Oxford Handbook of the Ends of Empire*, edited by Martin Thomas and Andrew Thompson, 357–72. Oxford: Oxford University Press, 2018.

Marković, Mihailo. *From Affluence to Praxis: Philosophy and Social Criticism*. Ann Arbor: University of Michigan Press, 1967.

– "Humanism and Dialectic." In *Socialist Humanism: An International Symposium*, edited by Erich Fromm, 84–97. New York: Anchor Books, 1966.

– "Introduction." In *Praxis: Yugoslav Essays in the Philosophy and Methodology of the Social Science*, edited by Mihailo Marković and Gajo Petrović, xi–xxxvi. Dodrecht, NL: D. Reidel Publishers, 1979.

– "Tragedy of National Conflicts in 'Real Socialism': The Case of the Yugoslav Autonomous Province of Kosovo." *Praxis International* 9, no. 4 (1990): 408–24.

Marković, Mihailo, and Gajo Petrović, eds. *Praxis: Yugoslav Essays in the Philosophy and Methodology of the Social Science*. Dodrecht, NL: D. Reidel Publishers, 1979.

Marković, Mihailo, and Robert Cohen, eds. *Yugoslavia: The Rise and Fall of Socialist Humanism*. Nottingham, UK: Bertrand Russell Peace Foundation for Spokesman Books, 1975.

"Marks i mladezhta: Diskusiia." *Problemi na mladezhta* 3 (1984): 17–49.

Marks, K. "Podgotvitel'nye raboty dlia 'Sviatogo semeistva.'" In *Arkhiv K. Marksa i F. Engel'sa*, vol. 3, 247–86. Moscow and Leningrad: Gosudarstvennoe izdatel'stvo, 1927.

Marks, K., and F. Engel's. *Iz rannikh proizvedenii*. Moscow: Gosudarstvennoe izdatel'stvo politicheskoi literatury, 1956.

– *Sochineniia*. Vol. 1, 2nd ed. Moscow: Gosudarstvennoe izdatel'stvo politicheskoi literatury, 1955.

Martin, Terry. *Affirmative Action Empire: Nations and Nationalism in the Soviet Union, 1923–39*. Ithaca, NY: Cornell University Press, 2001.

Marx, Karl. *Economic and Philosophic Manuscripts of 1844*. Translated by Martin Milligan. Moscow: Foreign Languages Publishing House, 1959.

Marx, Karl, and Friedrich Engels. *Gesamtausgabe*. Abt. 1, bd 3, 1932.

– *Marx-Engels Collected Works*. 2nd ed. New York: International Publishers, 1975–2004.

Matusevich, Maxim. "Black in the U.S.S.R: Africans, African Americans, and Soviet Society." *Transition* 100 (2009): 56–75.

– "Journeys of Hope: African Diaspora and the Soviet Society." *African Diaspora* 1 (2008): 53–85.

– "Probing the Limits of Internationalism: African Students Confront Soviet Ritual." *Anthropology of East Europe Review* 27, no. 2 (2009): 19–39.

Mbembe, Achille. "African Modes of Self-Writing." *Identity, Culture and Politics* 2, no. 1 (2001): 1–39.

McKittrick, Katherine, ed. *Sylvia Wynter: On Being Human as Praxis*. Durham, NC: Duke University Press, 2015.

Medarov, Georgi. "Komunizmut e zlo." *Sotsiologicheski problemi* 1–2 (2015): 227–51.

– "Mezhdu (anti)avtoritarizma i demokratsiiata: Vuzmozhnostta za liberalen avtoritarizum." *Godishnik na Sofiiskiia Universitet "Sv. Kliment Okhridski," Filosofski Fakultet* (Kniga Sotsiologiia) 104 (2013): 7–28.

– "Zagubeni v protivorechiiata na prekhoda." *DVersia* 8, 9 February 2017. http://dversia.net/2473/zagubeni-v-protivorechiata-na-prehoda.

Memmi, Albert. *The Colonizer and the Colonized*. Boston: Beacon Press, 1991.

Merleau-Ponty, Maurice. *Adventures of the Dialectic*. Evanston, IL: Northwestern University Press, 1973.

Mervart, Jan. "Czechoslovak Humanist Marxism and the Revolution." *Studies in East European Thought* 26 (2017): 111–26.

Mezzandri, Alessandra. "On the Value of Social Reproduction: Informal Labour, the Majority World and the Need for Inclusive Theories and Politics," *Radical Philosophy* 2, no. 4 (2019): 33–41.

Mies, Maria. *Patriarchy and Accumulation on a World Scale: Women in the International Division of Labor.* London: Zed Books, 1986.

Mignolo, Walter. *The Darker Side of Western Modernity: Global Futures, Decolonial Options.* Durham, NC: Duke University Press, 2011.

– "Sylvia Wynter: What Does it Mean to Be Human?" In *Sylvia Wynter: On Being Human As Praxis*, edited by Katherine McKittrick. Durham, NC: Duke University Press, 2015, 106–23.

Milevska, Suzana, ed. *The Renaming Machine.* Ljubljana: Parasite Institute, 2010.

– "The Renaming Machine in the Balkans As a Strategy of Accumulation by Dispossession." In *EU, Europe, Unfinished: Mediating Europe and the Balkans in a Time of Crisis*, edited by Zlatan Krajina and Nebojša Blanuša, 78–92. London: Rowman and Littlefield, 2018.

Minchev, Dobrin. *Makedonskiiat vupros i bulgaro-iugoslavskite otnosheniia 9.IX.1944–1949.* Sofia: Universitetsko izdatelstvo "Sv. Kliment Okhridski," 1994.

Mirza, Heidi Safia, ed. *Black British Feminism.* London: Routledge, 1997.

– "Introduction: Mapping a Genealogy of Black British Feminism." In *Black British Feminism*, edited by Heidi Safia Mirza, 1–28. London: Routledge, 1997.

Mitev, Petur-Emil. "Deset godini institutsializirani izsledvaniia na mladezhta." *Problemi na mladezhta* 5–6 (1978): 3–23.

– "Filosofski predshestvenik na marksizma." In *Foierbakh: Istoriia i aktualnost*, edited by Petur-Emil Mitev, 35–90. Sofia: Nauka i izkustvo, 1972.

– ed. *Foierbakh: Istoriia i aktualnost.* Sofia: Nauka i izkustvo, 1972.

– "Formiraneto, razvitieto i razprostranenieto na filosofskite vuzgledi na Marks i Engels." In *Antologiia po istoriia na marksistkata filosofiia: ot vuznikvaneto na marksizma do leninskiia etap*, edited by Petur-Emil Mitev and Emiliia Mineva, 7–94. Sofia: Nauka i izkustvo.

– *Mladezhta – problemi i izsledvaniia.* Sofia: Narodna mladezh, 1985.

– ed. *Ot sotsialniia problem kum svetogledni otkritiia: Evristichnata logika na marksistkata filosofiia.* Sofia: Nauka i izkustvo, 1984.

– "Problemi na aktivnata zhiznena pozitsiia na mladata lichnost." In *Mladezhta – problemi i izsledvaniia*, edited by Petur-Emil Mitev, 134–45. Sofia: Narodna mladezh, 1985.

– "Sotsialnoto tvorchestvo na mladezhta." *Problemi na mladezhta* 4 (1978): 4–12.

Mitev, Petur-Emil, and Emiliia Mineva, eds. *Antologiia po istoriia na marksistkata filosofiia: Ot vuznikvaneto na marksizma do leninskiia etap.* Sofia: Nauka i izkustvo, 1981.

Mitev, Petur-Emil, and Ventsel Raichev, eds. *Izsledvaniia vurkhu istoriiata na marksistkata filosofiia*. Sofia: Nauka i izkustvo, 1973.

Mizov, Nikolai. "Etnoreligiozni aspekti na vuzroditelniia protses." In *Problemi na razvitieto na bulgarskata narodnost i natsiia*, edited by Georgi Iankov, Strashimir Dimitrov, and Orlin Zagorov, 166–82. Sofia: Bulgarska Akademiia na Naukite, 1988.

Mohanty, Chandra Talpade. *Feminism without Borders: Decolonizing Theory, Practicing Solidarity*. Durham, NC: Duke University Press, 2003.

– "Under Western Eyes: Feminist Scholarship and Colonial Discourse." *boundary* 2 12, no. 3 (1984): 333–58.

– "'Under Western Eyes' Revisited: Feminist Solidarity through Anticapitalist Struggles." *Signs: Journal of Women in Culture and Society* 28, no. 2 (2002): 499–535.

Mohanty, Chandra Talpade, Ann Russo, and Lourdes Torres, eds. *Third World Women and the Politics of Feminism*. Bloomington: Indiana University Press, 1991.

Moneva, S. "Abortut po zhelanie." *Zhenata dnes* 5 (1972): 18.

Moore, David Chioni. "Is the Post- in Postcolonial the Post- in Post-Soviet? Toward a Global Postcolonial Critique." *PMLA* 116, no. 1 (2001): 111–28.

Moraga, Cherríe, and Gloria Anzaldúa. *This Bridge Called My Back*. Albany: SUNY Press, 2015.

Morgan, Jennifer. *Laboring Women: Reproduction and Gender in New World Slavery*. Philadelphia: University of Pennsylvania Press, 2004.

Morley, David, and Kuan-Hsing Chen, eds. *Stuart Hall: Critical Dialogues in Cultural Studies*. London: Routledge, 1996.

Morozova, V.A. "Sochineniia K. Marska i F. Engel'sa." In *Bol'shaia Sovetskaia Entsiklopediia*, vol. 24, part 2, 261–3. Moscow: Izdatel'stvo Sovetskaia Entsiklopediia, 1976.

Mouffe, Chantal, ed. *Gramsci and Marxist Theory*. London and Boston: Routledge and Kegan Paul, 1970.

– *On the Political*. London: Routledge, 2005.

Muños, José Esteban. *Cruising Utopia: The Then and There of Queer Futurity*. New York: New York University Press, 2009.

Mutafchieva, Vera. "Iashar Shaban." Interview with Yaşar Şaban. In *Istoriiata naselena s khora: Bulgarskoto obshtestvo prez vtorata polovina na XX vek*, vol. 2, edited by Vera Mutafchieva, 745–56. Sofia: Gutenberg, 2006.

Nadasen, Premilla. "Domestic Worker's Rights, the Politics of Social Reproduction, and New Models of Labor Organizing." *Viewpoint Magazine*, 31 October 2015. https://www.viewpointmag.com/2015/10/31/

domestic-workers-rights-the-politics-of-social-reproduction-and-new-models-of-labor-organizing/.
– *Welfare Warriors: The Welfare Rights Movement in the United States.* New York: Routledge, 2005.
Narskii, I.S. "Ob istoriko-filosofskom razvitii poniatiia 'otchuzhdenie.'" *Filosofskie nauki* 4 (1963): 35–46.
– "Za istoriko-filosofksoto razvitie na poniatieto 'otchuzhdenie.'" In *Izsledvaniia vurkhu istoriiata na marksistkata filosofiia*, edited by Petur-Emil Mitev and Ventsel Raichev, 108–19. Sofia: Nauka i izkustvo, 1973.
"Nasilieto ne se zabravia lesno." *Demokratsiia* 138, 17 June 1993, 6.
Nelson, Cary, and Lawrence Grossberg. *Marxism and the Interpretation of Culture.* Urbana: University of Illinois Press, 1988.
Nelson, Jennifer. *Women of Color and the Reproductive Rights Movement.* New York: New York University Press, 2003.
Neuburger, Mary. *The Orient Within: Muslim Minorities and the Negotiation of Nationhood in Modern Bulgaria.* Ithaca, NY: Cornell University Press, 2004.
Nikolchina, Miglena. "The Seminar: *Mode d'emploi.* Impure Spaces in the Light of Late Totalitarianism." *Differences* 15 (Spring 2002): 96–127.
Oglesby, Carl, ed. *The New Left Reader.* New York: Grove Press, 1969.
Oizerman, Teodor I. *Formirovanie filosofii marksizma.* Moscow: Sotsekgiz, 1972.
– *Problema otchuzhdeniia i burzhoaznaia legenda o marksizme.* Moscow: Znanie, 1965.
Ong, Aihwa. *Neoliberalism as Exception.* Durham, NC: Duke University Press, 2006.
Oyěwùmí, Oyèrónkẹ́. *The Invention of Women: Making African Sense of Western Gender Discourses.* Minneapolis: University of Minnesota Press, 1997.
Parla, Ayşe. *Precarious Hope: Migration and the Limits of Belonging.* Stanford, CA: Stanford University Press, 2019.
Parmar, Pratiba and Valerie Amos. "Challenging Imperial Feminism." *Feminist Review* 17 (Autumn 1984): 3–19.
Parreñas, Rhacel Salazar. *Servants of Globalization: Women, Migration and Domestic Work.* Stanford, CA: Stanford University Press, 2001.
Patterson, Orlando. *Slavery and Social Death.* Cambridge, MA: Harvard University Press, 1982.
Pavlov, Todor. *Teoriia na otrazhenieto: Osnovni vuprosi na dialekticheskomaterialisticheskata teoriia na poznanieto.* Sofia: Narizdat, 1945.

Pazhitnov, L.N. *U istokov revoliutsionnogo perevorota v filosofii. "Ekonomichesko-filosofkie rukopisi 1844 goda" K. Marksa.* Moscow: Sotsekgiz, 1960.

Pence, Kathereine, and Paul Betts, eds. *Socialist Modern: East German Culture and Politics.* Ann Arbor: University of Michigan, 2008.

Pešić -Golubović, Zagorka. *Problemi savremene teorije ličnosti.* Belgrade: Kultura, 1966.

Petrov, Petur. "Bulgarskite mokhamedani protiv osmanskata vlast." In *Problemi na razvitieto na bulgarskata narodnost i natsiia*, edited by Georgi Iankov, Strashimir Dimitrov, and Orlin Zagorov, 74–93. Sofia: Bulgarska Akademiia na Naukite, 1988.

– "Iziava na bulgarska prinadlezhnost." *Nov Zhivot* 7 (1987): 8.

– *Po sledite na nasilieto: Dokumenti i materiali za nalagane na isliama.* Vols 1–2. Sofia: Nauka i izkustvo, 1987–88 [1972].

Petrov, Petur, and Mustafa Miusliumov, eds. *Druzhni i edinni prez vekovete: Sbornik istoricheski dokumenti i spomeni za turskoto naselenie.* Sofia: Izdatelstvo BKP, 1966.

Petrović, Gajo. "Man and Freedom." In *Socialist Humanism: An International Symposium*, edited by Erich Fromm, 84–97. New York: Anchor Books, 1966.

– *Marx in the Mid-Twentieth Century: A Yugoslav Philosopher Considers Karl Marx's Writings.* New York: Anchor Books, 1967.

Pismeni dokumenti za bulgarskiia kharakter na naselenieto ot iztochnite Rodopi. Kurdzhali, BG: OK na BKP, 1985.

Pistotnik, Sara, and David Alexander Brown. "Race in the Balkans: The Case of Erased Residents in Slovenia." *Interventions: International Journal of Postcolonial Studies* 20, no. 6 (2018), 832–52.

Popescu, Monica. "Lewis Nkosi in Warsaw: Translating Eastern European Experiences for an African Audience." *Journal of Postcolonial Writing* 48, no. 2 (2012): 176–87.

– "On the Margins of the Black Atlantic: Angola, the Eastern Bloc, and the Cold War." *Research in African Literatures* 45, no. 3 (2014): 91–109.

– *South African Literature Beyond the Cold War.* New York: Palgrave Macmillan, 2010.

"Poseshtenieto na dr. Todor Zhivkov v India. Vazhen etap v ukrepvashtata druzhba mezhdu dvete strani." *Narodna mladezh*, 25 January 1969, 1, 4.

Prashad, Vijay. *The Darker Nations: A People's History of the Third World.* New York: New Press, 2007.

"Predislovie k pervomu tomu." In K. Marks i F. Engel's, *Sochineniia*, vol. 1, xv–xvi. 2nd ed. Moscow: Gosudarstvennoe izdatel'stvo politicheskoi literatury, 1955.

"Predislovie ko vtoromu izdaniiu." In K. Marks i F. Engel's, *Sochineniia*, vol. 1, x–ix. 2nd ed. Moscow: Gosudarstvennoe izdatel'stvo politicheskoi literatury, 1955.

Puteva, Svoboda. *Mladata zhena*. Sofia: Profizdat, 1983.

– "Mladata zhena i neinoto svobodno vreme (Sotsiologichesko prouchvane v Stara Zagora)." *Mladezh* 7 (1970): 40–7.

– "Mladata zhena – trud, bit, otdikh." *Problemi na mladezhta* 5 (1977): 25–35. Republished in *Mladezhta – problemi i izsledvaniia*, edited by Petur-Emil Mitev, 167–76. Sofia: Narodna mladezh, 1985.

– "Mladiiat chovek – liubov, brak, semeistvo." In *Moeto budeshto semeistvo*, edited by Pavlina Popova, 52–65. Sofia: Narodna mladezh, 1984.

– "Problemi na realizatsiiata na mladata zhena." *Problemi na mladezhta* 4 (1979): 23–8.

– "Razvitieto na devoikata i mladata zhena v sotsialisticheskoto obshtestvo." *Problemi na mladezhta* 4 (1972): 34–49.

– "Spored vutreshnite potrebnosti i interesi." *Mladezh* 8–9 (1985): 70–2.

– "Svobodnoto vreme i kharmonichnoto razvitie na mladata lichnost." *Problemi na mladezhta* 5 (1984): 9–25.

– "Svobodnoto vreme na mladata zhena." *Problemi na mladezhta* 4 (1985): 40–53.

Quist-Adade, Charles. "Paternalism to Ethnocentrism: Images of Africa in Gorbachev's Russia." *Race and Class* 46, no. 4 (2005): 75–89.

"Ravenstvo, razvitie, mir." Interview with Elena Lagadinova, Chair of the Committee of Bulgarian Women. *Mladezh* 3 (1975): 14–15.

Renault, Matthieu. "The Idea of Muslim National Communism: On Mirsaid Sultan-Galiev." Translated by Patrick King. *Viewpoint Magazine*, 23 March 2015. https://www.viewpointmag.com/2015/03/23/the-idea-of-muslim-national-communism-on-mirsaid-sultan-galiev.

– "The Revolution Decentered: Two Studies on Lenin." Translated by Patrick King. *Viewpoint Magazine*, 1 February 2018. https://www.viewpointmag.com/2018/02/01/revolution-decentered-two-studies-lenin.

Reno, Matiu. "Detsentrirana revoliutsiia: Dva etiuda vurkhu Lenin." Translated by Momchil Khristov. *Novi Levi Perspektivi*, 27 November 2017. http://www.novilevi.org/publications/313-lenin1917.

Republika Bulgariia. Natsionalen suvet po etnicheski i demografski vuprosi. "Natsionalen doklad suglasno chl. 25, al. 1 ot Ramkovata konventsiia za zashtita na natsionalnite maltsinstva." January 2001.

Roberts, Dorothy. *Killing the Black Body: Race, Reproduction, and the Meaning of Liberty*. New York: Vintage Books, 1997.

Robertson, James. "Imagining the Balkans as a Space of Revolution: The Federalist Vision of Serbian Socialism, 1870–1914." *East European Politics and Societies and Cultures* 31, no. 2 (2017): 402–25.

– "On Czech Marxism: An Interview with Ivan Landa and Jan Mervart." *LeftEast*, 6 September 2016. http://www.criticart.ro/lefteast/on-czech-marxism.

Robinson, Benjamin. *The Skin of the System: On Germany's Socialist Modernity.* Stanford, CA: Stanford University Press, 2009.

Robinson, Cedric J. *Black Marxism: The Making of the Radical Tradition.* Chapel Hill: University of North Carolina Press, 1983.

Rosaldo, Michelle. "The Use and Abuse of Anthropology: Feminism and Cross-Cultural Understanding." *Signs: Journal of Women in Culture and Society* 3, no. 5 (Spring 1980): 389–417.

Rozental', M.M. *Dialektika Kapitala Karla Marksa.* Moscow: Mysl', 1967.

– ed. *Istoriia marksistkoi dialektiki. Ot vozniknoveniia marksizma do leninskogo etapa.* Moscow: Mysl', 1971.

– *Voprosy dialektiki v Kapitale K. Marksa.* Moscow: Gospolitizdat, 1955.

Rubin, Gayle. *Deviations: A Gayle Rubin Reader.* Durham, NC: Duke University Press, 2011.

Said, Edward. *The Edward Said Reader.* Edited by Moustafa Bayoumi and Andrew Rubin. New York: Vintage Books, 2000.

– *Orientalism.* New York: Vintage Books, 1979.

– *Reflections on Exile and Other Essays.* Cambridge, MA: Harvard University Press, 2000.

Sangari, Kumkum, and Sudesh Vaid. *Recasting Women: Essays in Indian Colonial History.* New Brunswick, NJ: Rutgers University Press, 1990.

Satterwhite, James. *Varieties of Marxist Humanism: Philosophical Revision of Postwar Eastern Europe.* Pittsburgh: University of Pittsburgh Press, 1992.

Scarboro, Cristofer. *The Late Socialist Good Life in Bulgaria: Meaning and Living in a Permanent Present Tense.* Lanham, MD: Lexington Books, 2011.

Schultes, Hannah. "Under Assault: Class and Gender in Bulgaria and Europe Today." An interview with LevFem Collective members Zhivka Valiavicharska, Neda Genova, and Raia Apostolova. *Political Critique*, 21 February 2019. http://politicalcritique.org/cee/2019/class-gender-bulgaria-europe/.

Schwartz, Marie Jenkins. *Birthing a Slave: Motherhood and Medicine in the Antebellum South*. Cambridge, MA: Harvard University Press, 2006.

Scott, David. *Conscripts of Modernity: The Tragedy of Colonial Enlightenment*. Durham, NC: Duke University Press, 2004.

– "The Re-Enchantment of Humanism: An Interview with Sylvia Wynter." *Small Axe* 8 (2000): 119–207.

Scott, Joan. *Gender and the Politics of History.* New York: Columbia University Press, 1999.

Serra, Fulvia. "Reproducing the Struggle: A New Feminist Perspective on the Concept of Social Reproduction." *Viewpoint Magazine*, 31 October 2015. https://www.viewpointmag.com/2015/10/31/reproducing-the-struggle-a-new-feminist-perspective-on-the-concept-of-social-reproduction/.

Sharkova, Savina. "Sotsialisticheskata zhena mezhdu publichnoto i chastnoto (1967–73): Vizii, protivorechiia i politicheski deistviia prez sotsializma v Bulgaria." In *Godishnik na Sofiiskiia universitet "Sv. Kliment Okhridski,"* vol. 103, 61–80. Sofia: Filosofski Fakultet, 2011.

Shenabuddin, Elora. "Gender and the Figure of the 'Moderate Muslim.'" In *The Question of Gender: Joan W. Scott's Critical Feminism*, edited by Judith Butler and Elizabeth Weed, 102–42. Bloomington: Indiana University Press, 2011.

Sher, Gerson, ed. *Marxist Humanism and Praxis.* Buffalo, NY: Prometheus Books, 1978.

– *Praxis: Marxist Criticism and Dissent in Socialist Yugoslavia.* Bloomington: Indiana University Press, 1977.

"Shte razkazvam za suvetskite khora." *Narodna mladezh*, 18 September 1972, 3.

Sinha, Mrinalini. *Colonial Masculinity: The "Manly Englishman" and the "Effeminate Bengali" in the Late Nineteenth Century*. Manchester: Manchester University Press, 1995.

– "Historically Speaking: Gender and Citizenship in Colonial India." In *The Question of Gender: Joan W. Scott's Critical Feminism*, edited by Judith Butler and Elizabeth Weed, 80–101. Bloomington: Indiana University Press, 2011.

Sinha, Subir, and Rashmi Varma. "Marxism and Postcolonial Theory: What's Left of the Debate." *Critical Sociology* 43, nos 4–5 (2015): 545–58.

Sitnikov, Eduard M. *Problema "otchuzhdeniia" v burzhoaznoi filosofii i fal'sifikatory marksizma.* Moscow: Izd AON i VPSh pri TSK na KPSS, 1962.

Slatterwhite, James. *Varieties of Marxist Humanism: Philosophical Revision in Postwar Eastern Europe*. Pittsburg: University of Pittsburg Press, 1992.

Slezkine, Yuri. *Arctic Mirrors: Russia and the Small Peoples of the North*. Ithaca, NY: Cornell University Press, 1994.

– "The USSR as a Communal Apartment, or How a Socialist State Promoted Ethnic Particularism." *Slavic Review* 53, no. 2 (Summer 1994): 414–52.

Smith, Barbara. *Home Girls: A Black Feminist Anthology*. New Brunswick, NJ: Rutgers University Press, 2000.

Smith, Jeremy. "The Battle for Language: Opposition to Khrushchev's Education Reform in the Soviet Republics, 1958–59." *Slavic Review* 76, no. 4 (2017): 983–1002.

Smithers, Gregory D. *Slave Breeding: Sex, Violence and Memory in African American History*. Gainesville: University Press of Florida, 2012.

Smolentsev, Iu. M. "Problema cheloveka v tvorchestve K. Marksa." *Sovetskaia pedagogika* 5 (1968): 19–29.

Spade, Dean. *Normal Life: Administrative Violence, Critical Trans Politics, and the Limits of the Law*. Durham, NC: Duke University Press, 2015.

Spillers, Hortense. "Mama's Baby, Papa's Maybe: An American Grammar Book." In *The Black Feminist Reader*, edited by Joy James and T. Denean Sharpley Whiting, 57–87. Malden, MA: Blackwell, 2000.

Spivak, Gayatri Chakravorty. *In Other Worlds: Essays in Cultural Politics*. New York: Routledge, 1988.

Stalin, Joseph. *Works*. Vol. 6. Moscow: Foreign Languages Publishing House, 1953.

Stanoeva, Elitsa. "Vizualna lustratsiia ili krai na debatite za minaloto?" *Terminal* 3, 29 November 2016. www.terminal3.bg/vizualna-lustraciq-ili-krai-na-debatitie-za-minaloto.

Stefanov, Khristo, and Maksimiliian Kirov, eds. *Suvremenno bulgarsko monumentalno izkustvo 1956–1986*. Sofia: Durzhavno izdatelstvo D-r Petur Beron, 1986.

Stepanova, E.A. "O sobiranii i nauchnoi publikatsii v SSSR literaturnogo nasledstva osnovopolozhnikov marksizma." In *Iz istorii marksizma*, edited by L.I. Gol'man, 6–59. Moscow: Izdatel'stvo politicheskoi literatury, 1961.

Stoianov, Tsvetan. *Suchineniia v dva toma*. Vol. 2. Sofia: Bulgarski pisatel, 1988.

Stronsky, Paul. *Tashkent: Forging a Soviet City, 1930–1966*. Pittsburgh: University of Pittsburgh Press, 2010.

Subotić, Jelena, and Srdjan Vučetić. "Performing Solidarity: Whiteness and Status-Seeking in the Non-Aligned World." *Journal of International Relations and Development* 22 (2017): 722–43. https://doi.org/10.1057/s41268-017-0112-2.

Taha, Mai, and Sara Salem. "Social Reproduction and Empire in an Egyptian Century." *Radical Philosophy* 2, no. 4 (2019): 47–54.

Takhirov, Shukri. *Bulgarskite turtsi po putia na sotsializma*. Sofia: Izdatelstvo na otechestveniia front, 1978.

Thompson, E.P. *The Poverty of Theory and Other Essays*. New York: Monthly Review Press, 1978.

– "Socialist Humanism: An Epistle to the Philistines." *The New Reasoner* 1 (1957): 105–43.

Ţichindeleanu, Ovidiu. "Decolonizing Eastern Europe: Beyond Internal Critique." *IDEA Arts & Society* 38 (2011): 101–4.

– "Vampires in the Living Room. A View to What Happened to Eastern Europe after 1989 and Why Real Socialism Still Matters." In *Asking, We Walk: The South as New Political Imaginary*, vol. 3, edited by Corinne Kumar, 331–46. Bangalore, IN: Streelekha, 2013.

Tipukhin, V. *Metod voskhozhdeniia ot abstraktnogo k konkretnomu v "Kaptale" K. Marksa*. Moscow: Omskogo sel'skokhoziaistvennogo instituta im. S.M. Kirova, 1961.

Tlostanova, Madina. *Gender Epistemologies and Eurasian Boderlands*. New York: Palgrave Macmillan, 2010.

Todorova, Maria. "Balkanism and Postcolonialism, or on the Beauty of the Airplane View." In *Marx's Shadow: Knowledge, Power, and Intellectuals in Eastern Europe and Russia*, edited by Costica Bradatan and Serguei Al. Oushakine, 175–95. Lanham, MD: Lexington Books, 2010.

– *Bones of Contention: The Living Archive of Vasil Levski and the Making of Bulgaria's National Hero*. Budapest: CEU Press, 2009.

– "The Bulgarian Case: Women's Issues or Feminist Issues?" In *Gender Politics and Post-Communism: Reflections from Eastern Europe and the Former Soviet Union*, edited by Nanette Funk and Magda Mueller, 30–8. New York: Routledge, 1993.

– "Conversion to Islam as a Trope in Bulgarian Historiography, Fiction, and Film." In *Balkan Identities. Nation and Memory*, edited by Maria Todorova, 129–57. London: Hurst and Co., 2003.

– "Identity (Trans)formation among Bulgarian Muslims." In *The Myth of "Ethnic Conflict": Politics, Economics and "Cultural" Violence*, edited by Beverly Crawford and Ronnie D. Lipschutz, 471–510. Berkeley: University of California Press, 1998.

– *Imagining the Balkans*. New York: Oxford University Press, 1997.

– "The Ottoman Legacy in the Balkans." In *Imperial Legacy: The Ottoman Imprint on the Balkans and the Middle East*, edited by L. Carl Brown, 45–77. New York: Columbia University Press, 1996.

Todorova, Maria, and Zsuzsa Gille, eds. *Post-Communist Nostalgia*. New York: Berghan Books, 2010.

Topolova, Iordanka. "Promeniashtata se rolia na pola i sotsialnata politika na NR Bulgariia." *Sotsiologicheski problemi* 2 (1978): 109–16.

Totev, Anastas. "Za broia na detsata v semeistvoto." *Problemi na mladezhta* 5–6 (1978): 36–44.

Traykov, Bozhin. "From Anti-Communism to Fascism: Ideological Crusaders of the Bulgarian Passive Revolution versus Socio-Economic Reality." In "Decolonial Theory and Practice for Southeast Europe," edited by Katarina Kusic, Polina Manolova, and Filipp Lottholz. *DVersia* (special issue, March 2019): 101–28.

Trifonov, Staiko. "Miusiulmanite v politikata na bulgarskata durzhava (1944–89)." In *Stranitsi ot bulgarskata istoriia*, vol. 2, edited by Mikhail Gruev and Aleksei Kal'onski, 210–23. Sofia: Prosveta, 1993.

Tsing, Anna. *Friction: An Ethnography of Global Connection*. Princeton, NJ: Princeton University Press, 2005.

Tsoneva, Jana. "Komunizmut e greshka." *Sotsiologicheski problemi* 1–2 (2015): 252–70.

– "Of the Past Let Us Make a Crime: Anti-Populism and the Politics of Bulgarian Liberalism." *LeftEast*, 5 January 2017. http://www.criticatac.ro/lefteast/anti-populism-and-the-politics-of-memory-in-bulgarian-liberalism/#comment-202803.

Tsoneva, Jana, and Zhivka Valiavicharska. "Obshtinata planira da vurne pametnika na Purva sofiiska diviziia ot 1934 g. A iska li da vurne Sanstefanska Bulgariia i da razpusne Narodnoto subranie?" *Novi Levi Perspectivi*, 14 July 2017. http://novilevi.org/publications/309-1934.

"Ukaz za nasurchavane na razhdaemostta." *Durzhaven vestnik: Ofitsialen organ na narodnoto subranie*, 23 February 1968, 1–2.

"Ukaz za nasurchavane na razhdaemostta." *Durzhaven vestnik: Ofitsialen organ na narodnoto subranie*, 15 March 1968, 1.

"Ukaz za nasurchavane na razhdaemostta." *Durzhaven vestnik: Ofitsialen organ na narodnoto subranie*, 10 August 1973, 1.

"Ukaz za nasurchavane na razhdaemostta." *Durzhaven vestnik: Ofitsialen organ na narodnoto subranie*, 1 March 1974, 1.

"Ukaz za nasurchavane na razhdaemostta." *Durzhaven vestnik: Ofitsialen organ na narodnoto subranie*, 10 January 1975, 1.

Vaksberg, Tatiana. "Tekhnologiia na zloto (3): Modelut na sblusuka." *Sega* 32, 7 February 2001, 12.

Valiavicharska, Zhivka. "Herbert Marcuse, the Liberation of 'Man,' and Hegemonic Humanism." *Theory and Event* 20, no. 3 (2017): 804–27.

– "History's Restless Ruins: On Socialist Public Monuments in Post-Socialist Bulgaria." *boundary 2* 41, no. 1 (Spring 2014): 171–202.

– "How the Concept of Totalitarianism Appeared in Late Socialist Bulgaria: The Birth and Life of Zheliu Zhelev's Book *Fascism*." *Kritika: Explorations in Russian and Eurasian History* 15, no. 2 (Spring 2014): 303–34.

– "The Production of 'Leninism' and its Political Journeys." In *Futures of Lenin*, edited by Alla Ivanchikova and Robert Maclean. Albany: SUNY Press, forthcoming.

– "Smutnite ruini na istoriiata: Sotsialisticheskite obshtestveni pametnitsi v postsotsialisticheska Bulgariia." *Novi Levi Perspektivi*, 2 December 2014. http://novilevi.org/publications/209-valiavicharska-monuments.

– "Social Reproduction in the Making: Recentering the Margins, Expanding the Directions." *CLCWeb: Comparative Literature and Culture* 22, no. 2 (2020). https://doi.org/10.7771/1481-4374.3837.

Vaziulin, Viktor. *Logika "Kapitala" K. Marksa*. Moscow: Moskovskogo universiteta, 1968.

Velev, Ivan. "Interesi i deinosti v sferata na svobodnoto vreme." In *Mladezhta – problemi i izsledvaniia*, edited by Petur-Emil Mitev, 184–202. Sofia: Narodna mladezh, 1985.

Verdery, Katherine. *The Vanishing Hectare: Property and Value in Postsocialist Transylvania*. Ithaca, NY: Cornell University Press, 2003.

Vora, Kalindi. "After the Housewife: Surrogacy, Labour, and Human Reproduction." *Radical Philosophy* 2, no. 4 (2019): 42–6.

Vranicki, Predrag. "Socialism and the Problem of Alienation." In *Socialist Humanism: An International Symposium*, edited by E. Fromm, 299–313. New York: Anchor Books, 1966.

"Vulnuvashti sreshti s Andzhela Deivis." *Narodna mladezh*, 20 September, 1972, 1, 3.

Vygodskii, V.S. *K istorii sozdaniia "Kapitala."* Moscow: Mysl', 1970.

Wa Thiong'o, Ngũgĩ. *Decolonizing the Mind: The Politics of Language in African Literature*. Oxford: James Currey; Nairobi: EAEP; Portsmouth, NH: Heinemann, 1986.

– *Moving the Centre: The Struggle for Cultural Freedoms*. Oxford: James Currey; Nairobi: EAEP; Portsmouth, NH: Heinemann, 1993.

Wacquant, Loïc. *Punishing the Poor: The Neoliberal Government of Social Insecurity*. Durham, NC: Duke University Press, 2009.

Weeks, Kathi. *The Problem with Work: Feminism, Marxism, Antiwork Politics, and Postwork Imaginaries*. Durham, NC: Duke University Press, 2011.

Weheliye, Alexander. *Habeas Viscus: Racializing Assemblages, Biopolitics, and Black Feminist Theories of the Human*. Durham, NC: Duke University Press, 2014.

Whitener, Brian. "Detroit's Water Wars: Race, Failing Social Reproduction, and Infrastructure." *CLCWeb: Comparative Literature and Culture* 22, no. 2 (2020). https://doi.org/10.7771/1481-4374.3843.

Williams, Eric. *Capitalism and Slavery*. Chapel Hill: University of North Carolina Press, 1994.

Wolfe, Patrick. "Settler Colonialism and the Elimination of the Native." *Journal of Genocide Research* 8, no. 4 (2006): 387–409.

Wolff. Larry. *Inventing Eastern Europe: The Map of Civilization on the Mind of the Enlightenment*. Stanford, CA: Stanford University Press, 1994.

Wynter, Sylvia. "Unsettling the Coloniality of Being/Power/Truth/Freedom Towards the Human, After Man, Its Overrepresentation – An Argument." *CR: The New Centennial Review* 3, no. 3 (2003): 257-337.

Wynter, Sylvia, and Katherine McKittrick. "Unparalleled Catastrophe for Our Species? Or, to Give Humanness a Different Future: Conversations." In *Sylvia Winter: On Being Human as Praxis*, edited by Katherine McKittrick, 9–89. Durham, NC: Duke University Press, 2015.

X, Malcolm. "I Don't Mean Bananas." In *The New Left Reader*, edited by Carl Oglesby, 207–22. New York: Grove Press, 1969.

Young, Robert. *White Mythologies: Writing History and the West*. London: Routledge, 1990.

Yurchak, Alexei. *Everything Was Forever until It Was No More: The Last Soviet Generation*. Princeton, NJ: Princeton University Press, 2006.

Za izdigane roliata na zhenata v izgrazhdaneto na razvito sotsialistichesko obshtestvo. Reshenie na TsK na BKP ot 6 Mart 1973 godina. Sofia: Partizdat, 1979.

Zagorov, Orlin. *Bulgarsko sotsialistichesko suznanie: Problemi na formirane i razvitie*. Sofia: Nauka i izkustvo, 1989.

– *Edinenieto*. Sofia: Otechestven front, 1981.

– "Istoricheskо suznanie i vuzroditelen protses." In *Problemi na razvitieto na bulgarskata narodnost i natsiia*, edited by Georgi Iankov, Strashimir Dimitrov, and Orlin Zagorov, 183–99. Sofia: Bulgarksa akademiia na naukite, 1988.
– *Obshtuvane i dukhovno nasledstvo*. Sofia: Partizdat, 1987.
– *Vuzroditelniiat protses: Teza, antiteza, i otritsanie na otritsanieto*. Sofia: Ares, 1993.
Zarecor, Kimberly. *Manufacturing Socialist Modernity: Housing in Czechoslovakia, 1945–60*. Pittsburgh: University of Pittsburgh Press, 2011.
Zheliazkova, Antonina, ed. *Mezhdu adaptatsiiata i nostalgiiata: Bulgarskite turtsi v Turtsiia*. Sofia: Mezhdunaroden tsentur po problemite na maltsinstvata i kulturnite vzaimodeistviia, 1998.
– "The Problem of the Authenticity of Some Domestic Sources on the Islamization of the Rhodopes, Deeply Rooted in Bulgarian Historiography." *Etudes Balkaniques* 4 (1990): 105–11.
– "Sotsialna i kulturna adaptatsiia na bulgarskite izselnitsi v Turtsiia." In *Mezhdu adaptatsiiata i nostalgiiata: Bulgarskite turtsi v Turtsiia*, edited by Antonina Zheliazkova, 11–44. Sofia: Mezhdunaroden tsentur po problemite na maltsinstvata i kulturnite vzaimodeistviia, 1998.
Zhelubovskaia, E.A., ed. *Marks – istorik*. Moscow: Nauk, 1968.
Zhivkov, Todor. *Bulgaria: Ancient and Socialist*. Toronto: Progress Books, 1975.
– "Edinstvoto na bulgarskiia narod e grizha i sudba na vseki grazhdanin na nasheto milo otechestvo." *Trud*, 30 May 1989, 1.
– "Edinstvoto na bulgarskiia narod e grizha i sudba na vseki grazhdanin na nasheto milo otechestvo." In *Istinata za "Vuzroditelniia protses": Dokumenti ot arkhiva na Politbiuro i TsK na BKP*, edited by Georgi Atanasov, 38–44. Sofia: Institut za izsledvane na integratsiiata, 2003.
– *Memoari*. Sofia: Trud i pravo, 2006.
– *Uchenie i trud, zhizneradostnost i druznovenie. Pismo do TsK na DKMS*. Sofia: Partizdat, 1978.
– *Za Komsomola i mladezhta*. Sofia: Narodna mladezh, 1971.
– *Za novata konstitutsiia na Narodna Republika Bulgariia. Doklad pred XVI sesiia na peto narodno subraniie 7 mai 1971 godina*. Sofia: Nauka i izkustvo, 1971.
Zhivkova, Liudmila. "Bulgariia i kulturata." In *S aprilsko vdukhnovenie v borbata za mir, sotsializum, za edinstvo, tvorchestvo i krasota. Dokladi, rechi, statii i izkazvaniia*, vol. 2, 536–51. Sofia: Partizdat, 1982.

– "Da bude Bulgariia!" In *S aprilsko vdukhnovenie v borbata za mir, sotsializum, za edinstvo, tvorchestvo i krasota. Dokladi, rechi, statii i izkazvaniia*, vol. 2, 519–23. Sofia: Partizdat, 1982.

– "Dostoini za doverieto na svoia narod: Vstupitelno slovo pred natsionalnata konferentsiia na kulturata za rabotata s mladata khudozhestvenotvorcheska inteligentsiia." In *S aprilsko vdukhnovenie v borbata za mir, sotsializum, za edinstvo, tvorchestvo i krasota. Dokladi, rechi, statii i izkazvaniia*, vol. 1, 742–5. Sofia: Partizdat, 1982.

– "Igrazhdaneto na kulturata na razvitoto sotsialistichesko obshtestvo – nasha neposredstvena istoricheska zadacha (Doklad pred tretiia kongres na bulgarskata kultura, Sofia, 18 May 1977)." In *S aprilsko vdukhnovenie v borbata za mir, sotsializum, za edinstvo, tvorchestvo i krasota. Dokladi, rechi, statii i izkazvaniia*, vol. 1, 614–710. Sofia: Partizdat, 1982.

– "Opoznavaneto na zakonite na krasotata i kharmonichnoto razvitie na choveshkiia individ." In *S aprilsko vdukhnovenie za mir, sotsializum, za edinstvo, tvorchestvo i krasota. Dokladi, rechi, statii i izkazvaniia*, vol. 1, 156–78. Sofa: Partizdat, 1982.

– *S aprilsko vdukhnovenie v borbata za mir, sotsializum, za edinstvo, tvorchestvo i krasota. Dokladi, rechi, statii i izkazvaniia.* Vols 1–3. Sofa: Partizdat, 1982.

– "Trinadeset veka bulgarska durzhava." In *S aprilsko vdukhnovenie v borbata za mir, sotsializum, za edinstvo, tvorchestvo i krasota. Dokladi, rechi, statii i izkazvaniia*, vol. 2, 533–55. Sofa: Partizdat, 1982.

– "Znamenatelen iubilei." In *S aprilsko vdukhnovenie v borbata za mir, sotsializum, za edinstvo, tvorchestvo i krasota. Dokladi, rechi, statii i izkazvaniia*, vol. 2, 506–18. Sofia: Partizdat, 1982.

ARCHIVAL COLLECTIONS

Tsentralen Durzhaven Arkhiv (TsDA), Sofia

TsDA, f. 1b, op. 6, arkh. ed. 3645, 50–7. "Protokol na TsK na BKP ot [21 June] 1958 god. otnosno podobriavaneto na rabotata sred turskoto naselenie."

TsDA, f. 1b, op. 6, arkh. ed. 3645, 58–64. "Dokladna Zapiska. Otnosno: Podobriavane na rabotata sred turskoto naselenie [June 1957]."

TsDA, f. 1, op. 27, arkh. ed. 19, 4–14. "Do Sekretaria na TsK na BKP Drugaria Encho Staikov. Tuk prilozhen … materiala ot dr. Nazum Khikmet vuv vruzka s negovoto prebivavane prez m. septemvri 1951 g. v NR Bulgariia."

TsDA, f. 1, op. 28, arkh. ed. 10, 5–7. "Zaiavlenie ot Sami Iusufov Hodzhov, zhitel na grad P-v, zhivusht na ul. Patriarkh Eftimii 10."

TsDA, f. 1, op. 28, arkh. ed. 16, 1–7. "Izlozhenie na turchin do TsK na BKP vuv vruzka s nedovolstvoto sred turskoto naselenie ot reshenieto na partiiata za slivane na turskite uchilishta s bulgarskite [7 April 1960]."

TsDA, f. 1b, op. 5, arkh. ed. 353, 242–470. "Tsentralen Komitet na Bulgarskata Komunisticheska Partiia. Protokol ot plenum na TsK na BKP, sustoial se na 2, 3, i 4 oktomvri 1958 g."

TsDA, f. 1b, op. 6, 1298, 37–43. "Za podobriavane rabotata na Partiiata sred turskoto naselenie, [26 April 1951]."

TsDA, f. 214b, op. 1, arch. ed. 716, 1–73. "Otnosno turskiiat maltsinstven i izselnicheski vupros."

Index

Page numbers in italics refer to figures.

abortions: access to, 83; statistics of, 82
Afro-Asian Writers' Association, 178
Alexander, Franklin, 174
Alexander, Kendra, 174
alienation: capitalism and, 43; concept of, 40, 42; critique of, 43–4, 45; limits of, 42; private ownership of means of production and, 43; in socialist societies, 40, 42; Stoianov's treatise on, 45–6, 47
Althusser, Louis, 11, 16, 36, 37, 54, 57
Annals of Marxism, 30
anti-colonial liberation movements, 4–5, 11–12, 25–6, 182–3
anti-communism, 191–2
Atanasov, Georgi, 106, 107, 114
Atanasov, Petur, 187

backwardness: legacy of, 112; socialist meanings of, 110
Baczko, Bronisłav, 11, 40
Bagaturiia, Georgii, 8, 38
Balabanova, Angelika, 63
Balibar, Etienne, 37
Balkan socialist federation: idea of, 129
Bandung Conference (1955), 5
Batishchev, Genrikh, 8
Baudelaire, Charles, 45
Black Atlantic studies, 178
Black Power movements, 5, 25, 172
Boggs, Grace Lee, 4
Bogomils (religious movement), 104
Bourdieu, Pierre, 154
Bratska Mogila (Plovdiv), 186–7, *188*, 189
Braun, Lily, 63
Budapest School, 7
Bulgaria: anti-colonial liberation movements and, 25, 100, 181; child care, 76–7, 78–80, 81, 83; comparative study of, 19; Constitution of 1947, 23, 129–30, 147; Constitution of 1971, 77, 147–8; cultural life in, 99, 109, 112–14, 142; economic crisis, 164–5; educational reforms, 142; ethnic and religious diversity, 112, 113, 117;

European Union and, 195; family culture, 85–6; far-right parties, 193, 194; industrial development, 68, 112; international relations, 12–14, 22, 94–5, 120, 131–2, 167, 180, 185, 195; labour, 165–6; land collectivization, 127; languages, 122, 124, 126, 128–30, 143; minority politics, 19–23, 86, 93–4, 96, 105–6, 122, 124, 128, 139–41; national consciousness, 91, 93, 185; National Revival period, 106–7; Ottoman legacy, 86, 95; population management, 81–5; population statistics, 109; pro-nativist politics, 81–2; public services, 226n15; restoration of historical figures, 194; rights and freedoms, 129–30; socialist development, 13–14, 112–14; struggles for national independence, 25–6, 95, 182; three-child policy, 82–3; women's status in, 60, 62, 63, 65–6, 67; during World War II, 145, 194. *See also* Greater Bulgaria

Bulgarian Communist Party, 116–17, 199, 217n6

Bulgarian identity, 102, 115, 154

Bulgarian national history: materialist social analysis of, 104; milestone events of, 104; re-examination of, 105, 118–19; roots of, 103; as socialist history, 103–4; socialist narrative of, 118. *See also* Ottoman period

Bulgarian peoplehood: notions of, 182

Bulgarian Socialist Party, 199–200

Bulgarian statehood: foundation of, 118; political autonomy of, 120

Burudzhiev, Ivan, 193

Cabral, Amilcar, 5, 12, 182

Capital (Marx), 38

capitalism: alienation under, 43; *vs.* communism, 191; economic features of, 41–2; ideology of, 41; *vs.* socialism, 41–2, 47; third stage of, 41; transition to, 190–1

Castro, Fidel, 5

Césaire, Aimé, 5, 12

Christianity-Islam dichotomy, 22, 117

Club for the Support of Free Speech and Transformation, 161

Cold War: framework of, 176–80; political logic of, 6, 25, 40, 94, 127, 131–2; scholarship, 40, 64, 177–8

Collected Works of Marx and Engels, 15, 27, 34, 35, 36, 38

Committee of the Bulgarian Women's Movement, 68

communism: criminalization of, 193; liberal equation of Nazism and, 189–90; post-Stalinist visions of, 50, 51

Complete Works of Marx and Engels, 35

Dalchev, Liubomir, 187, 188

Dalcheva, Ana, 187

Dalla Costa, Mariarosa, 69, 209n1

Davis, Angela: acquittal of, 172; campaign in support of liberation of, 170; influence of, 174–5; International Dimitrov

Award, 175; international tour, 172, 174; political cartoon commenting on arrest of, *173*; political views of, 152–3, 175; press reports about, *171*, 172; visit to Bulgaria, 170, 172, 174–5
democracy: socialist view of, 108–9; transition to capitalism and, 190
Derrida, Jacques, 150
Dialectical Materialism (*Diamat*), 31–2
dialectical method, 11, 48–9
Dialectics of the Concrete (Kosík), 7
Dimitrov, Georgi, 129, 139, 175
Dimitrova, Blada, 134–5, 136
Dinkova, Maria: on child-care centres, 77; on family relations, 85, 86; on feminism, 63; on motherhood, 74, 75; on pro-nativist politics, 82; on socialist development, 67–8; on women in socialist society, 66, 67, 70, 73–4, 80, 198–9
domestic work: gendered division of, 69–70, 73, 76
Dostoevsky, Fyodor, 45
Druzhba Rodina organization, 128, 145, 194
Dukhteva, Penka, 66, 67, 69
Dunayevskaya, Raya, 4, 39, 40, 41
Dunov, Petur, 24, 96
Dunovists, 96, 97

Eastern Europe: Marxist-humanist ideas in, 5–6, 7, 27–8, 41, 44, 48–9, 55; political and economic development of, 8, 199, 200; socialist legacy of, 200–1
Economic and Philosophical Manuscripts (Marx and Engels), 8
1844 Manuscripts: American edition of, 39; first full version of, 15; influence of, 27–8; interpretations of, 36, 38; political and historical relevance of, 39; publications of, 28, 30–1, 206n23, 207n39; Soviet editions of, 36; studies of, 14–15, 37–8; translations of, 15, 27, 35, 39, 206n23, 207n39
Engels, Friedrich: archive of, 30, 34; early works of, 27
ethnicity: religion and, 116, 117; socialist concept of, 153
ethnic minorities: assimilation policy, 20, 86, 114, 147, 168, 181; birth rate, 86; communist education of, 114; constitutional rights, 130, 147–8; expropriation of property, 163; government policy toward, 124–5, 127–8, 139–40, 217n6; marginalization of, 117; mass expulsion of, 162–3, 164, 167; social and cultural well-being of, 112–14; xenophobic discourse, 114
ethnocentric statism (ethnostatism), 24, 96, 120–1
ethnonationalism: anti-colonial politics and, 176; assimilationist politics of, 65; call for "unity" and discourse of, 101, 102; continuities and discontinuities of, 21–2; development of doctrine of, 21, 92, 100; as expression of political autonomy, 127; in the global sphere, 24; humanism and, 19, 20; national history and, 94–5; in post-Stalinist Bulgaria, 19, 29, 83–4, 87–8,

91–2, 94; roots of, 93–4, 95, 184–5; socialist doctrine of, 91, 95, 108, 120
Europeanization process, 192–3

Family (Parikian, 1981), 79
Fanon, Frantz, 5, 12, 182
fascist symbols, 189
Federici, Silvia, 209n1
femininity: socialist construction of, 59, 80–1
feminism: communist movements and, 63; in East European context, 64–5; negative connotations of, 63–4; opposition to racism and, 62; periodization of, 60, 62–3; in socialist countries, 16, 60, 61, 62; social reproduction and, 57–8, 86–7; Western narratives of, 16, 60, 61, 63
Fetscher, Iring, 40
Feuerbach, Ludwig, 33
Fire, The (Stefanov, 1981), 98
First Bulgarian Kingdom, 118
Foucault, Michel, 57, 58
Frank, Louis, 63
Frankfurt School, 4, 52
Free Angela and All Political Prisoners campaign, 174
freedom: humanist concept of, 49, 52, 55
free time: capitalism and, 71; leisure and, 17, 71, 73; socialism and, 28, 53, 59, 71–2
Fromm, Erich, 4, 44; *Marx's Concept of Man*, 39; *Socialist Humanism*, 40

Gandhi, Mahatma, 185
gender: denaturalization of, 75; motherhood and, 81; scholarship on, 18, 58, 59; socialism and, 17, 56, 60, 61, 75, 85; social reproduction and, 58, 65, 77; under Stalinism, 59. *See also* sexuality
German Ideology, The (Marx and Engels), 36
global South, 178
Gogol, Nikolai, 45
Golubović, Zagorka, 44
Greater Bulgaria: vision of, 195, 226n14
Guillén, Nicolás, 135

Haggins, Erica, 172
Hasan, Türkan, 159
Hegel, Georg Wilhelm Friedrich, 4, 33
Hikmet, Nâzim: influence of, 135, 136; meetings with and rallies in support of, 135–6; report on Turkish minorities, 136–9; selected poems of, 137; visit to Bulgaria, 134–5
Historical Materialism (*Istmat*), 31–2
historical revisionism, 103–4. *See also* Bulgarian national history
History of the Communist Party of the Soviet Union (Bolsheviks) (a.k.a. *Short Course*), 31
Hodzhov, Sami Yusufov, 144–5
holistically developed person: ethnonationalism and, 101; feminist use of concept, 59; gender and, 56; humanism and,

15, 56; labour and, 97–9; leisure and, 56, 59; realization of, 101; socialist concept of, 15–16, 28, 51, 55, 58–9, 97, 153; socialist reproduction and, 56; women and, 59; youth and, 55, 56
human: equation of man and, 29, 47; hegemonic discourses of, 55, 56; notion of socialist, 11; post-Stalinist idea of, 8–9, 28
human agency, 10
humanism: anti-colonial struggle and, 5; concept of freedom, 49; concept of praxis, 49; critique of alienation, 44; dialectical thought and, 48–9; ethnonationalism and, 19, 20; feminist directions of, 29; gender and, 58; hegemonic, 10, 11–12; international dialogues, 40; nationalist elements of, 87–8; post-Stalinist, 17, 91, 99, 110, 120; rise of, 4, 5–6; socialist, 29, 41, 52, 108; state-centric, 24; Yugoslavian, 44, 48–9
Hungarian uprising of 1956, 7

"*Iablanska* Commune," 159–60
Iakova, Violeta, 193
Ianchev, Zhivko, 84
Iankov, Georgi, 100, 106, 115
Ilyenkov, Evald, 8
Independent Association for the Defence of Human Rights, 161
Independent Committee for Religious Rights and Freedoms of Conscience, 161
Independent Syndicate Podkrepa, 161
Institute of Marxism-Leninism: collections of, 30; establishment of, 29–30; publications of, 30–1, 34, 36
international solidarity, 62
Islam: Christianity and, 117, 166; persecution of, 116–17; socialist government and, 106, 115, 158; theories of mass conversions to, 101, 105
Iz rannikh proizvedenii (*From the Early Works*) (Marx and Engels), 27, 35, *37*

James, C.L.R., 4, 41, 182
James, Selma, 69
Johnson-Forest Tendency, 4, 41

Kalivoda, Robert, 8
Khristov, Khristo, 106
Kierkegaard, Søren, 45
King, Martin Luther, Jr., 172
Kołakowski, Leszek: *Towards a Marxist Humanism*, 8
Kollontai, Aleksandra, 63
Konstantin Asen, Tsar of Bulgaria, 104
Kornishki events, 156
Kosík, Karel, 40; *Dialectics of the Concrete*, 7
Kurdzhaliiski region, 113
Kyrgyz people, 126

labour: as creative activity, 52–3; as form of personal realization, 54, 72, 97–9; freedom and, 52; free time and, 17, 53; gender and, 69–70, 73, 76; Marxist notion of, 61–2, 110;

socialist-humanist notions of, 17; social value of, 53; time budget and, 72, 73; unwaged, 61–2
Lagadinova, Elena, 63, 174
land communes, 97
Lapin, Nikolai: on alienation, 42–3; *Molodoi Marks (The Young Marx)*, 36; scholarship of, 8, 37; study of *1844 Manuscripts*, 37–8, 42
Lefebvre, Henri: *Dialectical Materialism*, 33
leisure: dichotomies between work and, 17, 51; free time and, 17, 71–2, 73; holistically developed person and, 56, 59; socialism and, 17, 26, 77, 87, 147
Lenin, Vladimir: Hegel's influence on, 33; on national question, 125, 182; *Philosophical Notebooks*, 33, 39; popularization of works of, 4; on principles of national self-determination, 13, 182; on state monopoly capitalism, 41
liberation, 10, 28, 55
Lion, the (Memorial to the First Sofia Division of the Bulgarian Army, 1934): installation of, 195–7; symbolism of, 195, 197–8; view of, *197*
Lorde, Audre, 174
Lotus (journal), 179
Lukács, György, 7
Lukov, Khristo, 193

Macedonians: national identity, 140, 218n21; relations with other ethnic groups, 117
Mamardashvili, Merab, 8
"man": concept of, 11, 12, 29, 47
Marcuse, Herbert, 4, 40, 41, 44, 52
Marković, Mihailo, 9, 11, 19, 33, 34
Marx, Karl: archive of, 30, 34; categorical apparatus of, 39; collected works of, 34; "Contribution to the Critique of Hegel's Philosophy of Right," 36; *Critique of Hegel's Philosophy of Right*, 31; on crude versions of communism, 50; early works of, 14, 15, 27–8, 36, 206n23; *Economic Manuscripts*, 38; evolution of political thought of, 36–7, 38; on free time, 72; *The Grundrisse*, 28, 36, 38; Hegel's influence on, 33; humanism in works of, 14, 28, 37–8; "Jewish Question," 36; publications of, 8; Russian translations of, 30–1; *Theories of Surplus Value*, 28, 38; "Theses on Feuerbach," 36. *See also 1844 Manuscripts*
Marx-Engels Archive, 15, 30–1
Marx-Engels Gesamtausgabe (*MEGA*), 31, 35
Marxism-Leninism, 8, 31, 33, 100
Marxist humanism: anthropocentrism of, 10; anti-Stalinist movements and, 7; central categories in, 9–10; critique of Stalinist Marxism, 4; development of, 28–9, 55; dialectical method of, 11; in Eastern Europe, 5–6, 7; ethnonationalism and, 19, 20; as foundation for political reforms,

8; global politics and, 4; during post-Stalinist period, 3–4, 8–10; representatives of, 4; rise of, 14
May Events of 1989, 160
Mitev, Petur-Emil, 10, 11, 38–9, 50, 53
Mizov, Nikolai, 106, 107
modernity(ies): alternative, 110–11; "multiple," 26; socialist visions of, 26, 180
monism, 21
motherhood: biological notions of, 75; in gender relations framework, 81; naturalization of, 59–60, 80–1; population management and, 81–5; prestige of, 75; as social duty, 74, 75, 81; state policies of, 75–8, 81, 83, *84*

Narodna mladezh (socialist youth newspaper): *America: Black and White* column, 172; coverage of Angela Davis trial and visit to Bulgaria, 170, *171*; coverage of international events, 172; "Unity of form and content" satirical drawing, *84*
nation: socialist concepts of, 116
national consciousness, 115, 117, 182–3
national identity, 117
nationalism: anti-colonial revolutionary, 183; evolution of, 91; post-colonial, 183; post-Stalinist, 94, 146, 181, 184–5; studies of, 182–4
national self-determination, 13, 125, 182
National State Archive, 140
Nehru, Jawaharlal, 185
neo-fascism, 189–90, 192, 193
Neruda, Pablo, 135
New Reasoner (*New Left Review*), 9
Newton, Huey, 40, 172
Nietzsche, Friedrich, 45
Non-Aligned Movement, 5
North Macedonia: frictions over territory of, 14; in visions of Greater Bulgaria, 195
Nyerere, Julius, 184

Oglesby, Carl: *The New Left Reader*, 40
Oizerman, Teodor, 36, 43
On Raising the Role of Women in Developed Socialist Society resolution, 65, 76
Ortega y Gasset, José, 45
Orthodox Church, 125, 129, 133, 134
Otechestven Front regime, 22, 23, 130–1, 132, 147
Ottoman period: colonial narrative of, 84, 85, 111; as cultural anachronism, perception of, 21, 106, 111–12; family and gender relations during, 86; nationalist theories of forced Islamization during, 85; scholarly debate on, 105–6; socialist-feminist imaginaries about, 65

parental benefits, 76–7, 78–80, 83
Parikian, Nikolina, 79
Partsalev, Georgi, 78
Pax Ottomana, 105
personhood, 44. *See also* holistically developed person

Petrović, Gajo, 11, 49
Pomak minority: cultural assimilation of, 20, 128, 145, 149, 156; identity of, 106, 167, 216n78; in post-socialist Bulgaria, 167; relocation of, 132; renaming of, 155, 156, 168; shaming discourse, 108; state interference with religious practice of, 158
post-colonial nations: Cold War politics and, 178; historiography of, 176–80; modernity and, 180; socialist countries and, 176–7, 179–80
Power of Women and the Subversion of Community, The (James and Dalla Costa), 69
Prague Spring of 1968, 7
Praxis (journal), 7, 40
Praxis group, 7, 19, 20, 44, 49
progress: discourse of, 108, 109, 110
pro-nativist politics, 81–2, 83–4
Puteva, Svoboda, 52, 71, 72, 85

race: socialist concept of, 153, 180
religion: ethnos and, 116, 117; language and, 117; national consciousness and, 115–16; promulgation of freedom of, 114–15; separation between nation and, 115
renaming campaigns: ethnic assimilation campaign and, 153; historical role of, 153; protests against, 159; slavery and, 151–2; state administration and, 157, 221n30; waves of, 149
Reshet, Bekir, 133
Revival Process: culmination of, 100; definition of, 106–7; demographic politics and, 86; economic effect of, 164–6; ethnonationalist doctrine of, 21, 107; foreign media on, 164; goal of, 101–2, 166, 180–1; idea of progress and, 112; information blackout about, 159; interference with religious practice, 155, 158; justification of, 107–8; mass exodus and, 20, 127, 162–3, 164, 167; outcome of, 166–7, 168–9; political economy of, 147, 161; principle of unity and, 101–2; regional features of, 155–7; resistance to, 23–4, 148, 155–6, 159–62, 166; roots of, 19–20, 92; scholarship on, 93, 107–8; social and cultural effects of, 107–8, 166–7, 168; state violence and, 160–1, 168; victims of, 159, 160–1, 167–8
Riazanov, David, 31
right-wing nationalism, 192, 193–4, 200
Robstvo (Yoke) (Dalchev, Dalcheva, and Atanasov, 1974), 186, *187*
Roma people: assimilation of, 127, 149; discrimination against, 144–5; hostility toward, 198, 226n15; interference with the religious practice of, 158; renaming of, 155, 156, 157, 168
Russian nationalism, 45

Şaban, Yaşar, 157, 158

San Stefano Treaty, 226n14
Saville, John, 4
Schopenhauer, Arthur, 45
Seale, Bobby, 172
Senghor, Léopold, 40
sexuality, 47, 58, 81. *See also* gender
Shinkov, Liubomir, 188
Siromashko liato (film, 1973), 78
socialism: *vs.* capitalism, 41–2, 47; child care, 76, 77, 78, 80, 81; criticism of, 24, 44; *étatist* forms of, 24; family and kinship, 47; gender and, 17, 56, 60, 61, 75, 85; historiography of, 22, 176–8; industrial development, 17; legacies of, 200–1; post-Stalinist, 6, 14; social relations under, 46–7, 50–1, 53; visions of "developed," 17, 42; women and, 70–1, 77–8
socialist countries: African students in, 179; anti-colonial movement and, 24–5, 176–7; economic development of, 41–2; feminist movements in, 60; in global historical context, 26; international relations, 25, 56, 177–8; political reforms in, 8; religion and, 116; scholarship on, 177–8; socio-economic life in, 46–8, 50–1, 177; in Western liberal thought, 6, 7, 16–17
socialist humanism, 53–4, 55–6
socialist modernization, 21, 111, 112
socialist monuments, 189, 194, 195. *See also* 1,300 Years Bulgaria monument; Lion (Memorial to the First Sofia Division of the Bulgarian Army); Bratska Mogila (Plovdiv)
social reproduction: body and, 57–8; capitalist vision of, 71; concept of, 61–2; concept of "holistically developed person" and, 58–9; feminist view of, 56, 57–8, 86–7; gender and, 58, 65, 77; humanist view of, 58, 71; material infrastructures of, 75; meanings of, 18, 57; post-Stalinist scholarship on, 16, 17–18, 54; in socialist Bulgaria, debates on, 58–9; socialist framework of, 71, 86–7
Soviet Union: African students in, 179; foreign affairs, 13, 131, 178; hegemony of Russian culture, 126–7; nationality policies, 125–6; scholarship on, 177
Stalin, Joseph, 32, 126
Stalinism, 8, 9, 41, 44, 49, 126–7
Stalinist Marxism: critique of, 11, 33–4, 50; limitations of, 31, 34; logical contradictions of, 32–3; philosophical disciplines of, 31–2; positivist methodologies of, 32
Starchev, Valentin, 92
Stefanov, Khristo, 98
Stoianov, Tsvetan, 45–6, 47, 48
Stoichev, Ivan, 173
Sviták, Ivan, 8, 40

Tanzanian nationalism, 183–4
Tanzanian socialism, 184
Tashkent Film Festival, 178–9
Tatarliev, Ilko, 106

"Theses on the Work of the Party among the Turkish Population," 140–1
Third World literary and visual culture, 179
1,300 Years Bulgaria monument: demolition of, 92, 194–5; design of, 89–91; erection of, 89, 118; neglect of, 92; original condition, view of, *90*, *119*; protest against demolition of, *196*; public discussion about, 194–5; sculptural compositions, 91, 92
Thompson, E.P., 4, 9, 10, 40
time budget, 72, 73
Tolstoy, Lev, 24, 97
Tolstoyists, 96, 97
totalitarianism, 190, 191
Totev, Atanas, 82
Towards a Marxist Humanism (Kołakowski), 8
Tsonev, Nikolai, 137
Turkey: Cold War politics and, 94, 167; foreign affairs of, 131, 132; migration of Turkish minorities to, 133
Turkish language: banning of, 158–9, 160; as form of cultural resistance, 161
Turkish-language schools: reform of, 122, 142–4, 145; separation from the mosques, 144
Turkish minority: assimilation of, 141, 149, 150; ban on traditional clothing of, 158; confiscation of property of, 162, 222n54; cultural development of, 143–4, 148; discrimination against, 125, 128, 146, 148, 217n6; economic activities of, 138; government policies toward, 108, 130–1, 132, 139–41, 142–3; Hikmet's report on, 136–9; intelligentsia, 143; land co-operatives and, 127, 138; letter of complaint by, *123*; marginalization of, 139–40, 147; mass expulsion of, 20, 112, 121, 124, 127, 128, 134, 162–3, 164, 221n24, 222n52; migration to Turkey, 127, 133, 218n34; mixed marriages of, 155; nationalism of, 132; Otechestven Front regime and, 130–1, 132; personal identification numbers of, 157; political representation of, 138; public perception of, 127–8, 133–4, 146–7; religious consciousness of, 134; renaming of, 149–50, 156–7, 162, 168, 221n30; returnees, 168, 223n71; significance of personal names for, 154–5

UN Declaration on the Elimination of Discrimination against Women, 66
Union of Bulgarian National Legions, 193
United States: anti-war protests, 5, 172; civil rights movement, 25; labour movement, 4; racism, 172

Vaziulin, Viktor, 8
Vazov, Ivan, 37

Webb, Beatrice, 63
Western Marxist feminism, 17, 61–2
Wilde, Oscar, 45
women: in Bulgarian national narrative, 84–5; in capitalist world, 67; career aspirations, 73–4; domestic work and, 69–70, 73, 76; economic well-being, 66, 67; educational opportunities, 66, 67, 71; emancipation of, 73–4; ethnonationalist politics and, 18; feminist movements and political self-identification, 62; feminization of, 80; gender politics and, 56, 60, 75, 85; as holistically developed persons, 71, 72–3; living conditions of, 69; misogynistic culture and, 68–9; motherhood and, 59–60, 74, 75, 84; in professional workforce, 18, 66, 67, 68–9; "second shift" work, 69, 70; socialism and, 65–7, 69–71, 76, 77–8, 80–1; social support of, 18, 77; sociological research on, 68; work-life balance, 71, 73
women's revolution, 198–9
Wynter, Sylvia, 12

X, Malcolm, 5, 40

youth (socialist): concept of, 56; as new collective subject, 54–5; relationship between class and, 54
Yugoslavia: break with the Soviet Union, 13; comparative study of, 19; disintegration of, 20; multinational model of, 23; Serbo-centric visions of, 19; socialist project, 50

Zagorov, Orlin, 102, 106, 115
Zhenata dnes (women's journal), 68, 73, 83; "Let's Abolish the Second Shift!" article, 69–70; "Socialism and the Human" article, *53*; "The Other Mothers of Our Children" article, *76*
Zhivkov, Todor: ascendance to power, 23; domestic policy of, 23, 139–40; on religious practice, 115–16; "Unity" speech, 112–14, 115–16, 164; visit to India, 185
Zhivkova, Liudmila: on aesthetic development, 97–8; on arts and culture, 97, 99, 109–10; on creative labour, 98–9; death of, 99; eclectic humanism of, 100; on evolutionary progress, 110; on formation of socialist society, 103; on national project, 104; philosophical views of, 96, 97; portrait of, *98*; universalism of, 99, 100; writings of, 96, 181
"Zhivkova era," 89, 99